DOCTOR-TO-BE

DOCTOR-TO-BE:
Coping with the Trials and Triumphs of Medical School

James A. Knight, M.D.
Professor of Psychiatry, L.S.U. School of Medicine,
New Orleans, Louisiana;
Formerly, Dean, College of Medicine,
Texas A&M University, College Station, Texas

Foreword by Charles C. Sprague, M.D.
President, The University of Texas
Southwestern Medical School at Dallas
Dallas, Texas

APPLETON-CENTURY-CROFTS / New York

81 82 83 84 85 / 10 9 8 7 6 5 4 3 2 1

Prentice-Hall International, Inc., London
Prentice-Hall of Australia, Pty. Ltd., Sydney
Prentice-Hall of India Private Limited, New Delhi
Prentice-Hall of Japan, Inc., Tokyo
Prentice-Hall of Southeast Asia (Pte.) Ltd., Singapore
Whitehall Books Ltd., Wellington, New Zealand

Library of Congress Catalog Card Number 81-67387

Design: Piedad Palencia

PRINTED IN THE UNITED STATES OF AMERICA
0-8385-1722-6 (case)
0-8385-1721-8 (paper)

To My Medical Alma Mater
Vanderbilt University School of Medicine

CONTENTS

FOREWORD

This is a book about medical students—young men and women who have envisioned a remarkable life for themselves and who are busy translating that vision into reality. It is a book about their experiences as they are given the best available knowledge and skills, shaped into effective practitioners of medicine, and provided with a professional identity that enables them to think, act, and feel like physicians.

The setting for their activity, and hence for this book, is the academic medical center: not a specific medical center, but any of a number of typical academic medical centers in this country and abroad, where the culture of medicine is transmitted and its frontiers advanced.

In spite of the many recent changes in medical education, the reader will be impressed as he or she proceeds through this book with how unchanging are many of the concerns of the medical student. Both the historical perspective provided by the author and the experience of the reader emphasize that the abiding concerns—health, birth, death, fear, competency, identity, and self-mastery—are ever constant.

To put it more directly, the persons who choose medicine—whether they are of this generation or of any past or future generation—seek throughout life to gain a clearer understanding of what led them to medicine and what sustains them in its practice. Changes in curriculum or medical school organization do not modify in the least the students' need to learn to cope with a more total responsibility and a more unrelenting authority over the lives of others than is borne by any other profession. Nor do such changes spare them from learning to face, without anxiety, the most tabooed issues of their society. Much of the daily work for which they prepare is a transgression of the ordinary prohibitions and taboos of the community. From wrestling with ethical decisions to working with their own feelings about death, medical students are occupied daily with many personal tasks beyond the acquisition of technical skill. This book documents many of these tasks, shows their ageless nature, and defines the parameters within which other tasks arise.

Beyond such topics, as they are discussed succinctly and directly in this book, there is a softer theme running throughout: the hope that today's humanity-oriented medical students will bring renewal to the medical enterprise. Medical students, as Dr. Knight aptly sketches them, come through as courageous and dedicated in their efforts to identify the pressing problems of medical education and of society and to work effectively for constructive solutions. They are concerned especially with those groups in our society most likely to be without adequate medical care: the poor and sick in the ghetto, in the inner city, and in isolated rural areas. Also, they press their teachers to join them in helping correct individual and social ills. Medical students view their profession as a *calling,* not a trade, and hope to bring to it a breadth of charity and dedication credited to some of medicine's finer moments in the past.

This book will be of great value to a variety of readers. Medical students and teachers will be helped to see in better perspective certain facets of the student's professional growth that are often overlooked or taken too lightly. Husbands and wives of students can obtain from the book a realistic picture of their spouses' challenging work and the stresses that accompany it. With this knowledge should come a greater understanding of their participation in the medical career of their respective spouses. Also, premedical students will be introduced to many aspects of medical education that will serve them as anticipatory guidance or create in them a new openness for the real essence of the medical school experience.

More important than all of these, however, this book may serve as a means of introducing the first glimmerings of the concept of a medical vocation to young readers who might otherwise never conceive of medicine as an option for their lives. Medicine has long suffered from a limited input spectrum. The urban ghettos, the rural hinterlands, and untold thousands of America's solid middle-class homes often provide no direct path for those aspiring to become doctors, except for those fortunate few related to a physician or personally acquainted with one. The lightness of Dr. Knight's writing touch, his innate feel for humor, and his ear for a catch phrase may contribute significantly to this book's ability to reach such "outsiders" and grant them an enticing peek into the world of medical vocations.

Almost 20 years ago, when I was Dean at Tulane University School of Medicine, I persuaded Dr. Knight to accept the position of Dean of Admissions at that School, a position he held for 10 years. After that, he became Dean of the Texas A&M University College of Medicine, and then went to the LSU School of Medicine in New Orleans. During these years, I have had a part in encouraging Dr. Knight to grapple with the issues about which he has written in this book. Actually, many of the chapters deal with subjects that he and I have discussed. It was to be expected that he would write this book and present the fruits of years of working closely with premedical and medical students. Not only has he been active in the selection of students for medical school, but also after their admission he has continued to be a friend as well as an advisor. When confronted with personal or academic problems, these students have sought his counsel. They have visited with him often, not only to bring problems but also to share their plans and rich experiences. Thus, what he has written has that authentic quality of one who has gone through the medical experience and, in turn, followed countless others in their growth and training toward becoming physicians. By reading this book, you may join him in traveling this fascinating and highly human pathway.

Charles C. Sprague M.D.

PREFACE

Many years of working with medical students have given me the challenge and inspiration for writing this book about them and their preparation for the practice of medicine. The book is a blend of experience, reading, thinking, and the help of many student and physician colleagues. Medical students are acted upon by hidden and overt forces that are of great importance in their lives and destinies. They are in their own right persons with hopes, convictions, and ideals. Best of all, they are inherently educable with a great capacity for growth and change.

The student can be understood best if the emphasis is placed on the importance of "identity" as a principal motivation in one's life. In the concept of identity is the acknowledgment that much of what one does, whether rational or illogical, really has to do with what one strives to be and achieve as an individual among other human beings. *Identity*, as it relates to professional development, means the acquisition of character and skills through being, feeling, and achieving. It distinguishes each medical student from all others. In this quest for personal individuation, there is also the persistence of the qualities of teachers and peers with whom one shares one's very existence. Thus, the student's identity has two facets: one looking inward for a sense of uniqueness, and the other looking outward for a sense of community with colleagues and patients.

Although the major focus of this book is the medical student, the premedical student is not overlooked. Premedical and medical student concerns are often similar. In the new edition of this book, the first two chapters deal with the multiple factors that enter into the decision to become a doctor, a description of the selection process for students, and an identification of the qualities looked for in aspiring physicians. The book continues with a discussion of the inner growth and development of the medical student—that is, his or her professional socialization—a rich, intense, and multidimensional process. An unforgettable part of the *rites of passage* is the impact of dissecting a cadaver. The chapter, "Sex and Marriage in Medical School," opens a popular area for dialogue. While including the student's personal concerns and experiences with the subject, the chapter goes further in relating the student's sexuality to the broader dimensions of the doctor-patient relationship.

A pivotal chapter deals with the psychological problems of medical students. Students carry to medical school an array of personal problems, many of which are hidden. The various stresses in school bring to the forefront difficulties that may be covert, resulting in study interferences and disordered school relationships. The nature of the medical school environment permits students to be junior colleagues in a panoramic educational process unique in most aspects of learning. The movement through the training period is filled with challenges and pitfalls; and a knowledge of deans, their assistants, and how decisions are made regarding students is essential for survival and success. Thus, some sensitive and often misunderstood issues are dealt with in "The Student's Relationships with the Faculty," and the "Profiles of Deans and Help for the Student." Another chapter focuses on developing an ability to make crucial decisions about patients when only fragments of information are available.

Although enormous progress has been made in the recruitment of women into medicine since the first edition of this book, it seemed wise to retain the chapter on women in medicine. Problems and concerns still abound in this area, and many women encouraged the author to address these issues again in a revised chapter on the woman medical student. Further, a chapter has been added on minority and disadvantaged students. Efforts in recruitment and graduation of minority students have not been as successful as hoped for and expected. Thus, we must respond to this challenge with increased vigor.

Students wrestle with choosing a specialty from among the many career options open to them. Thus, one chapter is devoted to the considerations that go into specialty choice. Ethical decision making has become increasingly important with the new developments in medicine. "Sense and Sensitivity in Medical Ethics" is directed toward helping the student formulate an ethical stance appropriate for meeting each situation. Coming to terms with one's feelings about death is an especially urgent matter confronting each medical student. Unless we understand ourselves psychologically in relation to our own finitude, too much time is spent dealing with our own problems rather than those of our patients. The final chapter is a brief statement of where students find themselves in the magnificent tradition and heritage of medicine.

I have written frankly and realistically about medical students and their colorful and hazardous journey toward becoming doctors of medicine. To some extent these students are changing, and reflect the rapid and accelerating changes of our society. As a group, there are more women, blacks, mainland Puerto Ricans, American Indians, Mexican-Americans, Orientals, and other minorities in medicine than before. They bring to medicine different socioeconomic backgrounds and attitudes and enrich the medical profession with their diversity, as well as erode class lines.

Further, the students bring humanistic concerns and a deep social consciousness. While aware of the hypocrisies and shortcomings in the dominant value systems of today, they embrace a basic value that reaches far back in our history—respect and appreciation for the human being, a rare and precious creature—as beautifully expressed in Shakespeare's *Hamlet:*

> What a piece of work is a man!
> How noble in reason!
> How infinite in faculty!
> In form and moving how express and admirable!
> In action how like an angel!
> In apprehension how like a god!

It is hoped that the medical school environment will nurture this attitude of mind, and support the student as both a scientist and a healer.

March, 1981   James A. Knight, M.D.

ACKNOWLEDGMENTS

I am indebted to many friends and colleagues for their help in the preparation of the first and the second editions of this book. Several of my former Tulane University colleagues assisted in numerous ways and will have my gratitude always. Special thanks go to Dr. John E. Chapman, Dean, Vanderbilt University School of Medicine, for counsel regarding the entire book; to Dr. Charles C. Sprague, President, University of Texas Southwestern Medical School at Dallas for suggestions and the writing of the Foreword; to Dr. Lois DeBakey, Professor of Scientific Communications, Baylor College of Medicine, for general editorial counsel; and to Mr. Charles F. Chapman, Director, Editorial Office, LSU School of Medicine, for valuable assistance in the revisions for the second edition of the book. Dr. Jeanne M. Lagowski, Chairman, Health Professions Advisory Committee, University of Texas at Austin, offered many fine suggestions for the revision of several sections of the book.

Further, Dr. James R. Schofield, Director, Division of Accreditation, Association of American Medical Colleges, has shared with me, beginning during our years together at Baylor College of Medicine, many of the basic ideas included in both the first and second editions of this book. Also, Dr. Davis G. Johnson, Director, Division of Student Studies, Association of American Medical Colleges, has been a helpful guide for parts of both the first and second editions of the book. Drs. Dean Coddington, Diane Daum, Klebert Jones, and Ms. Diane Heim, my colleagues at the LSU School of Medicine, counseled me in the revision of specific sections of the book. Dr. Anna Cherrie Epps, Director, Medical Education Reinforcement and Enrichment Program, Tulane University Medical Center, and Mr. Alfred Fisher, Executive Vice-President for Administrative Affairs, National Medical Association, Washington, D.C., helped immeasurably with the chapter on minority and disadvantaged students. Dr. Rickey P. Martinez, during his senior year at LSU School of Medicine, worked closely with me in coordinating the medical student input in the book's revision. Ms. Doreen S. Berne, Executive Medical Editor, Appleton-Century-Crofts, skillfully guided the revision of this book and was available at all times for expert editorial assistance. Deep appreciation is reserved for my wife, Sally, who contributed to several phases of the development and revision of the book. And my warmest thanks to medical students too numerous to name, at Baylor, Tulane, Texas A&M, LSU, and other schools in whose debt I stand for ideas, illustrations, enthusiastic encouragement, and inspiration.

1
THE DECISION TO BECOME A DOCTOR

Blessed is he who has found his work; let him ask no other blessedness.
—Thomas Carlyle[5]

A crippled man and woman, gently supporting each other, made their way slowly toward the entrance of the medical school. Before entering, they paused to read an inscription over the doorway from Marcus Aurelius: "Men exist for the sake of one another. Teach them, then, or bear with them." In the lobby the couple lingered before a statue of Aesculapius, a history of medicine display, and a bulletin board announcing special lectures. Appearing more rested now, they asked to be directed to the office of the dean of admissions.

They stated to the dean that they were there on behalf of their son who was applying to medical school. They had not told their son that they were planning to visit the school, for they would not want him to interpret their interest as interfering in his affairs. They wanted only to put in "a good word" for their son, whom they described as strong, bright, filled with compassion, and wanting more than anything else to be a doctor. They knew that he would care for his patients as he had cared for them. They had each been crippled in early childhood by poliomyelitis; thus, their son had known them only in their crippled state. Their disability, they believed, had given special meaning to their son's life; and, in turn, his plans and hopes had brought extraordinary meaning to theirs.

Later, when the son visited the school, he proved to be as fine a candidate for the study of medicine as his parents had pictured him. In many ways, these parents and their son demonstrate something of the broad spectrum of motives, apparent and hidden, that enter into a person's decision to become a doctor. While avoiding too quick or too easy an analysis of motivation, in this situation or others, it seems essential that motivation be explored in a vocation such as medicine in the interest of the doctor and the patient.

QUEST FOR VOCATION

Many fortunate persons have the privilege of choosing a preferred life work, a choice that represents one of the most momentous decisions made by a human being. Others may be deflected from a desired vocational goal by cultural and economic limitations or by organic handicaps. Still others may be diverted because the choice is made too late. This is especially true of medicine, where the prerequisites and preparation are so extensive that the goal usually cannot be reached unless one gets a reasonably early start. This was painfully illustrated in the life of Morton F. Thompson, whose popular novel, *Not as a Stranger,* depicts the life and development of a physician. Thompson himself always longed to study medicine.

Consideration of a number of vocational options is a part of normal growth, and a final choice represents a series of decisions made over a period of years. First, there is a period of *fantasy choices* common in childhood, followed by a period of *tentative choices* between ages 11 and 17. Last comes the period of *realistic choices,* when a definitive selection is made.[18]

Since the definitive career choice is usually made during adolescence or early adulthood, two beliefs of persons in this age group deserve emphasis: the belief that they have the potential for doing everything and the belief that their life span is unlimited. Thus, adolescents' omnipotentiality, as Pumpian-Mindlin describes it, may lead them to believe that they have the talents to master any vocation.[40] As they mature, they begin to assess realistically their resources for attaining a particular vocational goal. At the point that they surrender their feeling that there is no limit to their ability or life span, they are ready for a firm decision. Their recognition of the fact that they will not live forever forces them to think seriously and immediately about how they are going to spend their life and the meaning of that life. They have to wrestle with questions about the purpose of their existence and what will bring them the highest fulfillment.

As already implied, the reasons for choosing a particular vocation are complex. A thorough explanation would require an intensive analysis of each person's life history to identify the positive forces behind one's choice as well as why each potential choice was not selected. Usually, one looks within to understand one's motives, but this approach is not the whole picture, for, as Karl Mannheim points out, motives and actions often originate from the situation in which a person finds himself or herself.[16] Any genuine commitment is accompanied by some anxiety and guilt, in part because of the rejection of other alternatives. These alternatives rise occasionally in the mind to question the commitment.

Today, a wide array of vocational opportunities is available. A century ago, talented young persons who wished to undertake a profession had only three choices: theology, law, and medicine. During the decades immediately following the Civil War, 28 percent of all college graduates went into medicine. In that era, the president of Johns Hopkins University, Daniel Coit Gilman, observed that the medical student was likely to be "the son of the family too weak to labour on the farm, too indolent to do any exercise, too stupid for the law, and too immoral for the pulpit."[30]

As persons apply to medical school, their understanding of their motivation for studying medicine influences their acceptance and indicates in part the chances of future success in medicine. They may identify in themselves a number of motives, many of which are held in common with others. A person's motivation is seen in better perspective if it is projected upon a broad pattern of motivational factors. These factors can be grouped into three categories: (1) motives stemming from inner needs; (2) motives stemming from vocational appeal; and (3) motives stemming from conceived purposes.

Motives Stemming from Inner Needs

Relationships with Parents.   Positive or negative relationships with parents may play a decisive role in a person's choice of a career in medicine. Sometimes an identification with a parent may be based on the desire to surpass him or her and at other times on the wish to follow, help, and emulate. A person may become a doctor not because the parent was one, but because the parent wanted the son or daughter to be one. Others seem to become physicians through a strong wish to please the mother (who may or may not have married a doctor) or from a strong identification with the mother as the healing, restoring, comforting member of the family.[53]

The aspirations of a domineering mother may influence her son's or daughter's career choice, especially when her ambitions for her children are fanned by her disappointments with a husband who' never lived up to her expectations. Such was the life situation of the mother of Sir Arthur Conan Doyle. Her son not only became a physician but a great writer, creating the character of Sherlock Holmes.[12]

When asked about the evolution of their interest in the study of medicine, many students mention that they have a parent or sibling in medicine and have therefore had considerable exposure to what a career in medicine is all about.[4] For some it seems natural to follow in the footsteps of a parent. Some do so without any conscious awareness of it. A pathologist stated to me that at age 18 the feeling suddenly overwhelmed him that medicine was the vocation for him. He had given no serious thought previously to what he wanted to do with his life. On questioning him about any significant event preceding this decision, he mentioned that his father had died 10 days before. His father was a physician specializing in pathology. Here one sees an important psychodynamic factor: a transfer of authority and power from the dead father to the son.

The question is often asked if students from medical families do better in medical school than those from nonmedical families. In medical school, academic and clinical performance are equivalent for the two groups.[20] Further, about 16 percent of students entering United States medical schools can be expected to come from families in which the mother or father is a physician.

Occasionally one sees an applicant, descended from a long line of doctors, who feels that this family heritage is the only credential needed to gain admission to medical school. Such was the case with a poorly qualified and intellectually limited student who was aghast that he should be rejected by all the medical schools to which he applied. His father stated in a letter that the rejection of his son was an outgrowth of medicine's present tarnished image. He further noted that we had admitted into medical school people who were not descendants of the sons of Aesculapius, and they had created many problems for the profession and society.* Fortunately, this doctor's view is not widely held or followed, for it would deplete medicine of its vitality.

Some students attribute to the physician parent a forceful strategy in attracting them to medicine. Karl L. Schleich, who introduced infiltration anesthesia in 1894, reveals in his autobiography how powerful an influence a domineering physician father can have on his children: "I was entirely under the spell of my honored and venerated father—a compulsion from which I could never free myself as long as I lived. . . . Medicine to me, was the inevitable tribute of love."[44]

Two prominent psychiatrists have written lucidly about the influence of their fathers upon their choice of a vocation. Franz Alexander's father was an academician and one of the intellectual leaders of Hungary. Although Franz Alexander was deeply attached to his father, he states that probably his adolescent groping for self-assertion and independence contributed a great deal to turning his interest toward a scientific career and away from philosophy and the humanistic disciplines represented by his father: "My choice served also as a rebellion against the overwhelming influence of my father, a representative of the humanistic tradition, which prevailed during the formative years of my life."[1] Leo Alexander enjoyed the same kind of strong, positive relation-

---

* The doctor wrote: "The degeneration of the doctor image in the public eye is due in part, I am sure, to the loss of family tradition in medicine. There is something of the art of medicine that can only be transmitted through generations of families in medicine."

ship with his father as did Franz Alexander. His identification rather than rebellion led him to medicine: "It is probable, therefore, that one of my strongest, unconscious motives for becoming a physician was a strong bond of identification with my (physician) father which I am sure in the long run tipped the scales of my occupational choice in medicine's favor, although there were strong competing interests which rather harmoniously blended into the pattern of the medical and scientific activity that came to be my individual life work."[2]

To Control an Excessive Fear of Death. A reason for the choice of medicine as a career may be the control of one's own excessive fear of death. By becoming a physician, the person secures himself or herself against the jeopardy of death and obtains dominion over his or her own anxiety by having the power to cure. This aspect of motivation has been studied thoroughly by Feifel.[15] A recent applicant to medical school included in his application this statement, which clearly sets forth his personal concerns about death.

> In the face of man's one great flaw, all occupations fade to insignificance, save that of the healer. For man's great flaw is death. Only the healer can confront death with his tools and knowledge and prolong or save the most precious entity, life. Only the healer can return to a sick body the physical equilibrium so necessary for the spiritual peace demanded for that soul's ultimate confrontation with his own flaw. I intend to achieve my own spiritual tranquility through the satisfaction of restoring to others this necessary physical unity.

Thus, an exaggerated fear of death in certain persons is a relevant variable in the choice of a medical career. In their training, these physicians secure prominent mastery over disease, to help control personal concerns about death. Their fear is translated into a fight against death. They seek to win many victories over death not only for their patients but in relationship to themselves. This motivational factor may have a harmful side effect on certain patients. In those instances where the physicians' professional narcissism comes under attack— particularly in encounter with the fatally ill—their reawakened anxieties about death may lead them unwittingly to disinherit their patients psychologically at the very time they increase attention to their patients' physiological needs.

Need to Rescue. While the need to rescue is not unique to the medical profession, the opportunity for its expression is great indeed in medicine. For many in medicine, the highest mission in life is rescue. Related to the rescue fantasy is the need to have and maintain power over others. Power does things to its possessor such as preventing self-examination. Such persons not only become convinced that they are using power in the best possible manner, but they inevitably come to the conclusion, like kings of old, that God gave it to them.[47] This combination of self-justification and conviction of divine appointment may lead to blindness and, at times, tyranny in relationships with patients and family, as well as with others.

Need to Be Needed.   The need to be needed is a multifaceted component of motivation with many of the facets emerging in a camouflaged fashion. This need may present itself as a liking for people. Actually, a liking for people may serve as a disguise for the physician's need to be liked. When this is an anxiety-driven need, it often complicates the helping process. Closely akin to the physician's need to be liked is the need to be admired—admired for knowledge and skill in helping the helpless.

The need to be liked may also be a component of the need to be emotionally dependent upon others, including one's patients. This is a reverse type of dependency, for on the surface the physician's dependency is not evident. Yet, when the sick, the lame, and the blind are gathered around the physician, the physician is not likely to be abandoned by this helpless group.

Motivation to enter medicine can be viewed through subsequent development of emotional problems and illness in physicians. Illness may be the result of a particular motivational factor that led the physician into medicine and into a particular type of medical practice. In studies of physicians with problems of alcoholism or drug addiction, psychological dependency needs emerge as one of the factors which tripped these physicians.[13, 35, 39]

The image of the physician is one of independence and strength. At times of illness and tragedy, the physician is expected to move confidently and swiftly and to render the necessary care while remaining unmoved emotionally. The success of this pose is seen in the not infrequent criticism of physicians as being cold and without feeling. In the eyes of the public, the physician is a tower of independence, giving strength and support to those in need of help. This is also the image the physician wants to convey.

Medicine is hard work, but it is harder work for those who use the profession vicariously to give solace to others when they desperately need the solace for themselves. Doctors need to be needed, but such a need is more taxing if it is an adaptation to earlier deprivation.

The physician shares with others certain dependency yearnings, although the idyllic picture of the independent physician says nothing of these dependency needs. For most persons, the adjustment from dependency to independence is adequate, and they find resources in the environment for fulfilling certain dependency needs. As physicians are not expected to have dependency needs, many appropriate areas in the environment are closed to them. Thus, alcohol or drugs are sometimes used as a temporary solution or a crutch on which to hang some of their personal and private needs.[7]

A most satisfying aspect of medical practice is the fact that the physician is "needed." The sense of feeling needed by someone is at the core of every person's sense of worth, for it gives meaning to one's life. It may have its origin in a number of unconscious drives and become an important force in molding one's personality and determining the quality of one's interpersonal relationships. The mind usually equates being needed with being loved, for love, in part, is a form of interdependency. An attempt at nurturing one's self-esteem is to seek society's approval through prestige and position. One way of accomplishing this is through becoming a physician.

When such a motive is uppermost in persons who choose medicine, they will seek to be important and needed by the people they serve. If they attempt to meet all of their patients' demands and are unable to say "no" to them, they soon become overwhelmed by their work. When they begin to fail their patients, they react with frustration and depression and experience an awakening of the old feelings of inadequacy.[17]

Need to Be Creative.   Many students with creative capacities enter medicine. These students feel the need to be more of an artist than a practitioner. Often the pressure of medical school courses and clinical training tends to suppress creativity in the student. A redeeming feature of medical training is exposure to the magnificence of nature as it is displayed in the form and function of the human body.

There are incalculable opportunities for thoughtful, curious, and determined physicians to make an original contribution to their profession. The opportunity exists in medicine to use one's mind as well as heart in an artistic combination that leads to creative effort. The significance of even a small contribution is emphasized by Aristotle, a physician's son who practiced medicine early in his career: "The search for Truth is in one way hard and in another easy. For it is evident that no one can master it fully nor miss it wholly. But each adds a little to our knowledge of Nature, and from all the facts assembled there arises a certain grandeur."[28]

William Carlos Williams, a practicing pediatrician and one of the most important American poets of this century, has written: "I am grateful at least that I studied medicine ... that I might know what goes on in myself as well as others. ... The real thing is the excitement of the chase, the opportunity for exercise of precise talents. ... Discovery is the great goal."[52]

Triad of Intellectual Curiosity, Professional Pride, and Ambition. G.H. Hardy, the late and gifted English mathematician, identified what he believed to be the three basic motives of the professional life:

> The first (without which the rest must come to nothing) is intellectual curiosity, desire to know the truth. Then, professional pride, anxiety to be satisfied with one's performance, the shame that overcomes any self-respecting craftsman when his work is unworthy of his talent. Finally, ambition, desire for reputation, and the position, even the power of money, which it brings. It may be fine to feel, when you have done your work, that you have added to the happiness or alleviated the sufferings of others, but that will not be why you did it. So if a [person] ... were to tell me that the driving force in his work had been the desire to benefit humanity, then I should not believe him (nor should I think the better of him if I did). His dominant motives have been those which I have stated, and in which, surely, there is nothing of which any decent man need be ashamed of.[23]

Hippocrates, the father of medicine, deserves our highest acclaim for being the first to subordinate the priestly aspects of the physician's profession to intellectual and technical skills. He urged the use of inductive reasoning in place of tradition and superstition, made astute clinical observations, carefully recorded case histories, and argued that the physician, rather than the gods, has the responsibility to interpose treatments in order to influence the course of disease. Medical practice abounds in difficult and thought-provoking problems. The person who has no interest in probing the intellectually provocative problems presented by sick patients would make a poor physician indeed.

The Sherlock Holmes dimension of medicine—the art and science of diagnosis—is the greatest challenge in medical practice for certain physicians. Diagnosis is a technique requiring the fullest use of doctors' hands, senses, mind, and intuition. Treatment is so standardized in medicine that diagnosis may call forth much more of doctors' problem-solving skills. They may see themselves as the "Magnificent Diagnostician."

Kampmeier comments that in many years of interviewing applicants for Vanderbilt University School of Medicine, he searched for the attributes of the scholar—curiosity, perseverance, initiative, originality, and integrity. In such a person, the capacity for problem-solving resides.[26] Among those attributes, curiosity is the most easily identified and becomes something of an index to the potential of an applicant to develop into a competent medical practitioner or a productive investigator who pushes forward the frontiers of medical science. Indeed, pleasure in solving problems that provide intellectual curiosity is a basic motive in the good doctor.

Physicians take pride in solving difficult problems with skill and style. When they use intuition and wisdom to solve diagnostic and therapeutic problems, they are satisfied with their performance and avoid the shame that overcomes one when work is unworthy of one's talent. Good physicians are not without their professional pride.

C.L. Sulzberger reports on an interview with General Charles De Gaulle during which he asked De Gaulle if he agreed with Stalin's view that the principal force motivating people is fear. Without hesitation De Gaulle replied: "One must draw a distinction between the individual and the collective masses. For the individual, it is ambition and a taste for adventure. I think the real motivation, the primordial motivating force for the individual is ambition; but for the masses it is fear."[50]

Quest for Security.   Many applicants speak of the economic security offered by a medical career. Reality dictates that one provide for self and family. Beyond its normal uses, money may become a screen behind which many emotionally and neurotically determined motives operate. Thus, choosing a medical career in order to make lots of money is seeing at best only part of one's motivation. The quest goes beyond money to many other things which money represents in our society, such as power, respect, emotional security, and self-esteem.[41] The quest then moves one into competitive struggles where financial success becomes a form of self-validation.

For some physicians, the desire for economic security or the need to escape the drudgery of manual labor may represent less complicated money motives than those previously mentioned. Some are attracted to medicine because it frees them from the struggles of the business world. Doctors are certain of a good income if they work at all. Similarly qualified persons could be in business, working quite hard, and doing poorly financially. There was no doubt in the mind of Franklin Martin, distinguished surgeon and founder of the American College of Surgeons, that a vision of comfort and the determination to escape the drudgery of manual labor were the factors that led suddenly to his decision to study medicine. On a hot day in early August he was binding freshly cut oats in a large, open field. Almost suffocating from heat, he straightened up to wipe the perspiration from his face. When he looked up, he viewed in the distance a scene which he has described as a vision from paradise:

> Driving leisurely along the road in the shade of the maples was Dr. Daniel McLaren Miller, then the famous family physician of Oconomowoc. He was dressed in white linen, his buggy had a white canvas top and open sides, and the horse was protected by a white fly net that extended over its whole body, even to its ears. Before my eyes was a picture that brought joy to my soul and envy to my mind. Instantaneously I dropped my rake and gazed until the apparition leisurely passed out of sight around the bend in the road. Yes, I will be a doctor. Why haven't I thought of it before?
>
> My work became automatic, for my mind was a maelstrom of plans and methods. The heat was no longer troublesome and by the call to supper my course of action had been fully determined upon.[32]

Preference for Certain Adaptive Techniques. Keniston emphasizes that medical students may be distinguished by a preference for certain adaptive techniques, styles, and defenses.[27] Of the many ways of adapting to stress and anxiety, three are prominent. First, medical students react to anxiety-provoking situations by vigorous efforts to master, overcome, or counteract them instead of trying to live with them or escape them. Second, they are oriented primarily toward changing their environment rather than themselves. Finally, medical students, like many other students with developed scientific ability, generally possess a considerable capacity to translate feelings into ideas, to manipulate these ideas, and at times to forget the feelings that originally underlay them. Thus, in the face of personal anxiety or a stressful situation, medical students are less likely to be interested in or aware of their own feelings than to be preoccupied with understanding intellectually what is happening, planning a rational course of action, or studying the theoretical implications of the problem.

Stated technically, medical students' adaptive style tends to be counterphobic and obsessive-compulsive. A number of studies agree on finding distinctive use of obsessive-compulsive defenses among medical students.[14, 36, 43] For most medical students, these techniques remain adaptive, but any discussion of the emotional problems of medical students will include situations where they become maladaptive.

Motives Stemming from Vocational Appeal

Great Models. The family physician is often seen by the child as a great hero and one he or she would like to emulate. When the actual person is not available, good biography and autobiography are valuable substitutes. Children, as well as most adults, are hero worshippers and hero emulators, and reading about those who have accomplished great things can provide motivating sparks of incomparable potency. Thomas Carlyle has said: "Biography is by nature the most universally profitable and universally pleasant of all things; especially biography of distinguished individuals."[6]

Many students speak of the influence of the family doctor in their choice of a medical career. They, or a member of their family, were sick, and in some profound or dramatic way this illness was relieved by the ministrations of the family physician, who came like a great healing god. Illustrative of this was a student's encounter with a chronic infection during childhood. On recovering, he concluded that his parents' power was limited, but that the power and magic of the physician were not. At this point in his life, he made a firm decision to study medicine.

To the child, the doctor embodies all of the magical, omnipotent, and mystical qualities that awe the child. The child's impression of what the doctor does, the unlimited powers as the bearer of life and death, the involvement with the mysteries of sex, babies, operations, and blood combine in fortuitous circumstances to make a profound imprint on the child. The doctor comes to serve as an ego ideal of the child and may remain so always.

Simmel has done studies of children playing at being doctors. He states that the "doctor game" is frequently combined with the game of "father and mother," the role of sufferer being allotted to a doll that represents children in general. Simmel goes on to say:

> From the child's point of view, a doctor is permitted actively to employ all the mechanisms of pleasure which are forbidden to the child. The physician pays no heed to clothing and does not feel shame. He is allowed to hear and see everything and to busy himself unpunished with urine and feces. He knows all the mysteries of the difference between the sexes and how children come, and he exercises a kind of omnipotence over the body of the patient.[49]

The family doctor, as wise counselor and friend, is occasionally asked for advice concerning a young person's choice of a career. Such a practice at times produces another recruit for medicine. Wilfred T. Grenfell mentions that his family physician, in describing the attractions of medical science, had only to show the young Grenfell a pickled brain to stimulate in him a sharp desire to study medicine.[21]

Others, through a job experience or a personal friendship, have become acquainted with a particular physician who served as a model for their lives. De Vighne attributes his inspiration for the study of medicine to a year he spent with a Dr. Moffett. During this time De Vighne also read widely the lives and philosophical comments of the old medical masters, in which "the essence of medicine stood out more clearly than its substance." He resurrects his youthful thoughts:

> To carry in a little black bag the magic potion of life or death, comfort or pain, hope, confidence, and well-being was a tremendous responsibility. To have my presence a welcome blessing in the innermost sanctuaries; to be a repository of inviolate trusts when fear, anxiety, and, perhaps, penitence force the doors of seclusion and reserve, was a rare privilege . . . what I wanted above all else was to be wanted.[10]

Medicine has had its share of great adventurers. One great adventurer, Dr. Gordon S. Seagrave, made his decision to study medicine at age 5, after meeting a "big chap" who fascinated him:

> Rangoon, 1902—I was about five years old. A great hulking Irishman stamped up the steps to the huge verandah of the house my great-grandfather had built to live in when, after the second Burmese War, the British took over all of Lower Burma as far north as Toungoo. It was a huge house, but it shook under the Irishman's footsteps. I came out to explore. The Irishman apparently loved children. He sat me on his lap and told me stories of wild jungles and great deeds: about service in the Royal Irish Constabulary as a young man; about his later adventures in Canada in the Royal Northwest Mounted Police; about stray rifle bullets that whizzed past him as he sat in his bungalow in the Shan States and that bored through the side of his bookcase; about the day his horse ran around the corner of a jungle path and almost plunged into a wild elephant, bucked and threw him to the ground; about walking 60 miles with both bones of his arm broken to find the nearest doctor. Then he grasped the top of a heavy dining-room chair in his teeth and swung it over his head. I was fascinated! I tried it out on my tiny nursery chair, but it didn't work; my teeth couldn't have been much better then than they are now. Then he asked me for a glass of water to quench his thirst, and drank it down—standing on his head. I was completely overwhelmed!

After he had gone I asked my mother who the big chap was. "He is Doctor Robert Harper, a medical missionary at Namkham on the border between the Northern Shan States and China." That made it still more romantic. "When I grow up I'm going to be a medical missionary in the Shan States," I declared.[46]

Image of the Physician.   Great drama and romance surround physicians, and stories related to their work possess lasting public appeal. Their automatic acceptance wherever they go and the privileges permitted them without question are impressive indeed. An aura of mystery surrounds their skills and experiences, and they are believed to be able to save lives and perform miracles. In spite of criticisms and disenchantment with many areas of medicine, doctors continue to enjoy tremendous esteem and respect for having endured so much hard work and suffering to qualify as a physician and for having assumed the responsibilities thrust upon them by the practice of medicine.

A Challenging and Versatile Vocation.   In comparing medicine with other vocations, I believe that there are fewer people in medicine who are bored or dissatisfied than in any other profession. Endless opportunities exist in medicine for a wide variety of careers, and a doctor is eligible for a multitude of jobs.

Medicine offers the individual on one hand the opportunity to function as the pure scientist widening the periphery of our knowledge and on the other to function as the family physician dispensing healing and comfort. The remarkable quality of the profession lies in the fact that one is not forced to confine oneself to either end of the spectrum. Many students entering the study of medicine are aware of this and are attracted by the many options. They are especially challenged by the opportunity for fulfillment of two of the most exciting human potentials: (1) the gratification of curiosity, that is, the urge to know and to understand the phenomena of nature and (2) the desire to be of service to humankind. Sigmund Freud himself fitted well this category. He stated that his attraction to the study of medicine came from a need to understand something of the riddles of the world in which we live and perhaps even to contribute something to their solution.[29] Harvey Cushing has summarized well the broad base of suitability for a medical career: "There is, in reality, little to be said, other than that medicine has become so many-sided that anyone with a good head, a good heart, or skillful hands, who is possessed of a spirit of service, who is not afraid of hard work, and who will be satisfied with a modest income, will find ample opportunity for happiness and for the exercise of his talents."[9]

Most students attracted to medicine have a strong interest in the sciences as these are related to human life. The famous medical historian Henry E. Sigerist could not bear to specialize in a small facet of science like chemistry or zoology and consequently chose the study of medicine, which he believed would provide him with the broadest view of science and human life.[48] I suspect most medical students today share Sigerist's view.

Job Freedom.   A decisive value that future medical students share is that of job freedom. Crites, who correlated occupational values with Strong Vocational Interest Blank (SVIB) scales for undergraduate students, found that the student who showed great interest in becoming a physician also manifested great desire for job freedom.[8] Crites concluded that the reason for wanting to become a physician is preference for a job that permits considerable self-direction in a relatively unstructured situation.

The American physician in private practice is an astonishingly free agent. Dr. Martin Cherkasky of New York has described the physician's job freedom in this manner: "In his characteristic fee-for-service solo-practice situation, he is the least supervised of any professional group."[22] Many physicians believe that the freedom they seek and expect in their practice is intimately tied by mystique to medical quality—to quality of health care.

Motives Stemming from Conceived Purposes

Need for a Caring Relationship.   Students attracted to medicine are frequently persons with a long-standing need for, enjoyment of, and capacity to tolerate being in a caring, providing, dispensing, nurturing relationship to other people. They may have gotten much practice of this role during their childhood and adolescence in their own family.* Also, such persons often possess a highly developed capacity to identify with those for whom they care. A secretary who worked for many years in a medical setting once remarked to me that it is easy to tell a doctor from a facsimile. She went on to say that the facsimile may be just as skilled and competent as the genuine product but that the feeling and caring that permeate every word and action of the genuine product set him or her sharply apart from the facsimile.

---

* Psychiatrist Jerry Lewis, one of the nation's leading family therapists, emphasizes that health professionals may not necessarily come from healthy families. He states the view: "The role of the therapist comes early in the dysfunctional family."[31]

A healthy determinant for the practice of medicine is identification with the sick. This identification develops, or at least is enhanced, because every doctor has had the experience of being a patient. The patient, seeing the medical student or doctor as a worker of miracles, is seeing him or her unconsciously in the role of a parent. A disturbance in professional efficiency may result if the medical student or doctor accepts the role, unaware of his or her identification with a parent and his or her own wish to create new life. This wish is symbolized by the caduceus, the bisexual snake, which connotes rebirth after death in sickness.[19]

Involvement with Human Suffering. Intimate personal contact with physical or psychological suffering, in themselves or others, seems to have disposed certain students toward a vocation in which their lives will be devoted to combat suffering.

It appears that these medical students share with Bertrand Russell what he describes as unbearable pity for the suffering of humankind:

> Love and knowledge, so far as they were possible, led [me] upward toward the heavens. But always pity brought me back to earth. Echoes of cries of pain reverberate in my heart. Children in famine, victims tortured by oppressors, helpless old people, a hated burden to their sons, and the whole world of loneliness, poverty, and pain make a mockery of what human life should be. I long to alleviate the evil, but I cannot, and I too suffer.[42]

To Fight Wasteful Death. It is not uncommon for a student to decide to become a doctor after the death of a family member or close friend, sometimes with the conscious desire to learn how to fight wasteful death.[3]

One of this country's most distinguished women physicians, the late Dr. Alfreda Washington, made her commitment to fight wasteful death when she lost her brother from tuberculosis. At the suggestion of Dr. Edward L. Trudeau, she had gone with her brother to live in the Adirondacks in the hope of helping him find health in this beautiful outdoor setting. She writes that on a strange yellow day in September, 1881, she followed a crude country wagon moving slowly out from the Adirondack woods, over the long rough road homeward—its burden her brother's body. These are her moving words:

> I felt completely adrift, my whole plan of life in sudden and overwhelming chaos. The thought kept recurring; if I had known more of illness and the means of combating it, I might have been able to

do more for him. Out of these emotions came the decision which
set the course of my life. I would become a doctor.[51]

An applicant told the poignant story of having lost both of his parents while he was in his teens. His mother died of a viral infection of
four days' duration when he was fifteen. Her doctor did not take her
illness seriously, and she died with little help from him. A year later,
the applicant's father died suddenly of a heart attack. The applicant
spoke of how often he wondered what he could have done to help prevent these untimely deaths. Although his interest in science had been
strong and enduring, a sustained emotional component in his motivation had been related to his parents' deaths and had pulled him like a
magnet to a career in medicine.

Vocatio Dei.   Seldom do persons today perceive their vocation as a
divine calling. In fact, so rarely is the concept expressed by a physician
or medical student that one is taken aback on hearing it. Stephen
Paget, surgeon and youngest son of the illustrious Sir James Paget,
writes that many doctors would be astonished to learn that they had
been called to be doctors, but that such may well be the case:

> There are times when they say, what call had I to be a doctor? I
> should have done better for myself and my wife and the children
> in some other calling. But they stick to it, and that not only from
> necessity, but from pride, honour, conviction; and heaven, sooner
> or later, lets them know what it thinks of them. The information
> comes quite as a surprise to them, being the first received, from
> any source, that they were indeed called to be doctors; and they
> hesitate to give the name of divine vocation to work paid by the
> job. Calls, they imagine, should master men, beating down on
> them. Surely, a diploma, obtained by hard examination and hard
> cash, and signed and sealed by earthly examiners, cannot be a
> summons from heaven. But it may be. For, if a doctor's life may
> not be a divine vocation, then no life is a vocation, and nothing is
> divine.[38]

Ideals and spiritual values form the foundation of the vocation of
medicine. The physician has a mission or calling with a core that tends
toward the sacred, that even may be sacred. It is the misfortune of our
medical profession that this very core may have been lost in the mate-
rialism of our era. It is believed by some that many of the students entering medicine today, because of their social consciousness, may help

the profession recapture much of what is implied in the concept of vocatio Dei.

In the Service of Love. About one-third of the applicants to medical school whom I have interviewed through the years mentioned altruism as a part of their motivation for wanting to enter the medical profession, although often they apologized for introducing a motive that seems suspect. In general, they are sincere but occasionally one of them stumbles over his or her rhetoric, as did the following student whose claim of altruism was false.

Once Dr. Charles Sprague and I were talking with an attractive, but not overly bright, young man whose family and friends were exerting considerable pressure for his acceptance to medical school. He spoke of his deep commitment to the service of humankind and how the medical profession would give him the opportunity to minister sacrificially to the sick and poor without thought of personal return. Later in our interview, we asked him what line of work he would enter if he were not successful in being admitted to a medical school. He replied without hesitation: "I would become a partner in my father's construction business which would give me a highly paid career and all the good things of life." Shakespeare has warned us: "All that glitters is not gold."

Sometimes when persons attribute their choice of medicine to altruistic motives, a more searching scrutiny reveals the presence of certain qualifications to their noble-minded idealism. An example is the following portion of a letter written in 1841 by James Hinton, shortly before this eminent English surgeon became a medical student: "I feel sometimes a deeper desire than I can express to be in some way or other the benefactor of my species, and yet I cannot help suspecting that pride and ambition have far more to do with that desire than philanthropy. I do not find in myself the same willingness to be useful in a way of unnoticed—perhaps despised—toil as I do in ones that should procure me respect and esteem and be gratifying to vanity."[24]

Altruism is devotion to the welfare of others, regard for others as a principle of action. It is the direct opposite of egoism or selfishness in which interest in one's own welfare to the exclusion of others remains the guiding principle of action. Applicants who mention altruism believe that they will find meaning and fulfillment in a service-oriented vocation.

Possibly our cynicism has led us to sell human nature short. The research of psychologists such as Abraham Maslow has shown that the person's higher nature includes the need for meaningful work, for responsibility, for creativeness, for being fair and just. To think of pay in terms of money alone is clearly obsolete in such a framework. Maslow states that lower need gratifications can be bought with money, but when these are already fulfilled, then people are motivated only by higher kinds of "pay"—belongingness, affection, dignity, appreciation, honor coupled with the opportunity for self-actualization, and the fostering of values such as truth, beauty, excellence, and justice.[33]

One of history's great examples of altruistic love, expressed through medicine, is the life and work of Albert Schweitzer. At the age of 30, already a renowned theologian and interpreter of the organ works of Bach, Schweitzer gave up these pursuits to study medicine at Strasbourg and to go later to equatorial Africa as a doctor. When Schweitzer was about 21, he had weighed in his mind the fortunate circumstances and happiness that had always been his and made the decision to pursue his personal interests in theology and music until he was 30 and after that to devote himself to the direct service of humankind. Nine years later he came across an article entitled "The Needs of the Congo Mission" in a magazine of the Paris Missionary Society. The author of the article expressed the hope that his appeal would bring some of those "on whom the Master's eyes already rested" to a decision to offer themselves for this urgent work among the natives in the Congo. Schweitzer states in a matter-of-fact manner: "Having finished the article, I quietly began my work. My search was over. . . . To become one day the doctor whom these poor creatures needed, it was worthwhile, so I judged, to become a medical student. Whenever I was inclined to feel that the years I should have to sacrifice were too long, I reminded myself that Hamilcar and Hannibal had prepared for their march on Rome by their slow and tedious conquest of Spain."[45]

Social Reformer Dynamics.   Some students are attracted to medicine because it can be a vehicle for social reform. The primary goal is the pursuit of humanitarian objectives and not the acquisition of medical knowledge and technique. They may have little interest in caring for individual patients. It can usually be said that these students are more interested in programs than patients, more interested in the healing of society than the healing of the individual.

I have interviewed a number of applicants who were seeking medicine as a means toward a particular end, namely, the reform or reordering of society in some way. Many had rather global and sometimes vague ideas of how they planned to use a career in medicine for "the healing of the nations." Hard, disciplined work such as that of the medical missionary seemed out of the question. They saw themselves as Moses standing with outstretched arms atop Mt. Sinai. They had no intention of coming down into the valley to do the hard, messy work associated with the care of the sick and wounded.

Some of these individuals possess intense anger. They vent their anger in their reform activity. In the care of individual patients this level of anger would be a serious handicap to the intimate care, concern, and patience needed to participate in the recovery of the patient.

Other students in the social reformer category actually show characteristics which limit their ability to relate warmly and in depth to people. They appear to love humanity in a general sense but continous care and commitment to an individual patient over a long period of time would be intolerable. The nature of such a problem is alluded to by Dostoyevsky in *The Brothers Karamazov*:

> That's exactly the same sort of thing a doctor told me a long time ago. . . . He was an elderly and undoubtedly clever man. He spoke to me as frankly as you, though in jest, but in mournful jest. "I love humanity," he said, "but I can't help being surprised at myself; the more I love humanity in general, the less I love men in particular, I mean separately, as separate individuals. In my dreams I am very often passionately determined to serve humanity and I might quite likely have sacrificed my life for my fellow-creatures, if for some reason it had been suddenly demanded of me, and yet I'm quite incapable of living with anyone in one room for two days together, and I know that from experience. As soon as anyone comes close to me, his personality begins to oppress my vanity and restrict my freedom. I'm capable of hating the best man in twenty-four hours; one because he sits too long over his dinner, another because he has a cold in the head and keeps on blowing his nose. I become an enemy of people the moment they come close to me. But, on the other hand, it invariably happened that the more I hated men individually, the more ardent became my love for humanity."[11]

What Dostoyevsky says in this passage implies or emphasizes a negative connotation in social reformer dynamics, as related to the motivation for the study of medicine. A genuine social consciousness is seen in many students. These students are concerned with the poor and sick who live in the ghetto, the inner city, and isolated rural areas.[37] They see the study and practice of medicine not as an end in itself but as a means to express their humanitarian ethic. Because they focus on the social, cultural, and economic facets of medical care, they may be accused of being uninterested in medicine or of exploiting medical issues for political purposes. Such students see no difference between treating the sick and organizing a campaign in the community to change anything considered objectionable or to bring about something desirable.

The value of medicine is seen by those students as instrumental, not institutional.*

CONCLUSION

Students are motivated by conscious and unconscious factors working in association. Motives for entering the field of medicine, as well as adaptations necessary in the transitional period before graduation, are influenced by the personal development and past experiences of the student. Highly respected motives such as noble ideals and service to humanity are only a segment of the influences that may lead the student into medicine.

The problem of determining which unconscious personality factors promote the development of an effective physician and which interfere with competent medical practice is a difficult one. The way particular factors are handled by the conscious and unconscious mind of the student may make the difference. For example, the student whose unconscious motivation is to save the life of a sick parent or to bring a deceased parent back to life may function differently as a physician from the student whose unconscious motivation is atonement by reaction formation for death wishes against a sick or deceased sibling. Thus, there are alternatives in the psychological handling of even the same motivation.

Ernest Jones discusses the difference between displacement and sublimation as methods of handling such unconscious motivating factors. He emphasizes that in sublimation the new activity absorbs the interest of the person, wheras in displacement the new activity merely symbolically represents the unconscious wished-for activity.[25] In other words, a student who is motivated by unconscious wishes to save the life of the sick parent may sublimate this into interest in saving the lives of others, and yet will be able to tolerate the reality that some patients will die despite all efforts. However, if the wish is only displaced, the loss of a patient will unconsciously represent the feared death of the loved parent, and intense psychological reactions may interfere with the ability to practice medicine.

The illustration above serves to show the extreme complexities encountered in understanding the motivating influences determining the wish to study medicine. Such factors, although difficult to take into consideration, are extremely important in the selection of students for

---

* By studying similar students already in medical school, one may be able to see in better perspective the dynamics operating in bringing such students to medical school.[34]

medicine and in the subsequent processes of adaptation through which students will go during their medical career.

REFERENCES

1. Alexander F: Why I became a doctor. In Fabricant ND (ed): Why We Became Doctors. New York, Grune & Stratton, 1954, pp 54–58
2. Alexander L: Why I became a doctor and why I became the sort of doctor I am. In Fabricant ND (ed): Why We Became Doctors. New York, Grune & Stratton, 1954, pp 75–79
3. Ashford BK: A Soldier in Science. New York, Morrow, 1934
4. Bruhn JG, et al.: A Doctor in the House. Galveston, Texas, University of Texas Medical Branch, 1978
5. Carlyle T: Past and Present, Book III, Chapter II. New York, Dutton, 1960
6. Carlyle T: Sartor Resartus. New York, Crowell, 1838, p 80
7. Coste D: The risky business of becoming a doctor. New Physician 27:29, 1978
8. Crites JO: Vocational interest in relation to vocational motivation. J Educ Psychol 54:277, 1963
9. Cushing H: The Medical Career. Hanover, Dartmouth College, 1929
10. De Vighne HC: The Time of My Life. Philadelphia, Lippincott, 1942
11. Dostoyevsky FM: The Brothers Karamazov. Translated by Magarshack D. Baltimore, Penguin Books, 1958
12. Doyle AC: Memories and Adventures. Boston, Little, Brown, 1924, p 17
13. Duffy JC, Litin EM: The Emotional Health of Physicians. Springfield, Ill, Charles C Thomas, Publisher, 1967
14. Eron L: Effects of medical education on medical students' attitudes. J Med Educ 30:559, 1955
15. Feifel H: Physicians consider death. Proceedings, 75th Annual Convention, APA, 1967, pp 201–202
16. Friedson E: Profession of Medicine. New York, Dodd, Mead, 1970, p 85
17. Garell DC: Some reflections on physicians' well-being. New Physician 27:32, 1978
18. Ginzberg E, et al.: Occupational Choice: An Approach to a General Theory. New York, Columbia University Press, 1951
19. Glauber OP: A deterrent in the study and practice of medicine. Psychoanal Q 22:381, 1953
20. Gough HG, Hall WB: A comparison of medical students from medical and nonmedical families. J Med Educ 52:541, 1977
21. Grenfell WT: A Labrador Doctor. Boston, Houghton Mifflin, 1919, pp 37–38
22. Gross ML: The Doctors. New York, Random House, 1966, p 19
23. Hardy GH: A Mathematician's Apology. London, Cambridge University Press, 1940, p 19
24. Hopkins E (ed): Life and Letters of James Hinton. London, Kegan Paul, 1878, pp 10–11
25. Jones E: Papers on Psychoanalysis. Baltimore, Williams and Wilkins, 1950

26. Kampmeier R: The past—guidepost, not hitching post. South Med J 58:31, 1970
27. Keniston K: The medical student. Yale J Biol Med 39:346, 1967
28. Kornberg A: Basic motives of a professional life. Perspect Biol Med 13:222, 1970
29. Kung H: Freud and the Problem of God. New Haven, Yale University Press, 1979, p 12
30. Lasagna L: Life, Death, and the Doctor. New York, Knopf, 1968, p 25
31. Lewis JM: Assessment of family mental health. Address given at Touro Infirmary, New Orleans, Louisiana, June 6, 1980
32. Martin FH: Fifty Years of Medicine and Surgery. Chicago, Surgical Publishing Co, 1934
33. Maslow AH: Toward a Psychology of Being. Princeton, New Jersey, Van Nostrand, 1962
34. Maxmen JS: Medical student radicals: Conflict and resolution. Am J Psychiatry 129:1211, 1971
35. Modlin HC, Montes A: Narcotics addiction in physicians. Am J Psychiatry 121:358, 1964
36. Molish HB, et al.: A Rorschach study of a group of medical students. Psychiatr Q 24:744, 1950
37. Mullan F: White Coat, Clenched Fist. New York, Macmillan, 1976
38. Paget S: Confessio Medici. London, Macmillan
39. Pearson MW, Strecker EA: Physicians as psychiatric patients. Am J Psychiatry 116:915, 1960
40. Pumpian-Mindlin E: Omnipotentiality, youth, and commitment. J Am Acad Child Psychiatry 4:1, 1965
41. Rado S: The Psychoanalysis of Behavior. New York, Grune & Stratton, 1958, pp 47–80
42. Russell B: The Autobiography of Bertrand Russell. London, Allen & Unwin, 1967
43. Schlageter CW, Rosenthal J: What are "normal" medical students like? J Med Educ 37:19, 1962
44. Schleich KL: Those Were Good Days. New York, Norton, 1936, p 100
45. Schweitzer A: Out of My Life and Thought. New York, Holt, 1949
46. Seagrave GS: Burma Surgeon. New York, Norton, 1943
47. Seidenberg R: Catcher gone awry. Int J Psychoanal 51:332, 1970
48. Sigerist HE: The University at the Crossroads. New York, Schuman, 1946, p 15
49. Simmel E: The doctor-game, illness and the profession of medicine. Int J Psychoanal 8:470, 1926
50. Sulzberger CL: Editorial. New York Times, Nov 14, 1970
51. Washington A: Mine Eyes Have Seen: A Woman Doctor's Saga. New York, Dutton, 1941
52. Williams WC: Autobiography of William Carlos Williams. New York, Random House, 1951
53. Zeitlin NG: Why I became a doctor. In Fabricant ND (ed): Why We Became Doctors. New York, Grune & Stratton, 1954, p 133

2

THE SEARCH
FOR THE IDEAL
MEDICAL STUDENT

The race is not always to the swift—nor the battle to the strong—but that's the way to bet.

—Damon Runyon

The search for the ideal medical student is a noble endeavor, containing the hope that society will be given an ideal physician. The bright and creative student with great potential, strong motivation, strength of character, and evidence of high-level performance is best suited to give society the medical care it needs and demands. Each medical school has its own strategy for identifying the type of student it hopes to attract.

The admissions process varies considerably from school to school, but certain guidelines are followed by all schools. The submitting of an application to medical school, usually through the centralized application service of the Association of American Medical Colleges, is probably the most significant action taken by a student in his or her life up to that time. In turn, the admission of a student is the most critical step a school takes in the education of a physician.

There is widespread interest in selection committees and how a school sets its policies for admitting new students. Usually the faculty of a school of medicine establishes the operating policies and methods of selection for the admissions committee, and these guidelines are followed carefully and diligently. The committee must rely heavily on objective criteria, such as grade averages (overall, as well as in science coursework), Medical College Admissions Test (MCAT) scores, appraisal by faculty from the applicant's college, special accomplishments and talents, the substance and level of courses taken in college, whether the academic performance has continually improved or suffered reverses, and physical and emotional health. If the students' academic records and faculty evaluations meet a prescribed standard, the students are usually invited to visit the school for interviews.

A word about the health of students under consideration for selection is indicated. The impact of federal legislation regarding the handicapped on admissions procedures has led to the elimination of most questions about health, especially those about previous emotional difficulties. The Rehabilitation Act of 1973 states, "No otherwise qualified handicapped individual in the United States . . . shall, solely by reason of his handicap, be excluded from the participation in, be denied the benefits of, or be subjected to discrimination under any program or activity receiving Federal financial assistance." DHHS rules and regulations address the issue of admission procedures: ". . . qualified handicapped persons may not, on the basis of being handicapped, be denied admission or be subjected to discrimination in admission. . . ." Further, the regulations "prohibit preadmission inquiries as to whether an applicant has a handicap. One may inquire after admission only so that the necessary accommodations can be planned."

Do regulations about the handicapped complicate the work of admissions committees? Yes, in some situations. One of Louisiana State University Medical School's finest recent graduates was a young man who was born without legs. This type of applicant furnished a selection committee no difficulty. On the other hand, what about an applicant who has had previous psychotic episodes yet managed to make good grades? One can see in these matters a consideration of two sets of rights—the rights of the individual and the rights or protection of patients. Silver and others have stated the matter clearly: "To the federal legislators and some members of the legal profession, the issue might be the civil rights of all individuals, including the handicapped. For medical educators the issue is the right to decide who can become a physician and what type of medicine an individual can practice so as to ensure the protection of patients."[25]

The task of the admissions committee is formidable, and service on the committee is not cherished by every faculty member. Medical students now serve on most of the selection committees in this country and also help with interviewing and other tasks related to evaluation and selection of candidates.

In the provocative book *Zen and the Art of Motorcycle Maintenance,* Robert Pirsig tells of the gifted scholar Phaedrus who lost his mind trying to define "Quality."[18] Each year the admissions committee in every medical school is similarly required to define "Quality." Professor Morowitz addresses the urgency of the task: "The issue is not an abstract one, but an immediate, pressing, tangible, existential reality, for each committee must select a small number of matriculants from a large number of applicants."[15] Generally, admissions committees do a remarkably good job. Yet, many committee members express nagging doubts about their work and wonder frequently if they did not reject, for example, "better candidates than the ones accepted." Further, many within and outside the medical school are at times critics of those selected. In response to this type of criticism, an admissions officer once said, somewhat facetiously: "One cannot expect the admissions committee to be perfect. After all, in a selection process of his disciples, carried out by Jesus Christ, he had an 8.3 percent attrition rate, and on several occasions, he was threatened with a higher rate. Should we expect better performance by the admissions committee than by Jesus?" Probably yes, because Jesus did not have Medical College Admission Test scores, grade point averages, letters of evaluation, interviews by several interviewers, or help from premedical advisors.

LETTERS OF EVALUATION OF THE APPLICANT

The usefulness of letters of evaluation varies some from college to college, and depends in part on how carefully the pertinent issues in evaluation have been identified and addressed. Most premedical advisors and their committees are skilled in their work and maintain a consistently good record of effectively evaluating their applicants for medical school.

Generally, admissions committees send guidelines to those who will be writing letters of evaluation. The admissions committee's expectation is usually set forth in a statement such as this one:

> In selecting applicants to medical school, the admissions committee depends heavily on evaluations of the applicants supplied by undergraduate faculty members. Since the number of qualified applicants to medical schools far exceeds the number of first year class positions available, the committee is anxious to select those individuals whose accomplishments, personal attributes, and abilities indicate that they have the greatest potential for medical training and practice. Therefore, you are asked to provide a thoughtful and completely frank appraisal of the applicant in relation to other premedical students you have known at your institution.

The following guidelines represent items that many admissions committee members and admissions directors emphasize: [3, 5, 22, 26]

Personal Attributes.   The emphasis should be on the applicant's personality and his or her interactions with others, as well as characteristics that indicate special promise or potential problems in medicine. Characteristics deserving comment are:

1. Motivation for medicine: how interest developed and how it has grown, genuineness and depth of commitment.
2. Maturity: personal development, ability to cope with life situations.
3. Emotional stability: performance under pressure, mood stability, constancy in ability to relate to others.
4. Interpersonal relations: ability to get along and work with others, rapport, cooperation, attitudes toward supervision.
5. Empathy: sensitivity to the needs of others, considerations, and tact.
6. Judgment: ability to analyze a problem, common sense, decisiveness.
7. Resourcefulness: originality, skillful management of available resources.
8. Reliability: dependability, sense of responsibility, promptness, conscientiousness.
9. Communication skills: clarity of expression, articulateness.
10. Perseverance: stamina, endurance.
11. Self-confidence: assuredness, capacity to achieve with awareness of own strengths and weaknesses.

Academic Achievement. Since transcripts are available, comments in the letter of evaluation should amplify or clarify certain items in the applicant's record such as the following:

1. Academic achievement relative to others in that institution, e.g., class standing.
2. Consistency of performance.
3. Extenuating circumstances which might account for atypical grade(s) or course load(s), such as illness, employment, or extensive extracurricular involvement.
4. Degree of difficulty of individual courses and overall course loads, e.g., upper-division courses taken during freshman year, honors section, and so on.
5. Approach to course work as it relates to gaining mastery of the material or in gaining a good grade and as it relates to working and thinking independently or merely following the crowd.

Employment, Extracurricular or Avocational Activities. Since this information is given in the application, elaborate only if some new dimension can be added. Activities which indicate motivations for medicine or concern for others are of special interest. If involvement in an activity was extensive, what was the effect on academic achievement?

Honors Received, Academic or Nonacademic. Specify what achievement the honor represents, and the competition for, or degree of selectivity of, such awards.

Overall Evaluation. Admissions committees find it helpful if the letter of evaluation contains a value judgment, or overall appraisal, of the applicant's potential for medical school and practice based on all attributes of the applicant, not merely academic performance.

The importance of letters of evaluation in the admissions process for medical school cannot be overemphasized. Admissions committees value most highly those letters that are frank and that present a fair and balanced picture of the applicant. Probably next to frankness, admissions committees appreciate specific examples of an applicant's behavior rather than generalities.

THE MEDICAL SCHOOL INTERVIEW

The medical school interview, because of its subjective nature, is usually of great concern to premedical students. They wonder how medical schools use the interviews and what they can do to ensure that their interviews will be the best possible.

The interview provides a means of assessing the personal qualities of applicants, and of screening out psychological misfits. Although the interview is of little value in predicting academic achievement, it does serve a number of useful purposes:

- It offers an opportunity to verify and clarify information obtained from the application and other sources about the student. It allows the student to explain any unique or complicated aspects of the application.
- The interview and the visit to the medical school offer the student an opportunity to learn more about the school and its educational program by meeting and talking with faculty and students and touring the school's facilities.
- The interviewers can see whether the applicant has obvious physical handicaps, gross deficiencies in personality, or emotional instabilities, and can determine if an applicant has the capacity to relate with warmth to another human being.
- Information can usually be obtained that will help the admissions committee decide which of the large number of qualified applicants are most likely to profit from a particular school's educational program.

- The interview permits the admissions committee to seek more information regarding the applicant's motivation, goals, and long-range planning.
- The interview humanizes the admissions procedure through the personal contact between the applicant and the faculty and students of the medical school.

Applicants usually seek advice as to how to conduct themselves during an interview. Those who have gone through interview experiences and those who do interviewing offer suggestions similar to these:

- During the interview, be yourself, for interviews can bring out betrayals of character.
- Try to communicate clearly and succinctly but do not be verbose.
- Be prepared to respond to all kinds of questions, many unrelated to the study of medicine.
- Be prepared to discuss your motivation for the study of medicine and any activity or experience which has tested or clarified this motivation. "Why do you want to be a doctor?" is usually *not* the way the question is asked. A more helpful phrasing of the question is: "Tell me about the development of your interest in the study of medicine and anything you have done to clarify or test your interest."
- Be appropriately dressed and groomed, as if applying for a job.
- Don't try to second guess the interviewer. Answer questions honestly.
- Avoid attempting to "butter up" the interviewer.
- If you don't know the answer to a question, say so.
- Explain your deficiencies honestly and don't offer mere excuses and rationalizations for lack of academic achievement.
- Don't be hesitant to ask questions, for the interview serves equally the purpose of the applicant.
- Be honest about your financial needs and discuss them freely.
- Don't be on the defensive or on the offensive.
- Don't judge the success of an interview by its length.

There are almost as many approaches to interviewing as there are interviewers. Although interviewers may follow a routine approach in establishing rapport and obtaining basic information from an applicant, they usually pride themselves on asking certain unique questions and on their evaluation of the responses to these questions. For example, one interviewer finds an insightful question to be: "What would you say is your weakest point?" This interviewer contends that a person honest enough to acknowledge shortcomings possesses an admirable trait. An admission of one's failure, the interviewer believes, is probably an indication of a humility necessary for real honesty and willingness to learn. One could question this conclusion, however. While some interviewers subject the applicant to stressful questions and situations, others would avoid these.[12] It is doubtful whether one approach bears greater fruit than the other. In other words, interviewers adopt an approach with which they are comfortable and that yields them the information they want. They should never forget, however, that the interviewee is *reacting* to the interviewer in every aspect of the interview.

SPECIAL QUALITIES

Pearl Rosenberg, in discussing academic excellence along with noncognitive factors as criteria for admission to medical school, emphasizes creativity and the capacity for independent work.[23] Yet, each medical school looks for the typical traits or qualities in the students it selects, but almost always it seeks to identify other qualities. Sometimes these qualities are implied in the usual ones such as those already mentioned in this chapter. Whether these qualities are new, different, or the same, they deserve further amplification. Five of these qualities are discussed here.

The first relates to the maturity that comes with a sense of accomplishment in some particular field. Has the student accomplished something significant in any field before applying to medical school? This field can be music, writing, sports, special studies, and so on. Some admissions directors of medical schools have identified this special accomplishment as a reliable indicator of success in medical school. A British study emphasized that such students with accomplishment in other fields, including experience in working with older colleagues, generally were able easily to establish the satisfactory interpersonal relations so necessary for the successful practice of medicine.[13]

The second trait relates to intense energy in the person. The student who is capable of doing an exceptional amount of hard work and also has time and energy to spend in activities other than studies possesses a trait in common with most successful physicians. In a study of a group of physicians who made distinguished contributions to neurology, Nathan found that the only characteristic or trait common to the 133 physicians studied was the unusual amount of energy each possessed.[10, 16]

The third quality relates to social consciousness. Today's students must be humanity oriented in the finest sense of the word. Not infrequently in the past, students and their physician-teachers focused sharply on the individual patient and neglected the complex social and psychological factors that influence sickness and health. A new set of demands confronts today's students. A deep social consciousness is essential if they are to prepare themselves to deal adequately with the change and ferment in medical education, the unavailability of medical services to many groups in our population, changing patterns of delivery of health care, and involvement in the social problems of humankind.

The fourth trait is "reasonable adventurousness." Heath, in a study of Princeton undergraduates, identifies six attributes which characterize the "reasonable adventurer": intellectuality, close friendships, independence in value judgments, tolerance of ambiguity, breadth of interests, and sense of humor.[11] Such attributes would make for a fully functioning human being, one who is open to new experiences in the changing world and would serve the person well in both the study and practice of medicine.

The fifth trait is creativity, a trait not easily defined or identified. In the light of what is known about creativity, however, the student possessing this quality brings to medicine a precious gift. Because of the increasing concern with identifying and nurturing the creative potential in students, some of the relevant dimensions of the topic are introduced here.

The distinguished physician and research scientist, Albert Szent-Gyorgyi, declares that the history of human progress is the story of a relatively small number of creative people—creative in art, science, or any other human endeavor. He goes on to say that as progress in the past depended on them, so it will in the future, and "the fate of any nation depends, to a great extent, on the question: How far does it produce creative minds?"[27]

Nobody will deny that medicine needs the creative person. Very little in medicine is routine, for each patient and each situation bring new challenges, as well as demands for problem-solving skills. Creative thinking may be the physician's most important weapon in coping with the emergencies and crises encountered daily in the practice of medicine.

Selection committees of medical schools have difficulty identifying the creative person and may actually screen him or her out because of showing too much independence in thought and action. The person who is expected to "fit in" and do the work "without causing any trouble" may be too highly prized in the selection process. Haskins speaks pointedly to this matter: "A society committed to the search for truth must for that very reason give protection to and set a high value upon the independent and original mind, however angular, however rasping, however socially unpleasant it may be. For it is upon such minds, in large measure, that the effective search for truth depends."[9]

The thorough study of a student's application to medical school and the formulation of appropriate questions in interviews with the student may reveal the presence or absence of factors usually found in the profile of the creative mind. These factors have been identified by a number of investigators and usually include the following:[2, 4, 6, 14, 24]

- A high degree of self-reliance and independence.
- Open to stimuli and a wide variety of interests.
- Intuitive, flexible, socially poised, and competent.
- Unconcerned about social norms although definitely not antagonistic to these (antiauthoritarian and unorthodox).
- A high degree of stability and a strong sense of responsibility.
- Curiosity, good judgment, and the ability to tolerate ambiguities without always needing the kind of certainty that more compulsively organized people seem to require.
- Ability to recognize problems and define them clearly.
- A need for recognition and praise.
- Intellectually curious and highly intelligent.
- Goal-oriented, not method-oriented.
- The emergence of these characteristics early in life.

Psychologist Paul Torrance sees creative talent as a cluster of traits. The traits he includes in the cluster are ones that admissions directors usually try to identify and evaluate: high sensitivity, capacity to be disturbed by problems; ability to see relationships in a flash; divergent rather than conformist thinking; and a powerful drive to take intellectual risks and push ability to the limit.[29]

In observing medical students whom their teachers identify as original and creative thinkers, one can easily note a few common denominators. These students are self-teachers, quick to raise questions about "facts" and "theories" in medicine that most people consider well established. They are better able than other students to live with uncertainty. They are profoundly aware of the brevity of life and the gravity of their purpose and feel impelled to strive. They yearn to change, to grow, to be different, and to escape from many of their human limitations. They possess personal courage which helps them stand aside from the social collectivity and often in conflict with it. Their courage is related to being themselves in the fullest sense.

Creative students bring to medicine a consistent and pervasive emphasis on innovation through science and a never-ending replacement of the old by the new in scientific progress. In the rich environment of hospital ward, laboratory, and classroom, these students receive the preparation needed to give expression to their creative talents. With eyes and ears that truly see and hear, exceptional observations may be made. As Louis Pasteur has put it, "In the field of observation, chance favors the prepared mind."

THE DEBATE OVER PREPARATION
FOR MEDICAL SCHOOL

Because of the limited number of spaces and the large number of highly qualified applicants, a kind of "guerilla warfare" among premedical students at the college level has developed. Some observers believe that this warfare that students engage in to eliminate their fellow competitors and supplement their own actual achievements is encouraged by the selection criteria the medical schools use.[8, 15, 21, 28, 30]

Dr. Stewart Wolf, a top clinician, researcher, and medical educator is concerned that we are bringing to medical school young men and women who lack the civilizing background in the humanities and who have spent their college years only learning the *right answers*.[30] Dr. Wolf tells of one university where the departments of English literature and sociology offer a course in the "sociology of medicine." The students engage in classroom discussion, as well as in reading and in writing essays. Each year most of the initial subscribers to the course are premedical students; most of them drop the course, however, before the grading deadline. "I enjoy the course," one student said to Dr. Wolf, "but I can't afford a 'B'." Dr. Wolf believes that it is high time to examine critically the validity of the criteria for medical school. He is afraid that our selection process screens out many of the students with the traits of creativity described earlier in this chapter.

Dr. Lewis Thomas, Director of Memorial Sloan-Kettering Cancer Institute, and Dr. Stewart Wolf are in strong agreement. Dr. Thomas would like to see developed in the college curriculum some central, core discipline, universal within the curricula of all the colleges, that could be used for evaluating the free range of students' minds, their tenacity and resolve, their innate capacity for the understanding of human beings, and their affection for the human condition.[28] Dr. Thomas describes the broad liberal education he would like to see applicants to medical school have as including Greek, Latin, the classics, philosophy, history, literature, and a number of other basic courses. Further, he believes that colleges should have much more of a say about who goes to medical school than the medical school itself: "If they know, as they should, the students who are generally bright and also respected, this judgment should carry the heaviest weight for admission. If they elect to use criteria other than numerical class standing for recommending applicants, this evaluation should hold."[28] It would be good indeed if Dr. Thomas' dream of what the undergraduate education of applicants to medical school should be came true. He is not optimistic, however, as he states in his essay on "How to Fix the Premedical Curriculum":[28] "There is still some talk in medical deans' offices about the need for general culture, but nobody really means it, and certainly the premedical students don't believe it."

THE REJECTED APPLICANT

Because there are far more highly qualified applicants than available places in medical school, rejection may have little to do with qualifications. In fact, a group of applicants the size of the group selected by medical schools in the United States and with quite similar credentials is left behind each year. Further, among those rejected are the late bloomers. Types of late bloomers such as George Bernard Shaw and Charles Darwin, who did not "wake up" until they were almost thirty, would be passed over by selection committees today. Thus, in the rejected group are many who fit the "ideal" category—many who are missed because their credentials do not tell the full story or who were rejected because the places were exhausted before they were accepted.

There are options and alternatives for students who are rejected. Dr. Carlos Pestana, a distinguished dean of admissions, has rendered both rejected applicants and medical schools a fine service through his practical guide and in-depth study of the rejected applicant: *The Rejected Medical School Applicant—Options and Alternatives.*[19] Dr. Pestana discusses pertinent topics such as reapplication, medical education abroad, and alternative careers. His work has been of great help to many who aspire to be physicians. His comments about credentials and reapplication deserve special emphasis: "Better credentials, academic as well as nonacademic, hold the key to success for most reapplicants. Except for the three-year applicants . . . , and the rare cases of bad luck among well-qualified candidates . . . , the difference between the 31 percent of reapplicants, who are accepted, and the 69 percent, who are not, lies in the extent to which they could move up in the competitive process of selection."[19] Pestana emphasizes further that he is not talking about unqualified candidates becoming qualified, because they start out fully qualified, but about candidates becoming a bit more competitive.

PREMEDICAL ADVISORS

Premedical advisors form an indispensable link in the "search for the ideal medical student." In general, premedical advisors bring to their work a spirit of concern and understanding for students planning and preparing for a medical career, for the undergraduate colleges from which the students come, and for the medical schools that make the final selection for admission. Much of the interface between undergraduate colleges and medical schools is through advisors. Fortunately, manuals have been and are being developed that describe the work of premedical advisors. An excellent example of such a manual is *Premedical Advising in Texas: A Manual,* recently produced by The University of Texas Medical School at Houston and the Macy Foundation.

One cannot overestimate the importance and value of premedical advisors' short-range and long-range contributions to the health care enterprise. Most advisors are scientists. Yet, while guiding and challenging students in their preparation for medical school, advisors must push aside a natural interest in getting students to follow a scientific career like their own. Because of their devotion to the human aspirations of students and their capacity to place in a secondary position some of their own personal goals, they project an image to students of warm, caring persons who skillfully perform their tasks. This image of the scientist is in sharp contrast to the popular archetype of the scientist as remote, detached, and devoted only to instruments and technology.

Communication between medical and undergraduate colleges is sometimes inadequate. In particular, medical schools often do not report to premedical advisors on the progress of their former students or on changes in admissions policies and curriculum, nor do they always request further information pertaining to unusual applications. Without that flow of information from the medical school, advisors cannot function at their best. Therefore, advisors must insist on the free flow of information in both directions. Without this reciprocity, advisors are handicapped, and their counseling does not attain its highest potential. Further, the medical college is handicapping itself. Thus, medical college admissions personnel and premedical advisors are mutually interdependent. Good working relationships, born of respect and trust in one another, will nurture the objectives of applicants and schools alike.

University administrations that support the premedical advisory programs make it possible for advisors to do their jobs effectively and successfully. Professors who serve as advisors need adequate budgets for support services as well as sufficient time allotments in their schedules to perform the multifaceted tasks of advising. We covet for all advisors a university administration that gives the advisory program a high priority in the allocation of money, space, faculty time, and other necessities or rewards.

While doing important tasks such as writing letters of evaluation, assisting students with their choice of courses, counseling in personal matters, or being involved in the hundred other responsibilities related to getting students ready for medical school, in an ultimate sense advisors render their greatest service in helping society get the type of doctors it really needs. What kind of doctors are needed? Of course, it is difficult to characterize or identify such persons, especially in their formative years. Yet, we know that we are not far afield when we identify students with characteristics such as integrity and emotional stability, a capacity for self-appraisal, sensitivity to the psychological and physical needs of others, the ability to detect and solve problems, and the ability to learn independently. Those who are attracted to a career in medicine generally start with an idealistic, humanistic commitment to the relief of suffering and an interest in people as persons. In the competitive, sometimes dehumanizing circumstance of getting ready to enter medical school, this commitment may be weakened or modified. Medicine is deeply indebted to premedical advisors who nurture the student's commitment, in those critical years of educational development, to a caring profession—a profession that seeks to improve the quality of life for those to whom it ministers.

CONCLUSION

Over a hundred years ago, the eminent British physician Sir James Paget published a report on a thousand medical students entitled "What Becomes of Medical Students?"[17] The title was taken from a story told of Abernethy, who on entering the anatomy classroom for an introductory lecture allegedly looked about and exclaimed "God help you all! What will become of you?" Paget found, in the 10-year follow-up, that only 720 of the students were still engaged in the practice of medicine. One hundred twenty-eight had died—25 of illnesses contracted in medical practice, 7 by suicide, 1 by "hanging." Thirty-one failed examinations at various stages of the educational program. Among the others were three who became actors and seven who became clergymen. One was imprisoned, five were guilty of "scandalous misconduct," and ten were lost through habits of intemperance or dissipation. If the losses are added, one finds the attrition rate among these students to be about 10 percent, augmented by another 18 percent who dropped out of medical practice within the period of inquiry. Although medical education remains a demanding endeavor, its outcomes are fortunately more positive than those set forth in Paget's report.[7]

Admissions committees are frequently urged to keep in mind the predictors of physicians' performance suggested by the Price-Taylor Study.[20] These predictors include realistic self-appraisal, coping ability, ethical behavior, evidence of staying behavior, evidence of orientation to lifelong learning, decision making ability, and compassion and sensitivity to interpersonal relations.

The medical profession attracts to its ranks students with a diversity of talents and interests. Some difficulty comes in trying to describe the exact qualities these students should possess. The word "ideal" has been used in the title of this chapter to emphasize excellence as the standard of measurement. Mistakes are made in the selection of some students, but the majority of those who become physicians prove themselves to be exceptionally fine persons.

Although medical educators possess considerable power in shaping the future of medicine, of much greater importance are the orientations and perspectives that students bring to medical school. Whereas the structure and character of formal training is undoubtedly important, its impact can only be understood in the context of initial student perspectives. Babbie's research in the area of values in medical training led him to conclude that good people make good doctors, and a person's goodness is largely determined prior to entering medical school.[1] Others before Babbie reached a similar conclusion, as witnessed by this inscription on the base of a statue at the University of Vienna: "Nur ein guter Mensch kann ein guter Arzt sein," which translates "Only a good person can be a good physician."

REFERENCES

1. Babbie ER: Science and Morality in Medicine. Berkeley, University of California Press, 1970, pp 181–183
2. Dallas M, Gaier EL: Identification of creativity: The individual. Psychol Bull 73:55, 1970

3. DeVaul RA: Personal communication from the Associate Dean for Student and Curricular Affairs, University of Texas Medical School, Houston
4. Flach FF: The reappraisal of the creative process. Psychiatric Ann 8:11, 1978
5. Fruen M, McGrath M: Tips on writing letters of evaluation. CAAHP, Vol. 1, No. 1, 1978
6. Garrett AB: The discovery process and the creative mind. J Chem Educ 41:479, 1964
7. Gough HG, Hall WB: An attempt to predict graduation from medical school. J Med Educ 50:940, 1975
8. Hackman JD: The premed stereotype. J Med Educ 54:308, 1979
9. Haskins CP: Report of President: Carnegie Institution Yearbook 1962. Bull Found Lib Ctr, 5:6, 1964
10. Haymaker W: The Founders of Neurology. Springfield, Illinois, Charles C Thomas, 1953
11. Heath R: The Reasonable Adventurer. Pittsburgh, University of Pittsburgh Press, 1964
12. Henig RM: Choosing the best of the brightest. New Physician 25:23, 1976
13. Lister J: Selection of medical students. N Engl J Med 298:1182, 1978
14. MacKinnon DW: Personality and the realization of creative potential. Am Psychol 20:273, 1965
15. Morowitz HJ: Zen and the art of getting into medical school. Hosp Pract 11:132, 1976
16. Nathan PW: Selection of future doctors—lessons from the past. Lancet 267:407, 1954
17. Paget J: What becomes of medical students? St Barth Hosp Rep 5:238, 1869
18. Pirsig RM: Zen and the Art of Motorcycle Maintenance—An Inquiry into Values. New York, William Morrow, 1974
19. Pestana C: The Rejected Medical School Applicant: Options and Alternatives. Second Edition. San Antonio, Texas, University of Texas Medical School, 1979
20. Price PE, Taylor CW, et al.: Measures and Predictors of Physicians' Performances. Salt Lake City, University of Utah Press, 1971
21. Rafalik D: Getting in—games applicants play. New Physician 25:21, 1976
22. Rankin BB: Personal communication from the Director of Admissions, Baylor College of Medicine, Houston
23. Rosenberg PP: Catch 22—the medical model. In Shapiro EC, Lowenstein LM (eds): Becoming a Physician—Development of Values and Attitudes in Medicine. Cambridge, Massachusetts, Ballinger, 1979, pp 81–91
24. Schubert DSP: Creativity and the ability to cope. In Flach FF (ed): Creative Psychiatry Series. New York, Life Sciences Advisory Group, 1975
25. Silver LB, et al.: Mental health of medical school applicants: The role of the admissions committee. J Med Educ 54:534, 1979
26. Steward JP: Letters of evaluation. The Advisor 7:2, 1971
27. Szent-Gyorgyi A: On scientific creativity. Perspect Biol Med 5:173, 1962

28. Thomas L: How to fix the premedical curriculum. N Engl J Med 298: 1180, 1978
29. Torrance EP: Creativity and its educational implications for the gifted. The Gifted Child Quarterly Summer: 67, 1968
30. Wolf ST: I can't afford a B. N Engl J Med 299:949, 1978

3
TO WEAR THE HEALER'S MANTLE

This is the School of Babylon
And at its hand we learn
To walk into the furnaces
And whistle as we burn.
  —Thomas Blackburn[2]

The educational life of medical students has been described as a constantly changing environment through which they navigate their way for four perilous years. They do walk through fiery furnaces, to use the symbolism of the poet Blackburn or the prophet Daniel.*

The unique purpose of the medical school is the transformation of laymen into physicians. Students have the right to expect that their education will equip them with the rudiments necessary for ultimate professional competence. Thus, the school must teach students the specific skills of medicine as well as the more general techniques for coping with the vocational anxieties that inevitably confront the healer.[7]

Students must learn attitudes, adaptations, and orientations of a kind that medical school catalogs rarely discuss. They are expected to assume responsibility for other human beings who cannot care for themselves—to take the lives of these people into their own hands. They must accept a more total responsibility for and authority over human lives than any other professional in our society—a kind of responsibility that can evoke guilt, anxiety, and profound feelings of inadequacy. They must learn to face, without anxiety, the most tabooed issues and activities of our society—"violating" the sanctum of another person's body; dissecting a cadaver; examining excreta; and confronting death, terminal illness, intractable pain, psychotic disintegration, and sexual functioning. Much of the daily work is a transgression of the ordinary prohibitions and taboos of the community. Their intellect is strained to encompass the knowledge expected of them. Their emotions are challenged to weather the transition between their pre-existing lay prohibitions and inhibitions and the role and characteristics of a physician.

---

* "Men loose, walking in the midst of the fire." (Daniel 3:25)

In medical school, students have many important learning or maturing experiences that cannot be duplicated elsewhere. They observe the entire range of human behavior in times of sickness and trouble, and learn by participation the defined role of the physician in dealing with these problems. This is the process of acculturation often called "professional socialization" or "rites of passage." Despite studies suggesting that socialization in medical school often results in acquisition of the culture of the medical student rather than that of the physician, I believe the crucial part of the student's identity as a healer is established in medical school.[1]

The medical educational process poses a succession of developmental and adaptive tasks with which students must deal as they progress through medical school. Often certain factors within students interfere with successful adaptation. When those who help students in their professional growth emphasize the reality components of the students' stress, they help them recognize the issues with which they are struggling. Usually students are helped in reducing whatever emotional stress is present by realizing that the difficulties in adjustment which they are experiencing are common to other students.[7]

The medical student world is more than an academic one. Students are presented with a broad, often bewildering array of demands to be met and opportunities to be used. While studying and being taught, they interact in myriad ways with the life of an elaborate, intricately formed, and curiously specialized world.[4, 9, 18, 24]

Students must deal with many problem issues over the course of their school experience. The issues constitute role tasks to which the students must respond as a result of both external pressures and inner need. Among the issues are: problems of ambiguity and uncertainty in a profession that prides itself on its rationality and competence; problems relating to the fact that students' technical knowledge cannot be as detailed and extensive as the faculty demands or as they themselves would like; problems of forming a student subculture for purposes of mutual protection and assistance or for providing a measure of autonomy from authoritative demands; and problems of choosing a specialty.

The medical school strongly influences the student's approach to these tasks. The school helps the student find a balance between cold detachment and anxious concern in relation to patients. It offers ample training for decision making in the presence of uncertainty, as well as numerous opportunities for exploring what is involved in the various specialties. The students' effort to resolve these issues, while influenced by environmental demands and opportunities, is ultimately their own. Students selectively assimilate and integrate pressures that impinge upon them from all sides. In the process, their inner fantasies, character traits, talents, and personal commitments are also involved. Thus, students' professional growth is a function both of the external socializing system or environment and of personality.[3]

Professional development or socialization is multifaceted and involves a variety of tasks, as mentioned in the opening paragraphs of this chapter. Because the tasks vary in importance in the overall socialization process, some will be discussed in much greater detail than others.

WHAT IS PROFESSIONAL SOCIALIZATION?

Professional socialization involves the process of induction into a professional role, within the context of a socializing organization. The central question in socialization is: What kinds of relatively enduring, professionally relevant changes do students experience under various socializing conditions? Critics have described medical education today as training students so that they are well prepared to be medical students, but not physicians. Olmstead and Paget draw from this criticism an urgent question: "To what extent and in what ways is the medical school experience a part of professional socialization, [in] contrast [with] socialization to the role of the student?"[20] In other words, while medical students are learning the facts and skills of medicine, are they acquiring the values, attitudes, and behaviors of the role they are to play as physician or of the role they are playing as student?

Although considerable professional socialization of students takes place in medical school, it continues after the completion of medical school in somewhat different contexts, namely, their residency or specialty training, and their own office when they enter practice. The book *Intern* shows that medical school prepared Doctor X to be a medical student, but did not prepare him fully for all of the eventualities of the internship.[5] If it had, there would have been no need for his internship.* And in certain ways his internship did not prepare him for office practice, which stands in vivid contrast to the emergency orientation of the hospital. Actually, the final steps in the young physician's professional socialization are likely to come from interaction with his or her own patients in the context of day-to-day care of them.

Fortunately, many medical schools are giving more responsibility for patient care to students and are permitting the practice of medicine to be learned in the medical school and its teaching hospitals. Being a student should imply that one is practicing the very activities for which

---

* The beginning year of residency and not internship is often used today to designate the first year of training after medical school.

one is preparing. Medical education is a form of supervised rehearsal of the various aspects of the total role the student is eventually to play in his or her medical career.

The personality of the incoming medical student is often overlooked as a major factor in determining the direction a student's socialization will take. This factor is succinctly discussed by Olmstead and Paget:

> From the perspective of professional socialization, entering medical students are products of socializing contexts which have emphasized dependence, authority, and structured demands. What is not shared equally, however, is the content of the personality or value core, which may vary widely among medical students, as it does among individuals in any group. Some, for instance, accept happily their dependence in relation to authority figures, while others chafe at the constraints it imposes. Some see science as a central value, while others see it as peripheral to themselves and their view of the world.[20]

The purpose of professional socialization is to induce change in those being socialized. It is to be hoped that what students experience in medical school produces enduring changes in them that are relevant to and preparatory for the professional role of doctor. In mediating the conflicting demands, students learn behaviors and reorder previously held values so that they become, to some extent, different persons. The change expected is the synthesis of what one knows and is assimilated into a more coherent and consistent behavioral pattern.

THE SEARCH FOR PROFESSIONAL IDENTITY

Most of the literature on medical student maturation emphasizes the high degree of anxiety encountered in medical students. Appropriate counseling and treatment facilities are one approach toward helping them master their anxiety. Probably more important is appropriate recognition of the readily understandable anxieties of students.

An overriding source of anxiety lies in the students' concern over their ability to perform as a physician in caring for the sick. They must face and attempt to master the difficulties encountered in the clinical situation, where the doctor must often act on the basis of insufficient data and meet the challenge of difficult patients. Students usually bring to medical school an expansive view of the physician as an omnipotent and omniscient healer. Their own self-image, once they are assigned to care for patients, stands in sharp contrast to their view of what a physician should be. Thus, they become anxious, guilty, and depressed.

The students' concerns regarding what doctors do and how they do it are further compounded in some medical schools by postponing meaningful clinical exposure until after the second year, when students have mastered the basic science material to the satisfaction of the faculty. Students are challenged more easily and adapt more successfully if they participate in carefully planned clinical experiences at the outset of their medical training, along with their basic science course work. And, fortunately, this is what happens in most medical schools today. A planned sequence of clinical exercises throughout the four years, with gradually increasing responsibility, brings into sharp focus the challenges of being a physician. Students do not develop a professional identity as physicians until they begin to deal with patients. Ascribed, assigned, and perceived roles become congruent only when the students actually begin to relate to patients.

No aspect of a medical student's work helps him or her acquire a professional identity as much as does the care of patients. A page from Somerset Maugham's *The Summing Up* portrays beautifully the impact of his student days, especially his care of patients, on all of his life to follow:

> I entered St. Thomas's Hospital in the autumn of 1892. I found the first two years of the curriculum very dull and gave my work no more attention than was necessary to scrape through the examinations. I was an unsatisfactory student ... but when, after two years, I became a clerk in the outpatients' department I began to grow interested. In due course I started to work in the wards and then my interest so much increased that when I caught septic tonsillitis through doing a post-mortem on a corpse that was in an unreasonable state of decomposition and had to take to my bed, I could not wait to get well to resume my duties. I had to attend a certain number of confinements to get a certificate and this meant going into the slums of Lambeth, often into foul courts that police hesitated to enter, but in which my black bag amply protected me. I found the work absorbing. For a short period I was on accident duty day and night to give first aid to urgent cases. It left me tired out but wonderfully exhilarated.
>
> For here I was in contact with what I most wanted, life in the raw. In those three years I must have witnessed pretty well every emotion of which man is capable. It appealed to my dramatic instinct. It excited the novelist in me. Even now that forty years

have passed I can remember certain people so exactly that I could draw a picture of them. Phrases that I heard then still linger in my ears. I saw how men died. I saw how they bore pain. I saw what hope looked like, fear and relief; I saw the dark lines that despair drew on a face; I saw courage and steadfastness. I saw faith shine in the eyes of those who trusted in what I could only think was an illusion and I saw the gallantry that made a man greet the prognosis of death with an ironic joke because he was too proud to let those about him see the terror of his soul.[14]

A part of the identity of a physician is in knowing who he or she is, and that identity has a relationship to the care of patients. As physician and ethicist Edmund D. Pellegrino has insightfully stated: "To be a physician is freely to commit oneself to the moral center of the relationship with the patient and to do so with one's whole person. . . . It is a daring and a transforming experience to heal another person. To do so is to penetrate in some way the mystery of that person's being, and that becomes disastrous unless we are clear about our own being."[22]

THE QUEST FOR COMPETENCE

Students' efforts to become adequate for handling the responsibility soon to be thrust upon them involve them in a series of adaptations. They will eventually have "absolute" responsibility for and power over many of their patients; yet they are fallible, sometimes ignorant, and at times careless human beings. They soon realize that it will never be possible to learn all that is known in modern medicine, and that in some areas little is known that will be of help to heal their patients. Just the same, these patients will place themselves in their hands and trust their abilities. And still more sobering is the realization that all of their patients will eventually die.

Nevertheless, students must make the attempt to become totally competent, knowledgeable, and skilled so that they can say with full confidence in any situation: "There was nothing more I or anyone else could have done." They are thus powerfully motivated to become proficient with the tools of the profession and often seek reassurance that they are learning.

In a field where no one can know everything, there lies the continual struggle to feel competent to cope with the life-and-death responsibility that is placed on a physician's shoulders. One may wonder whether the responsibilities of medicine may not push some students into a defensive attitude of omnicompetence with their patients (and others) that militates against their being humane physicians. Keniston makes this searching statement: "It seems possible that certain medical schools, with some students, help produce what we might term 'professionally patterned defects'—human and vocational disabilities that are informally 'learned' through the largely unexamined years of medical education."[10] Keniston is referring to such patterns of behavior as a defensive attitude of omnicompetence with patients, erection of barriers of cold detachment between doctor and patient, and a commitment to purely technical competence to the neglect of humane qualities.

In spite of their fears about their ability to care responsibly for patients, students want to get involved in patient care soon after getting to medical school. They want to learn to communicate with patients so that each hears the message of the other.[15] While wanting to have responsibility for patient care, students feel heavily the burden of the doctor's accountability for what happens to his or her patients.

In the professional socialization of the student, the responsibility perspective deserves serious analysis. There are difficult moral-emotional problems involved in the socialization of responsibility. The important question is: How does one find a middle ground between the sense of total responsibility (with the excessive guilt it produces when a patient dies) and an amoral responsibility in which the trait of self-criticism is lacking? Many unconscious wishes and fantasies can complicate this process: the wish to become an all-powerful healer; the wish to atone for past transgressions, real or imagined, by giving succor to the victims of disease; doubts about one's competence and one's moral right to assume such great responsibility; and the wish to use a professional role for purposes of self-aggrandizement.[13, 25] Students engage in a considerable amount of inner work on issues of this kind. This inner work is influenced by the character of the medical school environment and by the students' perceptions of integrity versus self-deception and moral callousness versus sensitivity in their teachers and peers.

As a rule, the student's anxieties about death or suffering are either repressed or quickly suppressed, and fears about one's competence to handle the responsibilities of medical practice are quickly channeled into efforts to learn the subject matter well. The student's quest for competence extends far beyond medical student days. It is in the first year or two after medical school, during residency training, that he or she is pounded and sweated into the shape and substance of a competent physician. For the first time, he or she must accept fully the burden of responsibility, and the handling of it determines his or her success or failure.

Doctor X writes poignantly about the first year out of medical school:

> He learns more about medicine in this year than in all the other years combined, and he learns, for the most part, by committing a long succession of colossal blunders and then having them corrected (if possible) by the experienced doctors looking over his shoulder. Many times the intern will do harm. Many times he will make things worse instead of better. The intern's triumphs—the brilliant diagnostic coups, the errors he catches in time, the occasions when he makes precisely the right move at the right time to save a life—are precious moments to him; but at the same time he will inadvertently kill the patient who might otherwise have lived, through stupidity, or blundering, or blind experience. His triumphs are soon forgotten. His errors he must live with; he cannot be allowed to forget them.[5]

ADAPTING TO STRESS AND ANXIETY

As noted earlier (page 10), three ways of adapting to stress seem especially prominent among medical students in their professional development.[10] First, many react to anxiety-provoking situations not by trying to live with them or escape them, but by strenuous efforts to master, overcome, or counteract them. When confronted with a problem, medical students usually head straight into it and try to eliminate it. Second, medical students, in general, are oriented primarily toward changing their environment rather than themselves. Compared with graduate students in other fields, medical students are notable for the speed and zeal with which they attempt to devise practical, well-organized plans for changing things. They are not strongly inclined to examine their own feelings, fantasies, and motives or to explore techniques of self-reform. Third, medical students, like other students with developed scientific ability, generally have an acumen for translating feelings into ideas, and for manipulating these ideas, and at times have considerable capacity to forget the feelings that originally prompted the ideas. In summary, when confronting a personal anxiety or a stressful situation, the medical student is less likely to be interested in or aware of his or her own feelings than to be preoccupied with understanding intellectually what is happening, planning a rational course of action, or studying the theoretical implications of the problem.

In other words, medical students' adaptive style tends to be counterphobic and obsessive-compulsive. Studies such as those of Molish, Schlageter, and Rosenthal agree in finding distinctive use of obsessive-compulsive defenses among medical students.[16, 23] For most medical students these techniques remain adaptive, but at times they become excessively rigid or collapse altogether.

Medical school coursework serves a dual function: to teach technical competence and to prepare students for the psychological hazards of their vocation. From the first incision in the cadaver to the care of their first terminal patient, students tend to respond in a similar way: an initial phase of anxiety or dread gives way to an effort to learn about the object of anxiety, to develop the intellectual knowledge and psychomotor skills to do a competent job, and to master the task at hand. The emotions are gradually detached from the work of medicine, and what remains in consciousness are the knowledge and skills of the physician. The process of learning how not to react emotionally to the confrontations of medicine gives added impetus to learning the subject matter of medicine. Thus, acquiring medical knowledge is not only a way of helping patients, but also a necessary defense against the personal anxieties that might otherwise be aroused in the medical student.

The heavy demands made upon students' time and, later, physicians' time, may save them from preoccupation with themselves or from excessive introspection. Although this may not serve always the students' best personal interests, it serves well their work and accumulation of technical knowledge. George Eliot depicts this characteristic in Lydgate, an able physician:

> Lydgate certainly had good reason to reflect on the service his practice did him in counteracting his personal cares. He had no longer free energy enough for spontaneous research and speculative thinking, but by the bedside of patients the direct external calls on his judgment and sympathies brought the added impulse needed to draw him out of himself. It was not simply that beneficent harness of routine which enables silly men to live respectably and unhappy men to live calmly—it was a perpetual claim on the immediate fresh application of thought and on the consideration of another's need and trial. Many of us looking back through life would say that the kindest man we have ever known has been a medical man, or perhaps that surgeon whose fine tact, directed by deeply informed perception, has come to us in our need with a more sublime beneficence than that of miracle-workers. Some of that twice-blessed mercy was always with Lydgate in his work at the Hospital or in private houses, serving better than any opiate to quiet and sustain him under his anxieties.[6]

PRESERVING SENSITIVITY AND
SOCIAL CONSCIOUSNESS

Professional development should involve preserving some of the finer qualities that students bring to medical school. The good physician should possess not only detachment and medical competence but also sensitivity, wisdom, and a high sense of social responsibility. More and more students are arriving in medical school with the latter qualities. The task of the medical school is to create a learning environment where the students will be able to preserve and strengthen these qualities throughout their medical education. The medical school experience should not serve to create, foster, or consolidate barriers of cold detachment and purely technical competence between future physicians and their patients. While these barriers are to some extent necessary in helping the student or physician deal with the anxieties inherent in a difficult vocation, they may become rigid, overelaborated, and inflexible, partly because their appearance is so automatic and unexamined. Keniston is right in urging medical schools to scrutinize carefully the human hazards of medical practice and the informal lessons of medical school and to help their students understand and examine their now largely automatic accommodations to the stresses of their vocation.[10]

In helping students retain sensitivity and social responsibility, the school will be opposing many of the most powerful trends of our society. Thus, such a task will not be easy. A proper beginning can be made by having the faculty and staff of the medical school and teaching hospitals treat patients and students in such a way that the humanitarian impulse, which students bring to medical school, will be recognized, saved, and nurtured. If the effort to teach competence could be supplemented with an effort to strengthen the entering students' sensitivity and openness to themselves and others, future physicians might be better supported in their desire to treat their patients not merely competently, but also wisely, responsibly, and humanely.

If faculty and staff have meaningful and authentic encounters with patients and by their behavior demonstrate a basic respect for the dignity of the individual patient, students are likely to follow with the development of a similar medical identity. Furthermore, if faculty and staff recognize the needs of their students, demonstrate a basic respect for their anxieties and concerns, and foster a feeling of self-esteem, students will have authentic models for helping them learn to interact with patients in a humanistic fashion.[28]

If medical schools would accept the advice offered by Dr. Paul Williamson, possibly more time would be allotted to the art and humanity of medicine. Williamson points out that the medical teaching and philosophy of today constantly emphasize the complex and difficult, whereas 99 percent of human ills are of a simple and direct nature. "It is a little foolish," he says, "to be an expert for one percent of one's practice and indifferently competent for ninety-nine percent of it. Yet, this can and often does happen."[29]

On the other hand, sensitivity and social consciousness need not be sacrificed because medical schools emphasize the complex and difficult—for example, the so-called "rare disease." Rare diseases do happen to people. It is small consolation to a patient that his or her disease is very uncommon and practically unknown. The rarer the disease a patient suffers, the greater the challenge to both the humanistic and scientific skills of the physician.

Williamson and others contend that the chance that the medical student will meet any of the rare diseases a second time in his or her life is too small to warrant full discussion. Actually, medical education should be more than training to cope with the frequent and the predictable. It should aim at creating physicians who are capable of helping any patient who consults them. The confrontation with a patient suffering from a rare disease—or a rare variant of a common disease—brings home to the medical student the ever-present need for painstaking observation and critical interpretation, as well as fosters the courage to dream unorthodox conclusions. This confrontation may also help the student to understand a fundamental fact of medical care—the uniqueness of each patient.

CHARISMATIC AUTHORITY: EARNED OR GIVEN

There is a quality of mystery in medicine, a gift of healing, which transcends the teaching-learning dimension of professional development. This quality relates to charismatic authority.

To comprehend the full dimension of charismatic authority, one should reflect on the definition of charisma: spiritual power and virtue attributed to a person who is regarded as set apart from the ordinary—set apart by reason of a special relationship to that which is considered of ultimate value.

In the definition of Max Weber, charisma denotes the "specific gifts of the body and spirit" possessed by those who become "the 'natural' leaders in times of psychic, physical, economic, ethical, religious, political distress."[8, 27] During the social development of Western civilization, charisma has become institutionalized within certain occupational groups, especially the clergy and physicians.

Medicine has two ancient links with charismatic authority. One is represented by the Biblical "power to heal sickness and to cast out demons" (Mark 3:15), which through the medical schools of the Middle Ages came to be conferred upon all those who completed the proper course of training. The other link is represented by ancient covenants, such as the Oath of Hippocrates, preserved from the time of pre-Christian healers, yet surviving as a source of authority in the modern medical profession.[26] The texts of such oaths have many variations, which are of no consequence, because the oath, like every ritual text, serves not in a literal but a symbolic meaning. Its essential point is that young physicians swear that they will lead a pure and holy life and, by this symbolic vow, assume charismatic authority as they enter the practice of medicine.

John Kosa, a social scientist, has given us some illuminating insights regarding charisma in the medical profession:

> One difference between medicine and other health-related professions (dentistry, nursing, and the different kinds of psychotherapists) is that the others have never been able to obtain the secret power of charisma, available since time immemorial to every physician. What is then the source of institutionalized charisma that makes the secret power available to one profession but denies it to the other? The Hippocratic oath, this simple rite of passage, similar to the rituals of old guilds celebrating the end of apprenticeship, cannot be the real source but only a ceremony marking the investiture with the authority of charisma. But the Hippocratic oath refers to that ability of healing and that mastery over death which no profession save medicine can claim. It does not matter whether or not that ability and mastery are real; at times of distress the public perceives and invokes them. . . . As long as medicine and magic were closely linked, such a contact was taken for granted; every medicine man knew an arcane lore full of magic elements, and this knowledge made a charismatic leader. But over the last century medicine has developed a rational body of knowledge that is transmitted to students, not in exclusive fraternities or apprenticeships, but in large institutions operating under public supervision. Yet, this scientific medical knowledge, immense, complex and efficacious as it is, strikes the public as overawing, arcane, and almost superhuman, and ensures the mark of charisma to anybody who is a legal posssessor of that knowledge.[11]

Kosa goes on to say that legitimation and investiture bestow charismatic authority upon a person but do not secure it. The authority may easily be obliterated and lost, and against such a danger the authority needs to be validated through regular exercise. The rational system of medicine has its built-in mechanism of validation. In regular medical practice, the physician discharges the four main charismatic offices: those of teacher, healer, leader, and general guardian of the public good. By their very nature, these offices validate the physician's authority.

The charismatic mark of any physician, according to Kosa, diminishes in the degree to which he or she is involved in a state system of medicine. A bureaucratic health care system indeed observes a formal routine in the doctor-patient relationship and defends this routine against the disturbing effects of individual charismatic relationships. In the United States, charismatic relationship survives as an important element in the private practice of medicine but is often lacking in the fragmented and impersonal service given by public clinics to low-income patients. Some of the present ventures of reorganizing medical care attempt to secure a bureaucratic form of charisma for the doctors of public clinics. For example, in the government-supported health centers in the urban slums, it was suggested that "The people should 'belong' to the center as they belong to a church."[12] Thus, the aim is to confer a charismatic aura to government-established health agencies in an effort to help them accomplish what private practitioners can.

Some social scientists believe that a curious transformation is taking place in our society wherein the physician appears to be losing some of his or her charisma. This charisma, however, is passing into the office he or she occupies. Today, applied science promises people almost unlimited possibilities of nearly magical proportions: "Increasingly, the glory of the doctor as a person fades, while his scientific practices glow with promise. Far from being seen as completely unique individuals, doctors are coming to be regarded as interchangeable because they all have approximately the same training—a belief, incidentally, which is self-consciously fostered by medical groups and institutions that socialize the practice of medicine."[19] This is what Max Weber identifies as the routinization of charisma, the gift of grace being transferred from the person to the position.[27] Thus, the physician is not accorded unquestionable authority; rather, the science being applied is the final authority. As medicine comes to be regarded as predominately science and little art, it follows that doctors are thought to be made rather than born. The mass media, in general, have a tendency to emphasize the doctor's scientific skills at the cost of his or her personal powers. This tendency may be indicative of the doctor's passage from the status of a charismatic hero to a cultural hero.[19]

As government's intrusion into the practice of medicine becomes greater every day, there is concern that all doctors will become civil service technicians, and as such, they will lose their charismatic authority. Many outside of medicine, especially in the social science fields as previously noted, also predict the secularization of American medicine and the erosion of the doctor's charismatic authority. The social scientists base their predictions on a number of factors; chief among them are the cooperative efforts of the community trying to improve its general health and determine the priorities of medical care. They state quite frankly that doctors will endure not as mediators of the mysteries of life and death, but as civil service technicians in the health enterprise.

Such predictions are partly nonsense. In our culture, the charismatic authority in medicine has to do with the possibility of death in any illness, which accounts for the seriousness of the medical enterprise. Also, there are too many unknown or unknowable factors in illness for medicine to rest entirely on technical skill. Furthermore, it is impossible to assess fully the knowledge of doctors or how, on behalf of the recovery of their patients, they will bring to bear their knowledge—with all its ramifications as to timing, quality, blending, intuitive insights, and exquisite awareness of the right amount for intervention. Because of these phenomena, doctors will always retain a great deal of their original priestly role. Patients know that medicine deals with powerful and mysterious forces which are not completely amenable to what is generally identified as scientific reasoning.

In spite of the new technologies for the prevention or treatment of disease, illness remains as threatening as ever as far as a particular sick person is concerned. The human condition which led to charismatic authority is still with us. Because of the frailty of mortal flesh, we ascribe to doctors a special more-than-human authority in the hope that they will intervene successfully on our behalf should we fall ill.

No matter what changes occur in the delivery of health care, there is no need for doctors to fear the loss of charismatic authority as long as they validate and renew it daily throughout their lives. How do they validate and renew it? They do so by reverting to the source of their authority: the conscientious concern for the well-being of their patients; a receptivity to their silent plea, "Don't let me die"; and the unbroken promise that they will wage an unrelenting battle against death in the patients' behalf. With such a commitment, their charismatic authority cannot be interfered with, for its validation and renewal will occur daily.

CONCLUSION

Formally, students' medical education begins when they enter medical school and continues throughout their lives, for continuing education is an essential part of physicians' professional growth. This in part accounts for the often-quoted statement that when the sun sets on the first day of school for beginning medical students, they will be behind in their work and will never catch up in their lifetimes. Such a statement is true. It is not meant to discourage, but rather to add challenge and anticipation to the lives of aspiring doctors. There will be no empty todays or tomorrows.

A career in medicine is anchored in responsibility, not in freedom. In fact, the M.D. degree is rooted in such enormous responsibility that new doctors may feel that bondage, rather than freedom, characterizes their lives. Yet, it is that kind of responsibility that truly brings freedom. When one's commitment is to others, when one's work comforts and heals, one finds meaning in life, and with meaning comes the only freedom worth cherishing.

Wise students and physicians develop an existential stance and try to live each day fully, for today is all they have for certain. When tomorrow comes, it will bring a new set of demands and opportunities and will permit the consideration of very little of that which was unwisely put off from yesterday. The great physician Sir William Osler speaks of an illuminating moment when he, as a young man, became acquainted with Thomas Carlyle's essay "Signs of the Times." A sentence in the essay captured his attention and became an obsession: "Our main business in life is not to see what lies dimly at a distance but to do what lies clearly at hand." Into each day Osler packed the ingredients of the full life and refused to fret or worry about yesterdays or tomorrows. Osler tells of his discovery and encourages others toward a similar life style in his essay "A Way of Life."[21]

Similar to Osler's counsel but with more emphasis on what can be done in a day when resolve remains firm are the words of Ernest von Bergmann. In a letter written about 1895 to his son Gustav, who was studying medicine, von Bergmann admonished: "No fortress is entered in one assault, but he who advances his trenches with firm resolve attains his goal. To this remain true!"

Oliver Wendell Holmes has written that there is something very solemn and depressing about one's entrance into the study of medicine, for the setting of one's learning is in the context of suffering, tragedy, death, and the symbols of death. Holmes goes on to say: "When I first entered the room where medical students were seated at a table with a skeleton hanging over it, and bones lying about, I was deeply impressed, and more disposed to moralize upon mortality than to take up the task in osteology, which lay before me."[17] He, like his classmates, soon found an interest in matters that at the outset seemed uninviting and repulsive, and after the first difficulties were overcome, began to enjoy his new acquisition of knowledge.

Today's students share with Holmes many of the same feelings and experiences in making their way in the world of medicine. "Medicine" implies not only what medical persons do, but also denotes a social science that uses the methods of the natural sciences to obtain the objectives of promoting and restoring health, preventing diseases, and rehabilitating the patient. The healer's mantle, which the students seek, imposes these responsibilities. It is to be hoped that the fiery furnace through which they must walk to receive the mantle burns away the impurities from mind and soul and leaves them worthy to tend the suffering.

REFERENCES

1. Becker HS, et al.: Boys in White: Student Culture in Medical School. Chicago, University of Chicago Press, 1961
2. Blackburn T: The School of Babylon. In Allen DC (ed): A Celebration of Poets. Baltimore, Johns Hopkins Press, 1967, p 131
3. Bloom SW: Socialization for the physician's role—a review of some contributions of research to theory. In Shapiro EC, Lowenstein LM (eds): Becoming a Physician—Development of Values and Attitudes in Medicine. Cambridge, Massachusetts, Ballinger, 1979, pp 3–53
4. Coombs RH: Mastering Medicine—Professional Socialization in Medical School. New York, Macmillan, 1978
5. Doctor X: Intern. Greenwich, Connecticut, Fawcett, 1966, p 10
6. Eliot G: Middlemarch, a Study of Provincial Life. Boston, Colonial Press, vol 3, p 189
7. Gaensbauer TJ, Mizner GL: Developmental stresses in medical education. Psychiatry 43:60, 1980
8. Gerth HH, Mills CW: From Max Weber. New York, Oxford University Press, 1958, pp 245–264
9. Jonas S: Medical Mystery—the Training of Doctors in the United States. New York, Norton, 1978
10. Keniston K: The medical student. Yale J Biol Med 39:346, 1967
11. Kosa J: Entrepreneurship and charisma in the medical profession. Soc Sci Med 4:25, 1970
12. Lee RV: Provision of health services. N Engl J Med 277:685, 1967
13. Levinson DJ: Medical education and the theory of adult socialization. J Health Soc Behav 8:253, 1967
14. Maugham WS: The Summing Up. New York, Doubleday, 1938, pp 61–63
15. Mayerson EW: Putting the Ill at Ease. New York, Harper & Row, 1976
16. Molish HB, et al.: A Rorschach study of a group of medical students. Psychiatr Q 24:744, 1950
17. Morse JT: Life and Letters of Oliver Wendell Holmes. Boston, Houghton Mifflin, 1896
18. Mullan F: White Coat, Clenched Fist—The Political Education of an American Physician. New York, Macmillan, 1976

19. Myerhoff BG, Larson WR: The doctor as culture hero: The routinization of charisma. Reflections 1:7, 1966
20. Olmstead AG, Paget MA: Some theoretical issues in professional socialization. J Med Educ 44:663, 1969
21. Osler W: A Way of Life. (Address delivered to Yale students, April 20, 1913) Springfield, Illinois, Charles C Thomas, 1969
22. Pellegrino ED: To be a physician. Texas A & M College of Medicine Convocation Address, October 14, 1977
23. Schlageter CW, Rosenthal J: What are normal medical students like? J Med Educ 37:19, 1962
24. Shapiro EC, Lowenstein LM (eds): Becoming a Physician—Development of Values and Attitudes in Medicine. Cambridge, Massachusetts, Ballinger, 1979
25. Sharaf MR, Levinson DJ: The quest for omnipotence in professional training: The case of the psychiatric resident. Psychiatry 27:135, 1964
26. Sigerist HE: Medicine and Human Welfare. New Haven, Yale University Press, 1941, pp 105–106
27. Weber M: The Theory of Social and Economic Organization. Translated by Parsons T, Henderson AM. New York, Oxford University Press, 1947
28. Webster TG, Robinowitz CB: Becoming a physician—long-term social group. Gen Hosp Psychiatry, 1(1):53, 1979
29. Williamson P: Office Diagnosis. Philadelphia, Saunders, 1960, p viii

4

THE CADAVER: COLD COMPANION, BUT IDEAL PATIENT

Mortui vivos docent. *

A student mentioned that a few days before he began his course in gross anatomy he had two dreams about cadavers. In the first dream he passed a haunted house with a cemetery in the front yard. As he was passing, fully dressed ashen gray bodies lifted themselves from the grave plots and swooped down upon him. He fought off their attack and fled. The next night he dreamed that he stood beside the table upon which rested the cadaver assigned to him. Beneath the covering sheet, the cadaver's arms lifted themselves. He interpreted these dreams as being offensive action on the part of the cadavers: "Since we students would be dissecting these cadavers, the cadavers were resisting this by attacking us before we could attack them."

Further comments by this bright and stable student showed that he saw himself as an "intruder in the dust" in his dissecting experience, as violating a taboo, as invading the privacy and rights of the dead. This is a feeling shared by many students, at least in the early days and weeks of their dissecting experience in gross anatomy.

The anatomy laboratory provides for many students a profound emotional shock. These students share with society the reverence and respect that is given the dead body, as well as the many unconscious and magical attitudes toward the dead. The human form on the dissecting table, heavy with the pungent odor of formaldehyde, often becomes the focus of intense anxiety. The jokes, naming the cadaver, uneasy laughter, and nonchalant attitude toward the dissection of the corpse are common experiences and are remembered by most physicians.†

---

* This inscription—"The dead teach the living"— has often been placed over the doorways of anatomy laboratories.
† Becker and associates in their study of medical students, *Boys in White,* did not find the anatomy laboratory and the dissection of the cadaver a source of trauma in the students they studied.[1] These investigators saw essentially none of the defensive behavioral patterns used by students in dealing with anxiety. Their observations appear to be atypical.

In addressing the incoming freshmen at the University of Buffalo Medical School in 1905, Dr. J. E. King alerted the students to one of the most unpleasant and upsetting events of the first year—their first time in the dissecting room. He went on to relate a story about one of the jokes played on a student by his classmates in such a room.[13] Dr. King's remarks about the trauma and the macabre humor related to the dissection of the cadaver are similarly expressed by a majority of physicians. Thus, the experience leaves an imprint that may never be completely erased.

The evidence of this imprint is found in the writings of many physician authors. For example, Arthur W. Epstein, neurologist and psychiatrist, builds his splendid and insightful novel about the human spirit, *The Dissecting Room,* around memories of the anatomy laboratory and a medical school class reunion. On the cover of the book are found these words: *"The Dissecting Room takes its origin from a key experience in every physician's life—an experience whose ripples touch many distant shores."*[8] Another example of the anatomy laboratory's imprinting is surgeon Marshall Goldberg's novel, *The Anatomy Lesson.*[11] The novel begins with these words: "Emotion is the imprinter of memory. The remembrance of that first day of medical school was forever after that like the unfolding of a bad dream for Daniel Lassiter, never objective or sequential but always beginning with a stark, haunting vision—the slow-motion opening of the doors to the anatomy lab, a faint odor of embalming fluid wafting to his nostrils, and then his sudden immersion into the macabre world of cadavers within . . . bodies of the working dead."

One could list a number of positive and negative factors growing out of the dissection of a cadaver. At times, however, it is difficult to decide whether a particular item should be listed on the positive or negative side of the ledger.

Students are immediately aware that the manual skill and knowledge they gain by dissecting are to be transferred later to living patients. They are supposed to be emotionally detached from the cadaver they are dissecting, and usually assume, uncritically, that they are. From a psychological standpoint, how could this be possible? Their relationship to the cadaver becomes an outlet for many sublimated drives, such as those of mastery and power. The cadaver, completely passive and unresistant to the dissector's intentions, easily comes to be the student's ideal of a patient in all respects and the prototype of all future patients in certain respects.[14]

The fact that the cadaver is dead is an attribute, a quality that is desirable to the student for many subjective reasons. That the cadaver was once alive is pushed aside psychologically by the student and is not assigned any importance. During the fourteenth century, in order to guard against the loss of humanistic awareness in students, the School of Salernum required students to celebrate mass each morning for the salvation of the cadaver's soul, thereby reminding students before they began their dissection that the cadaver was once a living person.[14, 20] Such an effort today to humanize the cadaver creates, for both student and faculty, serious problems with which it is difficult to deal effectively. For example, students have been asked to learn as much biographical material as possible about their cadaver before beginning dissection. Anatomy classes where this technique has been tried have had much higher dropout rates because of student anxiety, the breakdown of defenses related to detachment, and so on.

Experience with the cadaver helps students develop the *preclinical state of mind* where students remain as confident and unruffled with the use of scalpel on the living patient as they displayed with the cadaver. Along with the skills and knowledge, much of the psychological relationship to the cadaver is carried over unconsciously to living patients. Where these patients differ from a cadaver in failing to follow a treatment regimen or showing a will of their own, the students, in their clinical years, may feel a dissatisfaction or tension, which may be formulated as a longing for their original patient (the cadaver) that offered no resistances.

The wish that one were still working with a cadaver has probably played a part in promoting many technical advances or innovations in medical practice. The desire that the patient might be as amenable to dissection as the cadaver contributed to the invention of general anesthesia. Such, at any rate, must have been the thought behind the words of the illustrious Magendie, who startled his colleagues allegedly by opposing the use of ether in these words: "For some weeks, a certain number of surgeons have set themselves to experiment on man, and for an undoubtedly praiseworthy purpose—that of performing operations without pain—they intoxicate their patients to the point of reducing them, so to speak, to the state of a cadaver which one can slice and cut at will without causing pain. . . . As for myself, I should never allow my body to be handed over to a surgeon in a defenseless state."[17]

The transition from the preclinical "patient" (the cadaver), with whom one does not identify, to the human being in the clinic, with whom one does, is marked by conflict. The conflict between the "pure" anatomist's position and the humanistic one is the source of many extensive rationalizations.

In the conduct of medical practice, doctors must be sufficiently flexible to include both preclinical and clinical attitudes in their relationship with patients and must be prepared to shift from one to the other with the same patient. For example, surgeons treat the anesthetized patient as a quasi-cadaver during a surgical procedure but as a living person during convalescence. To understand a patient fully, doctors must identify with the patient. Thus, they identify or dissociate themselves from the patient, in accordance with the demands of rational diagnostic and therapeutic aims.

Renshaw speculates that the normal, healthy responses that students mobilize to cope with the stress of first exposure to the dead body may form the basis of subsequent mechanisms for coping with death and dying that are less adaptive because they create a gap between physicians, patients, and their families.[19] Actually, this gap may be accentuated because the dissection becomes a rite of passage that segregates developing professionals from their future public.[3]

The common opinion is that doctors are disturbed more by death than is the general population. Could this grow, in part, out of doctors' first clinical encounter with death, which usually occurs on their first day in medical school?* This encounter is not with a living patient but with the cadaver, the dead body, assigned the student in the anatomy laboratory. This anonymous person is an image of death. To some extent, everything the students learn in the years to come is designed to postpone having to look again into the face of death. Although they may be pleased with this completely passive and unresisting patient, possibly they enter into a declaration of war against death. While they dedicate themselves to healing and to facilitating health and life, part of the motivation is to defeat or at least delay death.

Students are usually not free of guilt in dissecting a human body and at some level of their thinking see themselves as "intruders in the dust." They seek to neutralize their guilt by giving special meaning to the dissection or by promising themselves to contribute much to society in return for having been granted this privilege of dissection. The serious application of their time and energies to learn from the cadaver is, to some extent, a symbolic wresting of life from death, for with this new knowledge they will win many victories over death.

An example of the thinking among students as to how they may be able to give special meaning to the cadaver's contribution to their

---

* From the beginning of their training, students must cope with the reality of death. In the anatomy laboratory, the reactions to death can be seen almost in caricature. Some students become depressed, while others display ghoulish or macabre humor. Some displace their impotent rage at death onto their partners at the dissecting table. A few drop out of school, and others let their partners do the work while they learn enough to get by, studying the illustrated text and preferring the disembodied illustrations to the real thing.

training follows. One of the four students dissecting a particular cadaver mentioned that this cadaver had been donated by a state mental institution and was that of a person who had no living relatives. Thus, the mental institution had donated his body to the medical school for teaching purposes. While dissecting, all four students expressed their awe at the marvelous and miraculous construction of the human body. One student became introspective and began to comment with reference to the cadaver: "It is a pity to die without friends and family. In college we read Tennyson's 'In Memoriam,' and I remember these lines:

> That nothing walks with aimless feet;
> That not one life shall be destroyed,
> Or cast as rubbish to the void,
> When God hath made the pile complete."

The student went on to say that these bodies, and possibly their lives, had ended as rubbish on a trash heap. Another student responded quietly but eloquently: "How can you imply that these bodies have ended on a trash heap? In the eyes of the world these people would have been considered unsuccessful—poor, ill, and alone. Yet, we do not know what lives they touched while living, what promises they fulfilled. And some student working with one of these bodies may be gripped by inspiration and insight that will lead him or her someday to the conquering of one of mankind's most dreaded diseases. God works in strange and mysterious ways to perform His wonders."

In line with what the last student said are the words of physician and poet Thomas P. Beresford, expressed in a poem entitled "Epitaph: For My Cadaver":*

> Wise, without breath,
> Teaching of death
> And of life's structures
> He gave to others
> What he had left:
> The final cleft,
> The selfless gift.[2]

Many students mention that a sense of awe and reverence like that of a religious experience sweeps over them at times, especially while

---

* By permission of the author and *Pharos* magazine.

dissecting the head or heart. Coupled with this religious experience may be a recognition of one's own mortality, the brevity of life, and the seriousness of one's purpose in vocational aspirations.

Some physicians, however, feel that one of the tragic errors of medical education has been making the dissection of the cadaver an initiation or rite of passage for the neophyte physician. A number of medical schools today are examining this old policy and modifying their curricula so that the medical student works first with the living, not the dead.

Two poignant voices coming from the distant past caution us against "dismembering and dissecting" as the initial approach in understanding the whole. These words are from *Amiel's Journal,* of about 1882:

> To understand is to possess the thing understood, first by sympathy and then intelligence. Instead, then, of first dismembering and dissecting the object to be conceived, we should begin by laying hold of it in its ensemble, then in its formation, last of all in its parts. The procedure is the same, whether we study a watch or a plant, a work of art or a character. We must study, respect, and question what we want to know instead of massacring it. We must assimilate ourselves to things and surrender ourselves to them; we must open our minds with docility to their influence and steep ourselves in their spirit and their distinctive form before we offer violence to them by dissecting them.[5]

Also, Polybius, in the second century B.C., spoke of the error of

> ... the notion that the contemplation of the *disjecta membra* of a once living and beautiful organism is equivalent to the direct observation of the organism itself in all the energy and beauty of life. I fancy that anyone who maintained such a position would speedily admit the ludicrous enormity of his error if the organism could be revealed to him by some magician who had reconstituted it, at a stroke, in its original perfection of form and grace of vitality. While the part may conceivably offer a hint of the whole, it cannot possibly yield an exact and certain knowledge of it.[5]

Most students are annoyed at the delaying of the appearance of living patients onto the medical school scene. A typical student comment is: "We start by dissecting a dead person, then spend long months in cold medical sciences. Why don't they walk us over to the hospital ward on the first day of school? At the same time that the students would be going to formal classes, they would be learning the art and science of medicine with patients. When you don't work with patients until your third year in medical school, it's too late—something has already died within you."

The student's objection to beginning his patient indoctrination with a cadaver instead of a hopeful, live person is supported by anthropologist Ashley Montagu. He writes in the *Journal of the American Medical Association:*

> A serious error, which is already beginning to be corrected in some medical schools is that instead of exposing the beginning student to health and vigorous life at its best, we expose him at the very outset of his medical training to the ravages of death and all that the preparator in the anatomy morgue can do to render the cadaver dissectible. The student is then supposed to reconstitute the cadaver as a living, functioning organism. This is absurd. The doctor should be prepared to minister to the needs of the living, and from the very first his studies should be conducted in relation to the living.[16]

Alan Gregg, the late medical educator and philosopher, held similar ideas to Montagu's and pointed out a major danger to lifeless medicine: a curious kind of callousness that need not be taken for maturity.[12]

Often the reason given for switching in medical school from the cadaver to a living patient is to spare students anxiety. Actually, there are better reasons, such as those given by Montagu and Gregg. To hope that students will be free of anxiety in their beginning work with the living is wishful thinking indeed. Psychoanalyst Cecily Legg mentioned that Anna Freud returned from a visit to a particular medical school enthusiastic about the school's new curriculum, where a student is introduced first to the birth of a baby and not to a cadaver.* Anna Freud gave the opinion that this new curricular approach would probably be much less anxiety provoking for the student. Dr. Legg asked if one experience would not be just as anxiety provoking as the other because of both conscious and unconscious factors. In the unconscious, opposites (for example, birth and death) often possess the same emotional intensity or capacity for causing anxiety.[9, 10] Anna Freud agreed with her and went on to say that evidently the rites of passage, whatever the approach taken, are laden with trauma, yet beginning with the living would seem to be a more reasonable approach in medical education and capable of bringing more positive benefits to the student.

Possibly we should listen to Dr. Henry Miller, vice-chancellor of the University of Newcastle-upon-Tyne, who urges a genuinely integrated

---

* Personal communication, January 18, 1972.

curriculum bridging the gap between the preclinical and clinical stages of training. He criticizes anatomists for their demand for inordinate hours of student time. He believes that the large amount of time devoted to human morphology, especially at the beginning of the curriculum, is not only logically indefensible but positively harmful to the student's motivation and enthusiasm. He writes, "For the average medical student it is a tedious and distracting chore, a penance to be undertaken before starting on his life's work. Much of what is taught is soon forgotten simply because it is irrelevant."[15]

Miller believes that the chief importance of anatomy is at the postgraduate level, where surgeons or other specialist physicians must learn the anatomy relevant to their practice. At this stage, however, they are more likely to learn it in the operating room or at the autopsy table than in the anatomy laboratory.

Anatomy seems destined to remain an emotion-laden topic for both student and faculty.[4] Constructive changes are taking place in many schools, but these changes have been slow to appear. Possibly we should not be discouraged, for changing an established pattern is difficult to bring about. Historian Robert Sobel says that the British created a civil service job in 1803 calling for a man to stand on the cliffs of Dover with a spyglass. He was supposed to ring a bell if he saw Napoleon coming. The job was abolished in 1945.[21] It is much easier to start something than stop it. Thus, gross anatomy as the starting point of medical education has been with us for a long time. Changing the initial emphasis from the dead to the living has been an almost impossible task.

Unfortunately, some of the many changes recommended appear rash and ill-conceived, such as the almost total abolition of gross anatomy. Few educators want the detailed course, popular only a few years ago, where students dissected out and learned the origin and insertion of every muscle or the distribution of every cutaneous nerve. Shorter textbooks have been written and are being used, and there is a de-emphasis on bones and muscle attachments and a greater concentration on function and on nerves and vessels. Furthermore, students are being taught how to learn anatomy and how to remember what they learn. The course is being evaluated from mere memorization to a visualization and an understanding of the body.[6]

George Engle, a psychiatrist and internist, emphasizes that the discipline of going through the structure of the human body in an orderly, systematic, and painstaking way gives knowledge that students will never forget.[7] Engle goes on to say that students may forget it in the sense that they cannot recall all the details, but their position in a few years will be vastly different from that of students who never knew it.

At what point in the student's progression through medical school should gross anatomy be taught? No agreement exists as to the correct answer. Should it be a student's initial experience in medical school? Parsons points out in his analysis of the social structure of medical practice that the dissection of a cadaver in the initial stage of medical training is not only an instrumental means of learning anatomy but is a symbolic act: "It is in a sense the initiatory rite of the physician-to-be into his intimate association with death and the dead."[18] As such, the situation is emotionally loaded and stressful for most students. Attitudes in the home, religious convictions, and other mental preoccupations determine the emotional response that attends the experience. It is to be hoped that *all* anatomy professors realize that the sights and smells that leave them unmoved may require the students to use a variety of emotional defenses.[4] Further, regardless of when anatomy is taught, a favorable environment ought to be created in the anatomy department where students can relate the daily experiences of anatomy to the humanistic, as well as scientific, values of the medical profession.

REFERENCES

1. Becker HS, et al.: Boys in White—Student Culture in Medical School. Chicago, University of Chicago Press, 1961
2. Beresford TP: Four poems. Pharos 42:23, 1979
3. Blackwell B: Medical education: Old stresses and new directions. Pharos 40:20, 1977
4. Blackwell B, Rodin AE, Nagy F, Reese RD: Humanizing the student-cadaver encounter. Gen Hosp Psychiatry, 1(4):315, 1979
5. Cantril H, Bumstead CH: Reflections on the Human Venture. New York, New York University Press, 1960, pp 14, 18–19
6. Crafts RC: Do we need anatomists or anatomy departments? J Med Educ 40:979, 1965
7. Engle GL: The implications of change in medical education. Hosp Pract 6:109, 1971
8. Epstein AW: The Dissecting Room. Gretna, Louisiana, Her Pub Co, 1978
9. Freud S: The antithetical meaning of primal words. Standard Edition of the Complete Works of Sigmund Freud. Translated by Strachey J. London, Hogarth Press, vol 11, 1953, pp 155–161
10. Freud S: On dreams. Standard Edition of the Complete Works of Sigmund Freud. Translated by Strachey J. London, Hogarth Press, vol 5, 1953, pp 659–665
11. Goldberg M: The Anatomy Lesson. New York, Putnam's, 1974

12. Gregg A: Challenges to Contemporary Medicine. New York, Columbia University Press, 1956, p 117
13. King JE: Student ideals. Buffalo Med J 62:184, 1906
14. Lewin BD: Counter-transference in the technique of medical practice. Psychosom Med 8:195, 1946
15. Miller H: Medical education and medical research. Lancet 1:1, 1971
16. Montagu A: Anthropology and medical education. JAMA 183:577, 1963
17. Olmstead JMD: Francois Magendie. New York, Schuman's, 1944, pp 243–248
18. Parsons T: The Social System. Glencoe, Illinois, Free Press, 1951, p 445
19. Renshaw DC: Death and the doctor. Chicago Medical Journal 82:153, 1979
20. Simpson MA: Medical Education—A Critical Approach. New York, Appleton-Century-Crofts, 1972, p 65
21. Quoted in Townsend R: Up the Organization. Greenwich, Connecticut, Fawcett, 1970, p 75

5

SEX AND MARRIAGE IN MEDICAL SCHOOL

Love is merely a madness, and, I tell you, deserves as well a dark house and a whip as madmen do: and the reason why they are not so punished and cured is, that the lunacy is so ordinary that the whippers are in love too. Yet I profess curing it by counsel.
—Shakespeare, *As You Like It*, Act III, Scene 2.

It has been frequently said that many medical students are neither sufficiently informed nor emotionally mature about sexual matters. Dr. Harold Lief's pioneering studies indicated that the majority of students led conservative sexual lives. He related this to the basic obsessive-compulsive personality type common among medical students, which he believed is more likely to be successful in a medical career.[11] Subsequent studies by Dr. Lief and others extend and modify these earlier findings. During the past 25 years, almost every medical school has made courses in human sexuality a part of the medical curriculum. While great strides have been made, much more needs to be done, for these courses vary widely in quantity, quality, and format. Further, the courses often fail to include adequate training for the treatment of sexual problems, although the courses may contain much useful information about human sexuality.[9, 13] Also, valid methods of evaluating these courses are only beginning,[24] and the results may turn out to be different from what was expected, as Schnarch and Jones have demonstrated.[19]

Of course, many authorities in sex education have pointed out that formal courses may not be the ideal method of instruction.[7, 12, 21] They are not suggesting that formal courses be de-emphasized but that new formats be developed in sex education and training. One format is the integration of sex education with rotations in obstetrics-gynecology and psychiatry during the clinical years.[6, 22]

Efforts are frequently made to compare the sexual knowledge or behavior of medical students with that of other students. In a 1970 study, 63 single male, sophomore medical students volunteered to respond fully and sincerely to a 352-item questionnaire covering approximately the same topics cited in Kinsey's *Sexual Behavior in the Human Male*. In addition to describing their own sexual behavior, the respondents, constituting a 57 percent sample of those invited to participate, indicated how they believed the average college man and woman would respond. The students appeared to believe that a double standard of sexual morality for men and women still existed. They displayed a generally conservative and proper "establishment" position, which suggested, as has been previously postulated, that they are inhibited and constricted in their behavior, and especially in their sexual behavior. However, comparisons between sexual activities reported by the students and those reported in the Kinsey report (for subjects of similar age with some college education) do not support the hypothesis that the sexual behavior of medical students is restricted. The medical students' estimates of the sexual activities of others were similar to the findings reported by Kinsey and did not suggest that they are naive and uninformed about sexual matters. Also, comparisons between students' descriptions of their own sexual activities and those they attribute to the average college student did not indicate that their concerns were different.[8]

A look at the present medical student population reveals a fair cross-section of the student types seen on the average university campus today. There are, however, situations in the social system of premedical and medical training that have potential for creating special problems in mate selection, marriage, and relationships with patients. Some of these problems will be reviewed in this chapter.

THE UNMARRIED MEDICAL STUDENT

The heavy demands of school hamper the social life of many students. Impending examinations, writing papers or case histories, and the care of patients leave little time for social life. When time is taken from studies for social activity, some students cannot enjoy this diversion. The thought of loafing while their classmates are studying or working detracts from the enjoyment of the occasion.

Since students are not able to anticipate when they can take an evening away from their studies, they usually cannot arrange or accept an invitation until the last minute. Eleventh hour planning limits the number of options available. Friends not in medical school may not understand the work situation of medical students and wonder why they often make plans at the last minute. The problem is further complicated when two or three weeks elapse before efforts are made to get together again. One may interpret such a long period of silence as an indication that the person doesn't care much for his or her company.

Under such circumstances, many of the relationships of students are superficial.

On the other hand, many are attracted to medical students and welcome dating opportunities, regardless of the circumstances. Medical students, male and female, are often looked upon as prize catches and sometimes for unexpected reasons. One college student stated that medical students are effective lovers, because in their anatomy courses they learn "what to feel" and in their psychiatry courses they learn "how to feel." Medical students ought to appreciate this testimonial, since their medical training is paying off in unexpected ways.

Among the positive changes brought by the increased number of women in medical school is the opportunity for medical students to date medical students. These students understand the setting and work situation of one another and share meaningfully on personal and professional levels that once were available to only a few in their medical training.

Medical students are often stereotyped sexually as either inhibited or dashingly romantic.[3] The mass media contribute substantially to keeping alive these stereotypes. Actually, one can find among medical students, male and female, essentially any type that one finds on the college campus. Probably the most typical is the serious student who puts his or her work first and deals with sexuality on a "catch as catch can" basis. Another type lives with a friend and enjoys the relationship without much guilt or concern about how others view living together without being married. Another type is active with multiple sexual partners and falls in the category that is euphemistically described as sexually athletic or macho. Again, the inference is to both male and female students. While *macho* is generally used to refer to the supermale, especially in regard to sexual matters, the female is not excluded from this category. For example, physician and movie producer Michael Crichton in a recent address spoke of feminine macho.[4] Thus, medical schools have both sexes represented in the macho group. Beyond those types described above, there are many students who fit none of these categories. Today a number of women who have been married and divorced are entering medical school, and they may or may not have children. The need to date is not strong in this group, for at some level they are saying, "We have put that activity behind us and are moving on to the fulfillment of other goals." They appear at ease, open, and nondefensive in this stance and enjoy good relationships with both sexes. One such student mentioned that when she does date, she is not searching for an enduring relationship, is comfortable dating an older or younger person, and can have sex with no interest in the possibility of a commitment. This student radiates a sense of warmth and renewal in her interpersonal relationships, as well as in the care of her patients. Many of the other students in this group possess this quality.

Sex Neutralizes Death

The students' immersion in death—cadavers, postmortem examinations, and dying patients—leads them to a variety of ways of dealing with their own fears of death and the fact that one day death will claim them. One of these ways is sex. Sex helps the medical students deny the painful transience of existence at a culturally permissible level. Since they are busy with the many academic and clinical responsibilities, they may feel justified in concentrating on the act of sex while escaping the commitments of love. They may become preoccupied with physical sex, although this is usually not the case. When such a preoccupation occurs, one wonders if it is not part of an effort to neutralize death, which stands as the symbol of ultimate impotence and finiteness. As Rollo May emphasizes in *Love and Will,* sex is the easiest way to prove one's vitality, to demonstrate that one is still young, virile and attractive, to prove that one is not dead.[14] In the sheer mechanics of sex, such students can prove, at least to themselves, that they are not alone. This type of sexual behavior is unhealthy insofar as it detaches one's sexuality from tender, long-term commitment to a member of the opposite sex. Usually the sex has no relationship to love. Shem, in describing sexual activity during his training in the hospital named "House of God,"* illustrates this point: "And I know now that the sex in the House of God had been sad and sick and cynical and sick, for like all our doings in the House, it had been done without love, for all of us had become deaf to the murmurs of love."[20]

Medical students are not the only students who may seek to transcend their immersion in or fear of death through sexuality. *The Wall Street Journal* carried an article about a college student who bought several old hearses from funeral homes and rented them to his fellow students as "dating buggies" or "jazz wagons." The hearses afforded privacy and a bed. The sexual act carried out in a hearse would seem to represent more than a convenient and inexpensive place for such activity.

---

* Shem uses a fictitious name, "House of God," to disguise the real name of the hospital where he interned.

MATE SELECTION

In this section, the emphasis is on those situations in the social system of premedical and medical training that have potential for creating special problems in mate selection and subsequently in marriage.

In general, medical students or physicians probably spend too little time in selecting a marriage partner. They are usually looking for a mate when their free time is highly compressed and contacts are limited. These two factors, plus the tendency to seek a supportive type, help to account for the fact that many doctors' spouses are health professionals.

Probably as many marital conflicts grow out of having selected the wrong mate as from the complications innate in the study and practice of medicine. In the best of circumstances mate selection is fraught with difficulties. The choosing of a mate is a confused step, not primarily because one inadvertently chooses a mate whose interests and habits are incompatible with one's own but because each of the pair is ignorant of the unconscious purposes that determine their respective choices.[10] Being in love does not guarantee that a wise choice has been made. Moreover, as George Bernard Shaw puts it in *Man and Superman:* "When two people are under the influence of the most violent, most insane, most delusive, and most transient of passions, they are required to swear that they will remain in that excited, abnormal, and exhausting condition continuously until death do them part."

Superficially, one would conclude that the nurse and physician would make an excellent marriage because each has great knowledge and understanding of the work and professional identity of the other. What is forgotten, however, is the "double dependency" which frequently brings them together and which at times interferes with their having a stable and mature marriage. The nurse-doctor double dependency is seen more often in the male physician than in the female. The nurse who is attracted to the physician is often one who has idealized the doctor as a helpful, giving, and understanding person like her parent or family doctor remembered from childhood. The nurse is confident that this type of man will soon meet her every emotional need. At the same time, the medical student or young physician is impressed by the efficiency and competence he sees in the nurse. His own feelings of awkwardness as a novice arouse his dependency feelings for the nurse, whom he may see in a motherly role, whatever her age. In many nurse-doctor marriages, this role confusion continues after marriage, with each partner expecting the strength and support from the other that existed in fantasy or perhaps in the hospital setting but was not transferable to the home.

In the sense that some persons are motivated toward the study of medicine to control an excessive fear of death, some persons are motivated toward marrying a doctor for the same reason. The fear of death in such persons is a type of death phobia. They seek out the medical student or doctor to marry as a counterphobic maneuver. The doctor has the magic to protect against death. They can acquire continuous protection through marriage to a doctor. This, at least, is their unconscious fantasy.

In the chapter, "The Decision to Become a Doctor," there is a discussion of the motivational factor of "the need to rescue." If medical students are gripped with a rescue fantasy, their highest mission in life is to rescue. This need to rescue may also guide their choice of a marital partner. They may rescue one whose "true worth" is not realized because of a low socio-economic status, one who is about to become a prostitute, one who is becoming mentally ill, or one who needs to be saved from the overuse of drugs or alcohol, to name a few extreme conditions calling for rescue. Like an evangelist, they move into action with this theme reverberating in the mind: "Soon will the season of rescue be over. . . . Haste then, no time for delay; but, throw out the lifeline and save a dear one today."

Both male and female medical students share a tendency in our society to divide the opposite sex into two distinct types: the sensual type with whom one can have sex and the other type from whom one can receive tenderness, love, and what a parent has to offer. This dichotomizing is done more sharply by males than females, which accounts in part for the use of the psychoanalytic term—the madonna–prostitute dichotomy—to describe this phenomenon.[5]

One medical student came to school with his new bride—a pale, retiring, virginal type—selected for him in part by his mother and sister. From the beginning, their sexual functioning was poor, and after a few months he was impotent with her. During his impotence he met a Comanche Indian nurse and became wildly potent with her while remaining impotent with his wife. The sexual games they played went beyond everything anyone always wanted to know about sex. After many months of this sensual abandon, he began to wonder why a wife could not also be a good sexual partner. At this point in his life, he began psychotherapy. As one would have expected, in a short time he gained psychological insight into his tendency to fragment women into two types and how this dichotomy had entered into his selection of one type of woman for a wife and another type for sexual pleasure.

An interesting behavioral pattern of some medical students sets the stage for their failure in mate selection. This group is characterized by students who are usually timid and shy in matters of sex when they arrive in medical school. They spent most of their time in college studying to assure medical school acceptance and neglected many of the tasks of growing up. Their sexual timidity in medical school gradually gives way to experimentation and then almost to compulsiveness in the satisfaction of sexual needs. As they contemplate becoming a doctor, these ideas come to mind: "I am going to be a physician and society expects much of me. I must be conforming, upright, and moral in every area of my life, including the sexual." Marriage *now* is the answer, they decide. And in no time they are married to some available person. They may be fortunate and get a good and suitable spouse. At times, however, they choose one who is innocent and immature or one who hardly has any identity of his or her own. Occasionally, male medical students unfortunately choose a partner with "a fast pelvis and a slow mind." As they get deeper into their medical career, they will find they have less time to quiet the restless pelvis or quicken the slow mind. Serious problems are inevitable. Women medical students may find a similar type in the male who is not tied down by job or other attachments and can follow them wherever they go. Medical students describe this type of male spouse with the words, "Have gun, will travel."

Because of the long period of costly training ahead of them, some students guard their independence and try to avoid serious romances. They may become so fixed in their pattern of running away from a developing in-depth relationship that the pattern operates spontaneously when they would prefer not to run. After losing a friend who had everything they wanted in a spouse, they suddenly awaken and try to win back the person. Often such persons have been hurt sufficiently in the previous disruption that they will not open themselves to another relationship with the injuring party. On the other hand, they may permit themselves to be won back; and in the new victory, the lover becomes ambivalent again and seeks postponement of marriage rather than running away as was formerly done. In such a situation one could say that progress toward marriage is being made but at a great emotional cost to both partners.

The previous remarks may lead one to believe that no medical students choose their mates wisely and carefully. Many medical students and physicians enjoy successful, happy marriages, in spite of the professional demands on their time and energies.

The Medical Student's Spouse

The trials and tribulations of medical students' spouses have been written about and spoken of so frequently that new spouses expect the worst. Usually they find the situation better than they anticipated. In general, one cannot help being impressed with the adaptive skills and attitude of most students' spouses. While striving for a good marriage now, they also are aware of the future promise of professional status, financial security, and diverse opportunities.

One must consider, however, the heavy costs and potential dangers to the marriage of any student pursuing a career in medicine.[2] One indicator of the impact of these pressures is the high divorce rate among medical students. Among the increased pressures are financial problems, which are generally more pressing among married students than single ones. Further, the spouse often bears a double burden of working full-time to support the family, as well as carrying the bulk of household duties, including child care if children are present. Other sacrifices required of many spouses are postponing or foregoing further schooling, delay in having children, and holding his or her own career or interests in abeyance. An engineer expressed genuine concern that if his medical student wife, now 30 years old, postponed much longer the having of children, they would end up with no children or children with Down's syndrome.

Another problem may be a widening gap between the intellectual levels of student and spouse. This need not be, however, for many spouses keep up with various facets of medicine and also develop their own talents to a high level of competence and self-fulfillment. Perhaps the greatest stress to the marriage relationship is the extreme limitation in the amount of time that student and spouse are able to spend together, as well as the forced separations that some couples must endure, especially during the clinical years of medical school. The husband of a medical student has written personally about the separations from his wife or limitations in time spent with her as "a spouse suffering the partial loss of a loved one."[17] He compares what happened to him and other spouses, male and female, with John Bowlby's account of the process of mourning and its resolution—protest, depair, and detachment.[1]

The male spouse may find himself in a more difficult situation than his female counterpart regarding some areas of the marriage. While assuming the role of breadwinner, he carries out also the less familiar and often conflict-producing tasks of running the household and childrearing. He may be forced to compromise his own career by relocation or give less to his work for the sake of his other responsibilities as a medical student's spouse. The outlook usually improves dramatically when his wife's formal training is over. Yet, in his marriage, as well as in many others today, gender does not automatically decide who does what in the relationship. The decisions that must be made require time, energy, and the patience of careful negotiation.

Success in Marriage

One may tend to see the medical student marriage as only a problem-ridden relationship. The testimonies of numerous students and their spouses indicate otherwise. "I would not have survived the trauma, loneliness, and heartache of medical school without the help of my spouse" is a statement often heard. The companionship and sharing in marriage are undeniable boons to a harried medical student who might otherwise feel lonely, unloved, and overworked. A spouse soothes the psychic wounds inflicted in the education process.

The spouses themselves have needs, and students smart enough to be in medical school should be able to figure out ways of meeting these needs while not seriously neglecting their work. Accomplishing this is not easy, but it is a goal worthy of commitment and sacrifice. At the same time, one cannot forget the sobering words of Dr. Christiaan Barnard's former wife that a member of the medical profession can only be a part-time spouse.

In discussing marriage with students who appear to have successful marriages, a few factors stand out sharply. One of these involves time spent with their spouses. They spend some time alone with their spouses and do so fairly regularly. And during these periods, they try especially not to let medical matters intrude.

Another factor stressed by these students is that each partner has a deep interest in helping the other grow emotionally and intellectually. Since medical students are immersed in an intense learning environment, they could easily grow intellectually beyond their spouses. At the same time, if spouses strive for both depth and breadth in their educational growth, they may attain a sense of being educated to a much greater extent than a partner who is narrowly focused on medicine. Thus, those students and their spouses, aware of how growth can take place in one another, avoid pitfalls and strive for intellectual and emotional growth in both partners.

A third factor observed in students with successful marriages relates to communication. These students appear to communicate in depth with their spouses and share with one another their feelings and innermost thoughts. Through effective communication they avoid becoming isolated. They experience intimacy and know how the needs of male and female may differ in priorities related to touching, closeness, physical sex, and orgasm. They search for the optimal distance and when to be close or move toward, and when to move away. They learn not to cling and be possessive, yet they learn how not to be detached. Above all, they learn to listen, which is a prime ingredient in communication. They may not want to hear about life-saving exploits at the medical center, especially as soon as one arrives at home. They may permit a brief period of isolation from one another on arriving at home for recovery from the "peopled out" feeling or for recharging emotional batteries.

They share in many of the mundane chores around the home. As one spouse has said, "It is salutary to see 'God' take out the garbage."

SEX EDUCATION IN MEDICAL SCHOOL

A frank 21-year-old girl mentioned to me how pleased she was to hear that medical schools today were trying to give their students some genuine human understanding in sexual matters. She told of being sent to her mother's gynecologist when she was 16 to see if everything was "all right." She was placed on the examining table and in stirrups by the nurse. The doctor seemed reluctant to examine her vagina, assuming it would not admit a speculum and assuming that the hymen was intact. "With me in stirrups," she went on to say, "and with one of his fingers up my behind, his opening question was 'How is your mother?' Who in heaven's name would want to talk about mother at a time like that. Is the female pelvis so disarming that it interferes with the doctor's asking relevant questions or doing a complete examination?" Fortunately, training programs today deal with all factors in the conduct of such an examination, so that the patient's welfare may be served to the fullest extent. Also, medical schools are making a serious effort to establish training in human sexuality for solving problems encountered in medical practice.[23] With adequate preparation in this field, future physicians should become both competent and comfortable in counseling their patients in sexual matters.

The changing attitudes toward sexuality in general have made it easier for medical schools to introduce sex education into their curricula. Also of help has been the more viable assumption behind an interest in sex education—that it should work to make sex a more rewarding part of people's lives. Thus, sex education is able to serve competence and not necessarily constraint.

A considerable part of managing sexuality also involves managing social relationships. Medical students' previous life experience may have given them little training in this component of sex education. If they had been totally dedicated to their premedical studies, they may have had little time to develop enriching relationships with the opposite sex. Before they could hardly realize their passing youth, they found themselves in medical school, without having come to grips with the usual tasks of adolescence. Because of this basic inadequacy in the social development of students, the medical school's task of training in sexuality has been rendered more formidable.

Medical students also mirror the usual distortions of sexuality seen in the public at large. When sex is mentioned, the mental image that comes to the average person is a physical one. When sex in marriage is discussed, one tends to focus on the sex act itself, to the exclusion of the many intangibles in the human psyche that are also involved. In sexual matters, the preoccupation of the medical student is similar to that of most people today—the performance of the sex act. Such a preoccupation may push to a peripheral position the qualities of love and intimacy in sex. This mechanization of sex introduces a confusion of values in sexuality and makes more difficult the personal and professional growth of medical students. In much of the training of students in sexuality, teachers confuse sex education with genital plumbing and engineered orgasm.

Medical students must deal with two broad aspects of sexuality in their interactions with patients. They are called upon to provide objective knowledge of sexual physiology, behaviors, and attitudes. Second, their interaction with patients embodies the psychosexual component of any interpersonal relation. The element of sexuality in the doctor-patient relationship has received little attention by medical educators.

In the courses in sex education now being developed by medical schools, sexual physiology is only one of the major components.[23, 24] Another dimension seeks to give students the capacity of understanding their own sexuality, especially their sexual motivations, feelings, and investments in doctor-patient relationships. Mudd and Siegel emphasize that physicians should be able to interact with their patients without serious inhibitions and in an entirely professional way. Besides being able to use and impart their knowledge with an objective, dispassionate attitude, they should be capable of integrating the inevitable sexuality of their relations with unimpaired professionalism and compassion.[16] Medical students have a strong desire for sex education both for their personal edification and to equip them to counsel patients.

There are numerous causes, many of them obvious, for students' anxiety in doctor-patient relationships. Sexual conflict has been identified as one of these causes, but it is rarely given proper attention in medical education. The medical students are suddenly thrust into situations in the doctor-patient relationship where protective or controlling social institutions such as clothing, taboo subjects, or rules for "decent" behavior are absent. Previously well-organized sociosexual inhibitions of behavior must be altered to permit incorporating the professional role of the doctor. The demand to construct artificially a code of values and behavior for a new professional role is difficult for almost any student since it tends to intensify or reawaken sexual ambivalence.[16]

In studying sexual conflicts of 75 students, Woods and Natterson found that a sense of sexual competence and confidence was indispensable to good doctor-patient interactions.[25] These investigators believe that the degree to which students' sexual anxiety is troublesome or detrimental to good doctor-patient communication depends on the extent to which students have resolved their own sexual conflicts and achieved a sense of sexual adequacy free of guilt, shame, or anxiety. This view would appear to be essentially valid, yet it might lead one to expect that students with the strongest feelings of sexual confidence or perhaps those with extensive sexual experience should be the least anxious in the professional situation. Data from a study of 397 male medical students at the University of Pennsylvania by Mudd and Siegel do not support this expectation.[16] A highly significant correlation was noted between feelings of confidence in social situations and number of coital partners. Mudd and Siegel go on to state that

> ... however, neither of these "social" measurements was found to correlate with decreased anxiety or with decreased propensity to anxiety in sexually provocative professional situations. In addition, the "profile" data revealed patterns of anxiety during various patient contacts that were remarkably *independent* of prior coital experience or feelings of social confidence. Apparently, then, students' experience or feelings of sexual adequacy in their "social" dealings do not endow them with a similar sense of adequacy and confidence during anxiety-provoking professional encounters. Even the most socially sophisticated and confident students experience sexual anxiety in their role as physicians.

Students, as they progress through medical school, gain a broader concept of sexuality. The concomitant decrease in sexual anxiety over the four-year period may be related to a number of factors, among them the assimilation of a professional role, independent maturation, and the acquisition of specific sexual knowledge. They become more comfortable and sophisticated in handling provocative confrontations.

Many special methodological problems are encountered in the teaching of sexuality to students. Students bring to medical school their own unique portfolio of beliefs and misbeliefs, information and misinformation, and varying proportions of anxiety, shame, and guilt. Teaching techniques must include more than the giving of information. Through the medium of repetitive supervised sessions with patients, students are helped to identify, understand, and cope with the inevitable and often irrational responses associated with the task of learning about the ontogenetic development of human sexual behavior—theirs and their patients'. Along with supervised sessions with patients, many schools present the students with lecture material covering the major areas of human sexuality. Also an effective teaching or learning method being made available to students is the seminar or small group for discussion of the students' own sexual concerns, as well as their many psychological stresses in the doctor-patient relationship. When these group discussions and seminars are included as a part of students' clinical rotations on services such as obstetrics-gynecology and psychiatry, their effectiveness is greatly enhanced. Not to be forgotten is the significance of the students' identification with their faculty. Besides respect, students need their professors' humanistic example.[15] Unfortunately, the establishment of appropriate dialogue directed toward the emotional needs of students and their patients is one of the most neglected aspects of humanism in medical education today.

CONCLUSION

When medical students seek counseling, their sexual and marital problems are not fundamentally different from those of other persons of the same age and social class distribution. They do seem, however, more hesitant than other students in seeking help about sexual problems. In all likelihood, this is based more on shame than on anxiety. As medical students, they believe that they are expected to know about these matters and therefore feel embarrassed to display their ignorance.

Unlike other students, their professional education requires that they be participant observers, not spectators. The medical students not only have their own problems to deal with according to their age and circumstance, but they must also learn to master the normal anxieties, shames, fascinations, and guilts associated with looking at and touching genitals. In addition, they must accumulate the data and develop the skills to make decisive judgments about the study, care, and treatment of the patients entrusted to them. Law students or divinity students do not have to do this, nor are they permitted to do so. This, then, becomes a task in the education of physicians, a task requiring proper and useful coping mechanisms to deal with ordinary shames, guilts, and anxieties so that students can acquire the compassionate objectivity specific to the healing role. This is included in what Romano identifies as "disciplining the capacity for human intimacy."[18]

The new training programs in human sexuality for medical students are expected to add greatly to their knowledge and skills and, in turn, enable them to be more effective in the care of their patients.

REFERENCES

1. Bowlby J: Processes of mourning. Int J Psychoanal 43:317, 1961
2. Bruhn JG, et al.: A Doctor in the House. Galveston, Texas, University of Texas Medical Branch, 1978
3. Coombs RH: The medical marriage. In Coombs RH, Vincent CE (eds): Psychological Aspects of Medical Training. Springfield, Illinois, Charles C Thomas, 1971, pp 133-167
4. Crichton M: Why work is work. Address given at the annual meeting of the American Psychiatric Association, San Francisco, June 6, 1980
5. Freud S: Contributions to the psychology of love. Collected Papers. Translated by Riviere J. London, Hogarth Press, vol. 4, 1953, pp 192-236
6. Friedman RC, Vosburgh GJ, Stern LO: Observed responses of medical students in a sex education seminar on obstetrics and gynecology. Int J Psychiatry Med 9:61, 1978
7. Golden JS, Liston EH: Medical sex education: The world of illusion and the practical realities. J Med Educ 47:761, 1972
8. Gottheil E, Friedman A: Sexual beliefs and behavior of single, male medical students. JAMA 212:1327, 1970
9. Green R (ed): Human Sexuality—A Health Practitioner's Text. Second edition. Baltimore, Williams & Wilkins, 1979
10. Kubie LS: Psychoanalysis and marriage: Practical and theoretical issues. In Eisenstein VW (ed): Neurotic Interaction in Marriage. New York, Basic Books, 1956, pp 10-43
11. Lief HI: Sexual attitudes and behavior of medical students—implications for medical practice. In Nash EM, Jessner L, Abse DW (eds): Marriage Counseling in Medical Practice—a Symposium. Chapel Hill, North Carolina, University of North Carolina Press, 1964, pp 301-318
12. Lief HI: Sex education in medical schools. J Med ED 46:373, 1971
13. Lief HI, Karlen A (eds): Sex Education in Medicine. New York, Spectrum, 1976
14. May R: Love and Will. New York, Norton, 1969
15. Mendel WM, Green WA: On becoming a physician. J Med Educ 40:266, 1965
16. Mudd JW, Siegel RJ: Sexuality—the experience and anxieties of medical students. N Engl J Med 281:1397, 1969
17. Robinson DO: The medical-student spouse syndrome: Grief reactions to the clinical years. Am J Psychiatry 135:972, 1978
18. Romano J: Teaching medical students about population, sexual practices, and family planning. J Med Educ 43:898, 1968
19. Schnarch DM, Jones K: Efficacy of medical school sex education. J Sex Marital Ther, in press
20. Shem S: The House of God. New York, Dell, 1978, p 12

21. Sheppe WM Jr, Hain JD: Sex and the medical student. J Med Educ 41:457, 1966

22. Stanley E: The way we teach—human sexuality. Med Teacher 1:184, 1979

23. Stayton WR: The core curriculum: What can be taught and what must be taught. In Rosenzweig N, Pearsall FP (eds): Sex Education for the Health Professional: A Curriculum Guide. New York, Grune & Stratton, 1978, pp 51-61

24. Whitbeck C: What are we teaching when we teach human sexuality? Conn Med 42:657, 1978

25. Woods SM, Natterson J: Sexual attitudes of medical students—some implications for medical education. Am J Psychiatry 124:323, 1967

6

PSYCHOLOGICAL PROBLEMS OF MEDICAL STUDENTS

Isn't the highest function of counseling to point out that the essential hurdles have to be cleared if one is to become a physician, and that most of them do involve pain and trauma, and the knowledge of good and evil, and guilt?
—Paul Haun[14]

Each step in the process of educating a medical student, of producing a physician, carries with it the potential of threatening the equanimity of the student, depending on his or her history and personality.[10]

Among medical students, one may apply, psychiatrically speaking, the same general diagnostic categories as one applies in any other academic community or even in the population at large. The psychodynamic factors pertinent to the development of the presenting emotional complaint, however, are often different. These factors relate to the problems unique to and inherent in the intimate nature of the medical educational process. Such problems often arouse latent conflicts as the students react to the unconscious significance that the particular problem may have for them. In other words, the content of their emotional reactions is colored by the subject matter under study at the time and by the unconscious meanings of events in their education.

Entering students have their deepest concern about their performance as students and their competence as individuals in interpersonal affairs. They want to establish a niche in their class and to know what their fellow students expect of them and what they can expect of their fellows in return. They are constantly assessing how they fit in the class and what kind of role their classmates are assigning them or they are assigning themselves. Will the role be a rivalrous sibling, clown, scapegoat, leader, teacher's pet, lover, helpful colleague, or nonentity?

Students bring to medical school an array of personal problems, many of which escape detection in whatever screening there is. They may or may not be aware of the nature of their troubles. The various stresses of medical school frequently bring these difficulties to the forefront, resulting not only in study interferences, but also in disordered school and personal relationships.[21]

Further, are any of the problems students have in medical school predictors of trouble later in the practice of medicine? Dr. Sander J. Breiner, with the help of a number of medical colleagues, has done a study of "impaired physicians" and looked at problems relating to early case findings in three categories: the medical student, the resident, and the young practicing physician. There was 75 percent to 100 percent agreement on the items that he and his colleagues identified as possible prodromata of a future "impaired physician" phenomenon. Only those items related to the medical student are relevant here:

> . . . any failure of the student to any degree in any area of medical education; few or no friends in his class, functioning socially as an isolate or misfit; social isolation in not dating the opposite sex; lack of freedom to laugh at oneself and at one's human condition of being a student, lacking the usual student's jocularity about his classes and professors; any regular use of mind-altering medication, including alcohol, to the point of mild inebriation or repeated or occasional episodes of marked excess of such drugs or alcohol; irregular or inconsistent grades, even without failure; irregular or poor class attendance; friction with the professor (even when the professor is the cause of the difficulty, the question must be asked, "Why did that student become the target of that professor?").[2]

Of course, the items about the medical student must be coupled with a group of items characterizing the resident and the young physician(less than five years past residency). Thus, if efforts are made to correct these problems during medical school, future impairment of the physician may be prevented.

RESIDUE OF TRAUMA FROM
PREMEDICAL PREPARATION

The emotionally traumatic and stressful process of preparation for medical school may become the anlage for later incapacitating anxieties during medical school. Because competition for admission is keen and places are available for only part of the well-qualified student group, selection policies of admissions committees give rise to a great deal of speculation and the perpetuation of the superstitions, myths, and legends that are indigenous to most undergraduate campuses. Particular science courses are emphasized to the exclusion of important courses in other fields. Grades acquire a disproportionate and frightening degree of importance. They supplant learning and preparation for later professional training as the goal of the medical student's education. Those students whose natural bent is not along the lines of the physical sciences find it necessary to work doubly hard to attain the necessary grades. The pre-existing substratum of anxiety that these students carry into medical school is easily aroused by the heavy scientific curriculum in the early years of their medical training.

College students need time to work through the adolescent problems that are a part of the life of this age group. Busy premedical students, using all of their time and energy to qualify and compete for admission to medical school, neglect their psychological maturation. Thus, they bring to medical school a host of unresolved adolescent conflicts to compound the numerous problems awaiting them there. The developmental tasks of late adolescence have been postponed. The total engulfment of their premedical studies usurps the usual and necessary period of late adolescence needed to resolve internal conflicts.

PROBLEMS WITH THE MEDICAL SCHOOL ENVIRONMENT

The medical school environment is a major factor in students' success or failure.[13] The same environment may be challenging to one student and stultifying to another. In spite of efforts to introduce flexibility into the medical school curriculum, the students move in lockstep fashion through most of their major studies. For the brilliant, creative students, lockstep curricula may contribute to their emotional breakdown. They find it almost impossible to conform to unimaginative teaching.[8]

Certain students prefer probing to great depths those courses in which they have a strong interest and treating superficially other courses. When students are forced to divide their time equally among all courses, without respect to interest or aptitude, some will be unable to tolerate the requirement. Thoreau would have been a casualty of the lockstep curriculum: "Why should we be in such desperate haste to succeed and in such desperate enterprises? If a man does not keep pace with his companions, perhaps it is because he hears a different drummer. Let him step to the music which he hears, however measured or far away."[28] For highly gifted students, the music they hear and follow is that which stimulates their rich imagination, deep and creative thinking, and unique ideas. They are not encouraged to use their creative talents in an environment that places high value on rote learning and visible performance.

A competitive environment is a source of problems for some students. Competitiveness varies from school to school, as well as from class to class. Some schools promote competitiveness, whereas in others the milieu is geared to play it down. Some classes of medical students generate a competitive atmosphere. Other classes quietly work out a modus vivendi that keeps competitive problems in check. Since competitive urges had a part in getting a student into medical school, these urges will continue to play a role in a student's actions and reactions. Competitive problems may grow out of or have some relationship to unsolved oedipal strivings, sibling rivalry, and rivalry with parent surrogates.

Cooperation is a far more rewarding trait in medical school than competition. Once a man, in a dream, visited heaven and hell. He was astonished to find both places similar in all respects except one. At each place there was a great banquet with tables covered with delicious foods of many varieties. In each place every person's arms were stiff and could not be bent at the elbows. In hell each person was hungry and scrambling to get food in his or her mouth because the stiff elbow prevented one's hand from reaching one's mouth. In heaven all were feasting with joy for they were feeding one another. The stiff elbow offered no resistance to putting food in a neighbor's mouth.

The majority of medical students have been identified, by studies too numerous to mention, as obsessive-compulsive in personality organization. Such students are attracted to medical school and are impressive to selection committees because of their high academic achievements.

Obsessive-compulsive students' traits of conscientious devotion to duty, perfectionism, capacity for hard work, and concern with detail usually serve students well in their preparation for the practice of medicine. In such anally-oriented students, however, some of these traits may be counterproductive. They are grade and rank conscious because tangible evidence of top performance may be for them a defense against the anxiety of insecurity and vulnerability. The frequent reassurance of instructors that one cannot learn all of the voluminous amounts of material dumped on one is of only transient value. It seems to impose the need to be able to discriminate, while attacking the obsessional need to know everything for the sake of security. What instructors are saying is tantamount to being informed that one cannot hope to defend oneself against one's anxieties.

The obsessive-compulsive character structure may contribute to success in certain areas while bringing failure to others. Such was the situation with a bright student whose compulsive behavior served him well in his studies and care of patients but was maladaptive in his marriage. He required of himself and his wife that they take a shower before and after having sexual relations. By the time he was ready to graduate he could have intercourse only while taking a shower. At this point, his wife insisted that they get psychiatric help. She was predominantly hysteric in character structure and was attracted to her husband by his high moral code, his worthy goals in life, and the esteem in which others held him. His problems were readily amenable to psychotherapy.

IN THE FOOTSTEPS OF THE PHYSICIAN PARENT

A question often asked is whether physicians' children have more academic and emotional problems in medical school than their classmates.[26] Some doctors' children develop a natural interest in medicine but do not have the necessary aptitudes. A more significant reason involves children who have had no real choice. They do not volunteer to go to medical school but are sent. Since children generally try hard to do what their parents want, physician parents may be late to realize that they have pressured their children. Also, sons and daughters may not recognize readily that they have been pressured.

Dean George Bryan of the University of Texas Medical Branch in Galveston has cautioned physician parents against imposing their dreams and expectations on their children who are struggling to establish an identity of their own. Dean Bryan asks the crucial question: Can physician parents be supportive of their children's innovativeness, although it does not fit the parents' image of where the children ought to be headed?[3] If parents would take that question seriously and discuss with their children alternatives to medical school if they are rejected or lack motivation for the study of medicine, their children and medical schools would be spared much grief.

A clear example of what Dean Bryan is pointing out is the physician's son whose weak performance in premedical studies raised questions in the premedical advisor's mind as to whether the son's pursuit of a medical career was the son's wish or the father's decision. The father exerted some "push and pull" to get his son in medical school and never took a close look at his son's motivation or qualifications for medicine. Only after the son dropped out of medical school during the first year did the father make some objective assessment of the situation.

Since the physician can be described as a charismatic individual, his or her child may be heir to some difficult problems of personal development. The child of an individual whom society has identified as charismatic may find it difficult to achieve the individuality and freedom for independent growth necessary for self-realization.

Ben Jonson has written: "Greatness of name in the father oftentimes overwhelms the son; they stand too near one another. The shadow kills the growth; so much, that we see the grandchild come more and oftener to be heir of the first."[15] Literature and life contain many examples of the kinds of forces which seem operative in instances where powerful parental figures not only are unable to see their own success and power reproduced in their children, but actually have served to preclude it. Further, in every person's life there is a time in which one struggles to attain emancipation from and certain objectivity concerning figures who are realistically powerful and important to him or her. The problem of acquiring a fuller objectivity and with it freedom for independent growth is made more complex and difficult when society also singles out a parental figure as standing above the masses.[19]

Many charismatic figures drive themselves powerfully and live with a high degree of anxiety, irritability, and inaccessibility. Their consciousness is captured by the events of their work, and their "great moments" are rarely with their family. While they have much to give, the giving is ordinarily to "the others." Time spent in teaching and inspiring their own children is highly limited. George Bernard Shaw has pointed out that "example is not the best way to train a child; it is the only way."

Children of physicians often view their parents in one of two ways. One way is to see the parent as a strong, omnipotent, excellent, and highly successful physician. They may be convinced that they can never become like that parent and will be only a poor specimen in comparison. The resultant sense of inadequacy, impotence, and low self-esteem keyed around the feeling that "I could never be half as good" can become a lifelong modus vivendi.

One medical student, intelligent and genuinely motivated, withdrew from school because of poor performance. His father and uncles were physicians and all nationally known. Competition with them created an intense anxiety that could only be relieved by a grandiose fantasy about becoming a greater name. This fantasy created guilt because to him it meant a literal annihilation of his competitors. Thus, his emotions would swing between feelings of utter helplessness and grandiosity. Only occasionally was he able to work effectively. When his competitive strivings related to his father and uncles took a prominent position, his anxiety level would rise and create an impasse. After leaving school, he entered psychoanalytic therapy and gradually came to grips with the conflicts that had created the climate of his failure. Later, he returned to medical school and distinguished himself without the guilt and anxiety that previously haunted him.

"Below average" is the other way a student may see the physician parent. "Good old Doc" is the way the people of the community described the physician parent. Often this assessment of mediocrity is not arrived at fully until the student is in the midst of his or her medical studies and learns what is meant by a competent physician. The student realizes that he or she will become a much better physician than the parent. The thought of overcoming or surpassing the parent can be anxiety producing for the child and lead to a fear of success, usually described as success phobia.

While the preceding paragraphs have focused on problems related to the offspring of physicians, one should remember that there are physicians' sons and daughters thriving in virtually every medical school. Their identity is clear, their motivation is sound, and their goals are realistic. Some will not equal the accomplishments of their parents, whereas others will accomplish much more. What lies ahead causes them no conflict.

PROBLEMS WITH PROFESSORS

The student–teacher relation in medical school is commonly compared with the child–parent relation. The teacher who adheres to this model feels that "Parent knows best." The medical student who accepts this model is likely to be either a passive good son or daughter or a rebellious adolescent. A more appropriate model is one of colleagueship or partnership. A true partnership is complementary, implying mutual recognition of individuality but not necessarily equality. Each party knows the needs of the other and what each can contribute.

The teacher who lives by the partnership model is less likely to create or mobilize psychological problems in students. Students do not feel threatened by such a teacher but want to be like him or her. Students get from the good teacher the feeling that they have learned something and also a sense of how to learn more by themselves.

Unfortunately, a vertical authoritarianism reigns in both curricular and administrative matters in certain medical schools. In such environments, students are not seen as junior colleagues, as Osler suggests, but as children to be taught and disciplined. This authoritarian atmosphere commonly provokes students to view each professor as having the power to block their advancement, thus interfering with the development of a basic trust between students and faculty. Although the professor's power may be benevolent, students see it as unrestrained and unregulated.

Students feel that Lord Acton, chief justice of the British Empire, was speaking for them when he said: "Power corrupts. Absolute power corrupts absolutely."* Some students expect to be "shot down" by an

---

* Psychiatrist Thomas Szasz has paraphrased Lord Acton's well-known dictum: "The corrupt seek power, and those most corrupt seek absolute power."

ultimate authority in medical school. Much of their complaining about stringent requirements is related in part to conflict with authority. At times, they expect and invite sadism from their professors.

Many learning difficulties grow out of problems with authority. One of our bright and well-informed students failed most of the first-year courses. He confessed that his instructors made him so angry that he did not answer the questions correctly, although he knew the answers. He acknowledged also that his biggest problem was with authority figures and that earlier someone had suggested that he get help with his problem before entering medical school.

A similar student found it impossible to produce anything on an examination, although he was prepared. In psychiatric treatment, a bizarre dimension of his toilet training came to light. Through age six he was not allowed to get off the commode or flush the toilet until his mother or the maid checked to see what he had produced. At medical school, in the laboratory and on examinations, when his instructors checked on what he had produced, he felt the same rage and frustration as he had when his mother or the maid checked on his toilet productions. He found it hard to produce for these instructors. Even in psychotherapy he felt the same frustration—with a therapist pushing him to produce. One night he dreamed that the analytic couch was a toilet and that he had left a stool on it.

Problems with authority in the learning situation call to mind a classification of teaching approaches similar to the stages of psychosexual development.[22] The anal stage is the relevant one for this discussion, with the key dynamic being "production-on-demand for others." The teachers expect the facts and theories fed the student to be digested and processed into scholarly lumps to be delivered at the assigned time for measurement, weighing, and evaluation. The teachers are impressed by the amount of paper or number of pages students, as well as colleagues, use to display their work. Often the bulk is equated with quality.

On the faculty of every medical school will be a number of unusual professors—prima donnas, eccentrics, saviors, and so on. Upperclassmen pass on to incoming students essential information on the care and feeding of the faculty.

Men and women do seem to differ in their approaches to the faculty. A female student is more likely to work to gain the acceptance or approval of her teacher, while the male student uses mastery as a test of his personal potency. In other words, a man is oriented to move immediately to figure out the problem or task, the woman to figure out the teacher. In medical school, however, the general consensus among all students, male and female, is that it pays to figure out the professor early in the game and to continue to do so.

OVERACHIEVING AND UNDERACHIEVING

Academically successful students often have as many problems as underachievers. Not infrequently, these are marital and family problems, resulting from the lack of attention, understanding, and responsiveness to the spouse's needs. This neglect is most often occasioned by demands of the medical curriculum and the student's obsessive concern for work. Such situations place a great deal of psychological stress on the spouse. These difficulties are accentuated by the fact that it often appears that the spouse, who is usually the breadwinner of the family, is being used with no thought given to the spouse's fulfillment. As such stresses increase, marital problems multiply; and these, if not faced and resolved, can and unfortunately do eventually lead to such serious consequences as suicide attempts by the spouse, as discussed later in this chapter.

Many overachievers become such slaves to the routines and rituals of school work that the nurturing of the cultural and aesthetic side of life is completely neglected. They give the excuse that there is no time at present, but that at some seemingly opportune future date such areas as spiritual growth, aesthetic appreciation, the cultivation of interpersonal relationships, and activities with the family will receive the attention they deserve. These students can often be brought to their senses if confronted with the fact that there can be no assurance that there will even be a tomorrow and that each day should, therefore, have some kind of completeness within itself. In such discussions students often begin to realize that the time they have set aside for really getting down to the business of living, namely, when they begin the practice of their profession, may well be more complicated and more crowded than their present state. Thus, their plan has no reality whatsoever. The realization slowly awakens within them that if they do not have time for certain avocational endeavors at present, they surely will not have time in the future. They recognize also that one makes a place for participation in the good things of life, regardless of the fullness of one's schedule.

Underachievers may be doing poorly academically because of the lack of ability, the presence of psychological problems, or because they are not willing to pay the price required to do well. Occasionally, the problem is one of faulty motivation. Students may have accepted the

challenge of getting into medical school to provide themselves with a
sense of worth, only to find in medical school that they are not interested in what a medical career entails.

Lack of academic productivity is often related to hidden psychological problems. For example, passive-aggressive rebellion against parents
may manifest itself in underachievement. When overtly or subtly pressured by parents to achieve in certain areas, students are able to hurt
and embarrass their parents by failing. Many superior students who are
underachievers have a passive-aggressive personality disorder. In the
family of the child who becomes passive-aggressive, one parent is
usually dominant and the other one submissive. The parents try to
force their children into a pattern of dependency and nonaggression.
Learning and achievement may actually be discouraged in an unconscious way, since these may be seen as aggressive behavior. Passive-aggressive children use indirect methods to express their hidden hostility
and anxiety. Underachievers often confuse the aggression that leads to
destructive, hurting expressions with the aggression that goes into
learning, success, and other productive and constructive enterprises.
The formulation may be condensed into the equation "to achieve is to
hurt." When their "productive" aggressions are proscribed and sub-
verted, learning indeed suffers.

The persistence of the grandiose self in narcissistic individuals may
lead to underachievement and academic failure, as carefully delineated
by Baker in his paper on "The Conquering Hero Quits."[1] School work
requires tolerance of trial and error incompatible with the omnipotent
demands of the grandiose self. Rather than working harder when confronted with difficulties, narcissistic students avoid their studies and
defensively pursue other activities that temporarily give narcissistic
gratification.

Low peformance may also develop from feelings of inadequacy and
fear of failure, leading students to give up studying completely in order
to "save face." Their inadequacy is hidden and those around them conclude that "they don't really want to be doctors."

A less obvious basis for underachievement may be fear of success or
the "success phobia" that is discussed more fully in the next section.
Success in medical school may represent for students outshining
everybody in their family in status and educational achievement. Their
guilt over leaving them behind in humbler circumstances may invoke a
pattern of self-sabotage.

Underachievers often seek help in determining whether or not they
have a psychological problem which is contributing to their poor performance. A psychiatric evaluation may reveal no evidence of an emotional abnormality. An effective way of helping such students, when it

has been determined that no psychological disability is present, is by not letting them hide behind a nonexistent emotional problem. They should be told very firmly, but supportively, to do their work or withdraw from school. This type of student will usually accept a frank analysis of his or her situation and then move ahead in improved performance as well as in personal maturity.

Garner and Jeans also call for a formal approach instead of passivity in this type of situation:

> The concept of a state of helplessness and of being in the clutches of forces of past experiences is too frequently fortified by the interpretation of the therapist's passivity as a confirmation of his feeling that he is incapable of taking any action to alter the situation. . . . Confrontation makes the patient unmistakably aware of the presence of the therapist as a person who has interfered with the blind acting out of his escape from freedom of choice, who has challenged the patient's solution to his conflicts in a decisive way, and made him think about it.[11]

SUCCESS PHOBIA

Academic failure of some students may relate to the fear of vocational success. The essential failure in adaptation in students suffering from the fear of success is an inhibition of aggression. Lionel Ovesey, who has discussed this problem psychodynamically, points out that this inhibition has its developmental origin in the early rivalries between the child and parents, as well as between the child and siblings.[23] These hostile struggles are unconsciously perceived by the child in symbolic terms of murderous violence. In the absence of any serious intimidation, such unconscious distortions are neutralized by a permissive environment that fosters the development of healthy patterns of aggression. Where intimidation is severe, however, either from the parental rival or from the sibling, or from both, the environment reinforces the symbolic equation between aggression and violence. Under such circumstances, the unconscious desire to destroy the more powerful rivals generates profound guilt and, at the same time, carries in its wake the certain threat of equally violent retaliation. The child begins to withhold aggression for reasons of conscience and also to avoid destruction by competitors, all of whom are seen as stronger than himself or herself. In this way, an inhibition of aggression gradually unfolds. Once this happens, the misconception that all aggression must be violent is symbolically extended to encompass assertion of all kinds, including accomplishment in one's studies. The child emerges from these struggles into adulthood, with ambitions intact, but with the capacity to take effective action seriously crippled. Competition, thereafter, is identified with the original rivalries of childhood, and success in any endeavor is unconsciously perceived as murder of the competitors. The person is beset by guilt, invokes the inhibition of aggression, and withdraws from competition to protect himself or herself from murderous retaliation. This is the nuclear conflict, and once it is fully established, the success phobia is set in motion.

PROBLEMS WITH PATIENTS

Students may develop a variety of hypochondriacal complaints when they study disease processes. Fears of physical illness appear in conjunction with the study of anatomic pathology and pathophysiology. Later, students may develop fears of mental illness when they have close contact with mentally ill patients. The nature of the symptom, precipitated by the subject matter under consideration, is most often related to the life experiences of the student and frequently may be traced to a personal or family history of disease.

As students advance in their training from minimal exposure to patients to intensive clinical work, new adjustments are required. Students' primary problems in patient care emanate from their feelings of insecurity and anxiety in attempting to apply the theory they have learned and from the loss of the structure that had previously been provided by lecture and laboratory courses. These feelings reveal themselves in the clinical situation as overt anxiety, indifference, hostility, and destructive argumentativeness or inability to carry out practical responsibilities. The students may experience guilt and a sense of helplessness when they are confronted with seriously ill or dying patients or worry about being faced with an urgent medical situation wherein their failure to have some information or skill at their fingertips might result in the death of a patient. How to protect themselves from too deep an emotional involvement with patients is a formidable task. Before developing enough detachment to function effectively, they may swing between exaggerated sensitivity and callousness.

In addition to guilt, some students are troubled by their inability to deal effectively with feelings of anger, inadequacy, and frustration growing out of their being the "gump" or the "low man" in the hierarchy of ward personnel. If the students are used primarily for unstimulating service functions and are given little instruction, their resentment grows toward all above them in the hierarchy. The crux of the matter is that unstimulating service functions are often required of them for which they are not paid and instruction for which they have paid is not given them.

In working with students, teachers and supervisors observe daily the complexities of student involvement with patients. At times the interaction of the patient and student in the so-called doctor–patient relationship is detrimental to growth toward "wholeness" in both patient and student. The student often identifies a personal or family problem with a particular difficulty that the patient has and can no longer be objective.

Gerald Caplan of the Harvard Medical School describes this difficulty as an intrusion of an interfering problem theme into the student's professional functioning.[5] Mentally retarded patients, alcoholics, accident victims, patients with sexual problems, patients with mental disorders, dying patients, and many others introduce for the student an interfering theme and cause him or her to mobilize certain defense mechanisms to cope with the situation. The core problem of the patient often symbolizes for the student some personal and crucial problem in his or her own life.

This symbolization may be illustrated by the case of a student who was assigned a cancer patient. Without any conscious awareness of what he was doing, the student communicated to the patient the impression that the condition was hopeless. In reality, the patient's malignancy was treatable, and the patient had been admitted to the hospital with the expectation that he would recover completely and return home, which he did. This student's sense of hopelessness stemmed from the fact that his father had died of cancer when the student was in his early teens.

In these sensitive clinical situations, effective teachers have their greatest and most frequent opportunity to push their students toward personal and professional maturity. With certain students one may openly point out what is happening and explore certain aspects of the students' personal lives to determine the cause of the difficulty with patients. In other cases one may meet resistance, if, for example, the student thinks the teacher is invading his or her privacy. With this type of student, one must respect the separation of the student's personal life from the work difficulty and not investigate the cause of the theme interference but rather focus upon defining the nature of the theme by a careful examination of its manifestations in the work context. This indirect approach is often very effective and has been used by many of the world's great teachers in the form of parables, illustrative material, and other peripheral mechanisms to stimulate growth and change in others.

THE STUDENT'S SPOUSE

Married students often feel guilty about not having the time or energy to be a good marriage partner. They find themselves relegating the spouse to a secondary place in life, for medicine is demanding and consuming. They are troubled by the spouse's loneliness, desire to have children without further delay, and financial dependency with its accompanying loss of self-esteem. They are never sure that the spouse understands the magnitude of the stresses, anxieties, and insecurities imposed upon them by the nature of their studies.

The spouse is troubled by an inability to compete with his or her partner's studies. Often the spouse spends evening after evening watching the partner occupied with studies to the point of almost total exclusion of any appreciation of the spouse's presence or desire for some attention. Later, during the clinical clerkship, the spouse is alone at home while the student is on duty at the hospital. Further, the spouse feels excluded from the challenging work of medicine since he or she can share only vicariously in bits of the experience. In reality, the spouse may feel rejected and compare the relative inattention and inactivity in the marriage to the romantically affectionate attentiveness of both before the wedding when they were suitors.

Several serious suicide attempts by the spouses of students, who are often overachievers, indicated a need for careful examination of what took place between husband and wife. A typical case is that of a beautiful and intelligent 23-year-old girl married to a third-year medical student who was close to the top of his class academically. He came home one evening and found his wife on the bathroom floor unconscious from a large amount of a sedative drug. Leaving a note of explanation for her action, she asked for his forgiveness and wished him well in his career:

> Please forgive me, but I can't stand myself any longer. I am just a weakling. Please, please forgive me. I have asked the Lord to forgive me, too. He will, for He is good and understands. No one is to blame but myself. I just couldn't accept my limitations. Now I know I couldn't be a good wife to anyone. I am too weak—too stupid. I don't want to be a drag on anyone any longer. I know you want to be a surgeon more than anything in the world. You are wonderful. I could never love anyone but you, and all I've done to you (and mother, too) is cause you heartache. I've tried to hold on to you, but it isn't fair to you. Be a good physician. I know you will. Love _____

What had happened between this medical student and his wife? She worked and earned most of the money for their maintenance. She saw little of him and missed his sharing with her some of the responsibilities associated with her role as wife and breadwinner. On numerous occasions she reached out to him for help. At first he responded fairly well but then gradually began to withdraw. His thinking was essentially along these lines: "Why doesn't she leave me alone? Her problems are far fewer than mine. Medical school is demanding more of me each day, and I need every ounce of my strength to accomplish my goal there. Surely her burdens are far lighter than mine."

As his wife's psychological stress continued to mount, she continued to ask for help. At this point he stopped trying to be supportive and responded to her with aggression. He enumerated his problems to her, compared the gravity of his situation with the superficiality of hers, and demanded to be let alone. Seeing that she could get no help from him, the wife decided in desperation to commit suicide. Any suicide attempt is a Janus-faced act; one face looks toward death and the other toward life. Thus, she was appealing to the wider human community for help.

In a similar situation, a medical student who was first in his class reacted to his wife's appeal for help with unconscious and covert aggression, mostly passive withdrawal. Rejected by her husband, the wife then made an effort to have an affair with a medical student who lived next door. He soon became frightened and withdrew from the relationship. When her cry for help was not heeded by husband or friend, she committed suicide by shooting herself in the head.

In general, spouses of medical students find their situation satisfying and meaningful. Often, their wives or husbands pay moving tributes to them and give the impression that fulfilling and glorious relationships can and often do exist in medical school between student and spouse. At times, however, spouses do experience emotional difficulty. This can usually be dealt with by the spouse's adjusting to a certain degree of loneliness, by developing satisfying interests, and by cultivating mutual support with spouse.

Major stresses for the spouse of the student are loneliness, limited finances, adjustment to irregular hours, the partner being home too little, as well as being under definite tension and pressure.[7] Adjustment to these stresses is facilitated by patience and understanding, as well as evolving personal ways of handling stresses.[6] Developing mutual support between wife and husband is crucial. Communication in depth must be maintained and nurtured with partner, family, and friends. The role is not easy and is well summarized by a medical student's wife: "One can have a wonderful life if one has the constitution of a mule, the patience of Job, and an appreciation of the literary works of Robert Burns—especially the lines about 'the best laid plans of mice and men.'"

THE OLDER STUDENT

Medical school has always attracted a number of older students. Although older applicants are admitted to medical school at a lesser rate than immediate college graduates, the difference in rate of acceptance can be accounted for by factors other than chronological age. Among such factors are lesser academic qualifications, lower or questionable motivation, less recent scientific preparation, and few applications filed per applicant.[24] Further, older applicants not infrequently base their late decision to enter medicine largely on economic motivation. In others, a lack of satisfaction with a first career choice or frank failure to succeed in it is evident. Probably the older students who make the best adjustment to medical school are those who see medicine not as a new field but as an extension or further fulfillment of what they were doing before entering medical school.

Anyway, certain mental health crises or emotional tasks confront these students in medical school. Some of the factors out of which crises arise are given here:

1. Inadequate material resources are a problem with most of these students. Often family responsibilities extend their budgets far beyond that of young, single students whose needs are limited.
2. Closely allied with inadequate material resources is the stress of coping with the demands or resentment of the spouse.
3. Rigidity learned from prior life and work habits multiply adjustment problems.
4. Achieving functional balance between the role as spouse or parent and the role as student is extremely difficult at first.
5. The lack of skill and discipline in study habits frequently makes it more difficult to keep up with younger classmates. Such students are often heard to remark: "I am late in starting. I'll always be behind."
6. Guilt feelings associated with the new role as student may drain emotional energy needed for more constructive pursuits.
7. A tendency to be overly absorbed in their studies may bring to the older students a sense of isolation, a feeling of being cut off from previously meaningful activities and relationships.

8. The tendency of the older student to use the school life and environment to solve adjustment problems that should be solved elsewhere gives others and the school the impression that this student is problem-ridden.

Fortunately, most of these crises are either situational or are related to self-perceptions and can be alleviated through counseling.

CRISES AND THE THREAT OF SUICIDE

In the medical student age group the three leading causes of death are accidents, malignant diseases, and suicide. In Simon's study, mortality rates from all causes and particularly from malignant diseases and accidents declined in the general population but increased among medical students.[25] Rates of death from suicide increased more rapidly among medical students than among the general population, matched as closely as possible for age, sex, race, and residence. These data are striking, since many medical students have their origins in the more favored socio-economic segments of the population, which generally have lower morbidity-mortality than for the general population.

The high suicide rate, as well as the frequent contemplation of suicide as a problem-solving device, would seem to indicate a need for earlier and more continuous counseling and surveillance. Communication to medical students and faculty of information about the problems and crises that can possibly lead to suicide may increase awareness, lead to earlier detection of high-risk persons, hasten effective intervention, and possibly prevent a significant number of these tragedies.

Separation anxiety, fear of homosexuality, depression, depersonalization, and fear of failure are some of the crises that bring to the forefront the threat of suicide. These will be discussed briefly for illustrative purposes.

Separation Anxiety

Separation anxiety is seen primarily in the entering freshman student and the graduating senior.

Entering freshmen may be away from their homes for the first time. Their high level of anxiety about being separated from home may become obvious only under certain circumstances. For example, a letter from home telling of the illness of a family member— even a minor illness—may precipitate near panic in the student. This is especially true if the illness involves the mother. On several occasions I have seen a student "rush home to save mother," and not return to continue his or her medical studies.

On superficial consideration, one may think that senior students are freer of problems than students in the lower classes. Yet this is the time of separation anxiety—the end of a dependency period, and a thrust into independence and increased responsibility, a time to serve and not be served. Unsolved problems from the past come to the surface and manifest themselves in some of these seniors. One student, two weeks before graduation, felt he could not accept the internship which he was under contract to begin in six weeks. Just before the Easter holidays he became depressed and often began to cry spontaneously. He stated, "I do not know why I would cry except that I felt so melancholic, alone, and trapped." During this period he considered committing suicide. He collected a lethal dose of barbiturates and kept them in his room. Also, since there were several guns in his fraternity house, he checked to see that ammunition for them was available. During the three-week period before Easter he lost twenty pounds. He gave a long history of home-sickness, feeling alone, wanting to be close to people, but desperately afraid of getting close. Fortunately he had joined a medical fraternity and lived in the fraternity house. This had given him a "sense of family" and enabled him to survive away from his home, according to the student. He begged that someone intervene to help him change his internship to his medical school's teaching hospital so that many of his previous relationships could continue unbroken.

This student was like a lonely depressed infant who cries for his mother. As he prepared to graduate and assume greater responsibilities in a new place, he was overwhelmed with separation anxiety. His emotional lability, enabling him to move quickly into a deep depression, coupled with his anxiety, made him a potential candidate for a serious suicide attempt.

The departing senior may find it difficult to separate from the school. One method of handling one's separation anxiety is to find fault with the school and severely criticize it. "Now I can leave, for this damn place is not worth hanging around any longer." This criticism often provokes anger in sensitive faculty and administrators who are unaware of the motive behind the student's attack on his or her soon-to-be alma mater.

Fear of Homosexuality

The fear of homosexuality is common among some students. These students at some level of awareness are afraid that they may be homosexual. This fear is usually not conscious and may bring forth peculiar behaviors as protective measures against homosexuality or against being homosexual. Occasionally this fear takes the form of homosexual panic. Although homosexual panic is not easily defined, Karpman gives a useful formulation: "It is latent homosexuality that is pressing to the surface for open expression, but is held in check by the dictates of the superego, with its sense of guilt. Finding himself between these two conflicting trends which he is unable to reconcile satisfactorily, the patient is thrown into an acute conflict of which the panic is the clinical expression, and preoccupation with paraphilia, the mental content."[16] Whether one sees acute homosexual panic as essentially an ego squeezed between id and superego is not of great importance. In many students the panic can denote a shattering ego disorganization in which a solution may be sought in suicide.

Such was the case with a student overwhelmed by fear of homosexuality. The disorganizing experience made him reach out so possessively and persistently for two of his male friends and fellow students that they became frightened and withdrew for a while. In the student's frantic efforts to reach one of his friends, he sent him a desperate note about his fears of killing himself and begged for psychiatric help. This student's plea for help was recognized early enough for effective intervention. His fellow students sensed the acuteness of the situation and participated in the rescue. Although a longitudinal history or a psychodynamic formulation of this student is not indicated, a few comments are necessary. The student had identified more with his mother than his father. Why the passive need for his father's love prevailed over identification with his strong father is not clear, unless he learned from his mother that passivity was more rewarding than independence. The father did not play a compassionate and understanding role in the student's development, and this threw him almost exclusively into the mother's zone of influence. In medical school, the fear of homosexuality developed in the predominantly male environment under the influence of both internal and external barriers to heterosexuality.

Depression

Almost all therapists in the field of student health emphasize the prevalence of depression. The depressive syndrome constitutes the most common serious medical diagnosis in many student health services. It causes acute and chronic impairment of the student's social and academic functioning. It also frequently results in withdrawal or dismissal from medical school. The threat of suicide is always present in these depressed students, and they are ready to speak of their suicidal ruminations.

Depressed students are often referred not for depression but for declining grades with concomitant difficulty in study and concentration. They report that they cannot absorb their reading and gradually lose interest in their studies. They feel guilty over their supposed laziness and for wasting time and their parents' money. Fatigue and lethargy are constant symptoms. They convey a sense of helplessness and hopelessness. They often ask about withdrawing from school. An overly depressed state is easily recognized and often by the student. Less easily recognized is the latent depressive state, which often escapes notice by patient or physician. Bychowski and others have described this state in detail.[4, 20] A student with a latent depression will show minimal obvious signs and symptoms of depression but complain of boredom, lethargy, preoccupation, and difficulty in studying. A group of latently depressed students studied by Grofe laughed at, doubted, or denied the possibility of depression, yet they unwittingly revealed their underlying depression by their word associations, character traits, and attitudes.[12]

Overtly or latently depressed students often find that their underlying emotional difficulty escapes recognition or their difficulty is ascribed to the pressure of the work load. Medical school officials then assume that such sudents are lazy or have poor work habits. The academic work load, however, is only the major situational stress of the moment for the depressed students, and they may hide their real emotional difficulty behind their studies. The academic work load only contributes to the burdens of depressed students and usually plays no actual part in the precipitation of the depression. The precipitating factor usually consists of an actual or fantasied rejection, resulting from a direct conflict with a parent or parent surrogate. The findings with depressed students usually corroborate the essentially Freudian theory of the depressive reaction as a reawakening of unconscious childhood feelings of rejection, which are triggered off by appropriate current stimuli.[9] It is remarkable how in so many cases the depressive affect is associated with the premature loss or absence of one or both parents in childhood or the conviction of rejection by a parent. The feeling of being unworthy of love is associated with the feeling of rejection.

Identification with a dead family member as an influence toward suicide has been mentioned in the literature as well as seen occasionally in clinical practice. It can be prominent in a male student whose father has died, especially if combined with despair at not living up to his image of what the father accomplished when he lived. Such an example was the student who appeared to have been strongly identified with his physician father, now deceased. He wanted very much to be a doctor also and committed suicide after becoming depressed in January of his senior year of college over not having heard from any of the medical schools to which he had applied.

Depressed students usually respond well to brief, psychoanalytically oriented psychotherapy. Unfortunately, the latent depression in many students tends to be overlooked and, therefore, psychotherapy may not be considered for these chronic underachievers who often have high intellectual ability. For such students, depression is their way of life, and they usually view the world as cold, prohibitive, and depriving. In avoiding close personal relationships out of fear of dependency, they seem isolated and regressed. This avoidance perpetuates their emotional deprivation. Brief treatment is often sufficient to help such students stem the depressive regression, acquire useful insights, and make some successful readjustments in work and interpersonal relationships.

Depression in medical students often causes them to appear schizoid in the sense that they seem isolated from those around them and unable to relate meaningfully. Recently, a colleague, working with freshmen, asked: "Why do we have so many schizoids among our freshmen medical students?"

Depersonalization

A suicide may be attempted while someone is in a depersonalized state. During depersonalization one becomes aware of changes in himself or herself that lead to feelings of strangeness or unreality, of numbness or not being able to feel. Descriptions may include expressions as "dead inside," "foggy feelings," "being asleep or in a dream," "make-believe."

During depersonalization, the defensive functioning or controlling forces of the ego are not operating with the same degree of effectiveness as in an unaltered state of awareness. In this dissociated state the person acts as both participant and observer and responds as though his or her behavior was being carried out by another individual. Thus, ordinarily unacceptable impulses and acts such as suicide are more easily permitted partial or complete expression. Whenever depersonalization is present, one can usually uncover, with careful interviewing, a history of previous suicidal ideation or behavior, evidence of death wishes, or a preoccupation with death.[29]

Thus, depersonalization, an incomplete withdrawal, is an unconsciously determined, stereotyped adaptation pattern of the ego to acute or chronic stress. In this altered state the individual may seek the maintenance of this oceanic feeling or complete escape, and self-destruction ensues. This situation is not infrequent in the suicide of the medical student.

Fear of Failure

Probably the two most anxiety-provoking situations for a medical student are situations that imply academic failure and those that have to do with death. The fear of failure concerns us here.

At times the wish to be in medical school (and at a *particular* school) springs more from the parents' motivation than the student's. Parental pressure for a particular life direction may alienate students from their own ambition. Hungry, however, for their parents' affection and appreciation, they strive for good grades. Thus, in this competitive milieu, even the receiving of love is tied to extraneous standards of performance. Probably students today are prepared more for the competitive world of an affluent society than they are for the opportunities for companionship, competence, and the sharing of ideas.

One such student comforted himself with the thought that he could always kill himself if he failed academically. He kept a cyanide capsule in his desk and threw it away on graduation. Another student, whose performance was marginal, expected to be dismissed just before the Christmas holidays. He mentioned that if this happened, he planned to wreck his car on the way home in a way that would appear accidental. Failing to get an M.D. degree, he acknowledged, would be far more disappointing to his parents than to him.

PREVENTIVE MEASURES

One of the deans at Harvard has stated: "When so many capable youngsters are on the beach, it makes good sense to have expert lifeguards when some of them go beyond their depth." The availability of psychiatric services is imperative. When services are available, students who need help usually seek it, although the students' willingness to seek or accept help may vary from year to year.[18] The rewards can be great for students, and, in turn, for future patients when help is received.

In making available psychiatric services to students, the school must protect the confidentiality of the doctor–patient relationship as carefully as crown jewels. The psychiatrist must not, as Thomas Szasz emphasizes, be a *double agent,* serving both student and college "in a conflict but owing real loyalty to neither."[27] The college is the psychiatrist's client only in the sense that the psychiatrist does his or her share to bring into being a community that is at once educational and therapeutic. Clearly, the psychiatrist is the student's advocate.

Usually when a psychiatrist works with a student, no report is expected to be made to anybody, and the student should know this. When a student is referred by an administrative officer for an evaluation, on the other hand, it is generally agreed that a psychiatric report is expected. Both psychiatrist and student should be clear on the exact reasons for and purpose of the referral, as well as the type of information needed for decision making regarding the student.

Anticipatory Guidance

Helping students anticipate what lies ahead is central in the maintenance of their equilibrium. Medical fraternities or similar student organizations function effectively in the field of anticipatory guidance. Thorough programs by the deans at the opening of school and at critical transitional points in students' training do a great deal to reduce anxiety and frustration.

Some deans regularly call class meetings at periods when the stresses are severe to discuss frankly the fears and gripes of the students, always guiding the interaction in constructive problem-solving channels. Since most classes have a clown, the clown may be used to help introduce some humor at the hard points. If only to comfort the distraught, such meetings are worth holding. A wise educator once said that one of a dean's duties is "to comfort the afflicted and afflict the comfortable."

The benevolent and perceptive teacher is the medical school's greatest asset in anticipatory guidance. The teacher's own observation of students and involvement with them become a valuable resource for the students in their growth toward maturity. Students are in need of face-to-face relationships with teachers who demonstrate their concern for the students both by support and by judgment. Sir William Osler said over 60 years ago:

> The successful teacher is no longer on a height, pumping knowledge at high pressure into passive receptacles . . . but he is a senior student, anxious to help his juniors. When a simple earnest spirit animates a college, there is no appreciable interval between the teacher and the taught—both are in the same class, the one a little more advanced than the other. So animated, the student

feels that he has joined a family whose honor is his honor, whose welfare is his own, and whose interests should be his first consideration.[17]

Developing Effective Study Habits

Working hard at studies every day, as is necessary in medical school, may be a new experience for students. Probably never before have they had to allocate time so carefully or discipline themselves to follow an essentially inflexible schedule. If they compulsively try to learn everything, they open the door to a host of troubles. Students learn that a better approach is to keep their ears and eyes open to discover what classmates are studying and professors are emphasizing. Students then integrate the information received from these two major sources and use it as a guide to studying.

The mass of material dumped daily on students can overwhelm them. Probably in college they did not learn how to seek out principles and stuctural content, how to determine the critical facts and with these data to reason rather than recall the answers. Maybe, for the first time their performance falters, and their fears of inadequacy begin to grow.

As first midsemester examinations approach, students' anxiety usually reaches its peak. At this time, attempts to reassure the students may provoke rather than allay their anxiety. They do not relish learning that one of their major defenses against anxiety—superior performance on examinations—is no longer expected of them in every test situation. Since they are still much too grade dependent to find solace in this view, the less said about their academic performance at this time, the better. Shortly after midyear, excessive anxiety in the majority of students abruptly disappears.

Successful students develop review techniques that help them keep vast amounts of material fresh in their minds. Dean Wilburt C. Davison of the Duke University School of Medicine encouraged students to use a review manual constructed on the principle of the brassiere, which only touches the high points.

Often students complain of studying for long periods and retaining nothing. Anxiety and other distractions interfere with the ability to concentrate or retain material. To avoid wasting time, students can develop the ability to do self-testing while studying. The shorter the time they can concentrate, the more frequently they should test themselves to see if they are absorbing the material.

Students should guard against excessive anxiety and not permit themselves or others to heap fuel on an already anxious state. A student may also relieve anxiety by displacing it on others. For example, a freshman student, white with fear, approaches a group of classmates and says, "I just heard that anatomy flunked 20 percent of the class last year." As the group becomes visibly shaken, the carrier of this bad news relaxes and appears free of fear.

An understanding of the situations that cause a person to need help may aid in prevention. A person's sense of adequate control may break down when assigned tasks exceed learning or skill or when previously developed capacities are reduced by illness, injury, or age. Another situation is created by the threat to every human being whenever those on whom one feels one must depend seem to desert or abandon one. A third kind of crisis may occur when deeply cherished value systems or beliefs are threatened. The universe for a time turns bleak and terrifying; when the threats are removed, hope and serenity return.

CONCLUSION

Rapid changes in medical education have added to the students' problems in the area of learning and personal development. With further revolutionary social changes about to take place in the field of medicine, the disruptive pressures on students will, in all probability, intensify as time goes on. In fact, some students are deeply concerned because they cannot predict what will be demanded of them by the changes occurring in the delivery of medical services. They are asking what the future holds regarding opportunities for self-assertion, creative thinking, and individual effort in medicine.

Many medical schools are shifting some of their attention from strictly academic considerations, such as grades, examinations, and curriculum reform, to the broader question of the schools' educational climate. This is being done in an effort to identify disruptive features and to learn how to eliminate them. Without neglecting academic standards or curricular matters, schools are paying closer attention to nonacademic factors in order to graduate physicians with not only great technological skills but with the maturity to use them wisely.

Attention to the educational climate of a medical school will readily illuminate the areas where students experience difficulty. Typically these areas are integrating the personal and professional dimensions of one's life; handling the frustration, anxiety, and consequent learning difficulties arising from the weighty requirements of medical school; and developing and maintaining social and emotional sensitivity.

A worthy goal for all in medicine is to seek to enhance their emotional health. An ancient epitaph found on an Athenian doctor's grave brings us a special message: "These are the duties of a physician: First to heal his mind and to give help to himself before giving it to anyone else."

REFERENCES

1. Baker HS: The conquering hero quits: Narcissistic factors in under-achievement and failure. Am J Psychother 43:418, 1979
2. Breiner SJ: The impaired physician. J Med Educ 54:673, 1979
3. Bryan G, Eiland DC: Are doctors' children assured a place in medical school? Tex Med 75:15, 1979
4. Bychowski G: The structure of chronic and latent depressions. Int J Psychoanal 41:504, 1960
5. Caplan G: Principles of Preventive Psychiatry. New York, Basic Books, 1964, pp 232–265
6. Derdeyn AP: The physician's work and marriage. Int J Psychiatry Med 9:297, 1979
7. Eagle JR, Smith BM: Stresses of the medical student wife. J Med Educ 43:840, 1968
8. Edwards MT, Zimet CN: Problems and concerns among medical students—1975. J Med Educ 51:619, 1976
9. Freud S: Mourning and melancholia (1917). Collected Papers. Translated by Riviere J. London, Hogarth Press, vol 4, 1925, pp 152–170
10. Gaensbauer TJ, Mizner GL: Developmental stresses in medical education. Psychiatry 43:60, 1980
11. Garner HG, Jeans RF: Confrontation techniques in psychotherapy: Some existential implications. J Existent Psychiatr 2:393, 1962
12. Grofe J: Depression in college students. College Health 11:197, 1963
13. Grover PL, Tessier KE: Diagnosis and treatment of academic frustration syndrome. J Med Educ 53:734, 1978
14. Haun P: Letter. J Med Educ 41:895, 1966
15. Jonson B: Timber, or discoveries made upon man and matter (1640). In The Works of Ben Jonson. London, Bickers & Son, 1875, p 147
16. Karpman B: Mediate psychotherapy and the acute homosexual panic (Kempf's disease). J Nerv Ment Dis 98:493, 1943
17. Keynes GL (ed): Selected Writings of Sir William Osler. New York, Oxford Press, 1951, p 173
18. Kligfeld M, Hoffman KI: Medical student attitude toward seeking professional psychological help. J Med Educ 54:617, 1979
19. Miller MH, Roberts LM: Psychotherapy with the children or disciples of charismatic individuals. Am J Psychiatry 123:1049, 1967
20. Nacht S, Racamier PC: Depressive states. Int J Psychoanal 41:481, 1960
21. Nadelson CC, Notman MT: Adaptation to stress in physicians. In Shapiro

EC, Lowenstein LM (eds): Becoming a Physician. Cambridge, Massachusetts, Ballinger, 1979, pp 201–215
22. Orlinsky DC: The integrity of psychotherapy and college teaching: A personal essay. Voices 6:98, 1970
23. Ovesey L: Fear of vocational success. Arch Gen Psychiatry 7:82, 1962
24. Sherman JF: The older applicant for admission to medical school. J Med Educ 53:215, 1978
25. Simon HJ: Mortality among medical students. J Med Educ 43:1175, 1968
26. Smith C: Why some doctors' sons do poorly in med school. Med Economics 41:98, 1964
27. Szasz T: The psychiatrist as double agent. In Strauss AL (ed): Where Medicine Fails. Chicago, Aldine, 1970, pp 157–160
28. Thoreau H: Walden; or Life in the Woods. New York, Dutton, 1908, p 287
29. Waltzer H: Depersonalization and self-destruction. Am J Psychiatry, 125:399, 1968

7

THE STUDENT'S RELATIONSHIPS WITH THE FACULTY

Charisma in a teacher is not a mystery or nimbus of personality, but radiant exemplification to which the student contributes a correspondingly radiant hunger for becoming.

—William Arrowsmith[1]

At the United States Marine Corps Recruit Depot, Parris Island, South Carolina, a large sign carries this admonition: "Let's be damned sure that no boy's ghost will ever say, 'If your training program had only done its job.' " With the changing of a single word this statement could become the challenging motto of the medical school faculty: "Let's be damned sure that no patient's ghost will ever say, 'If your training program had only done its job.' "

The numerous changes in curriculum and reorganization of medical schools detract at times from the essential ingredients of the educational process: the teacher and the student. The enthusiastic, stimulating teacher and the dedicated, open-minded student make an unbeatable combination not to be replaced by curricular gimmicks, teaching machines, and other adjuncts. If the teacher can communicate to the student a sense of enthusiasm, a devotion to knowledge, a zest for learning "why," and a compassion and care for patients, the student can overcome most other obstacles placed in the path to learning. Such a commitment to teaching led Tinsley R. Harrison to comment that he could not say which gives him the greatest satisfaction: "A smile of gratitude on a patient's face, a gleam of comprehension from a curious student, or the intellectual thrill of a new concept."[7] In his long career of teaching, patient care, and medical research, Harrison considers his most important medical contribution to be teaching.

Although vast reforms are under way in medical education, relatively little attention is being given to the teaching abilities of the faculty. The faculties of medical schools deserve the same reappraisal as the curricula have received in recent years. The complaint is widespread that teachers of medicine and those responsible for curriculum planning and program evaluation, despite exceptional skills as research scientists, usually bring no professional educational skill to their complex tasks as teachers and administrators. It has been suggested that we assure future medical students of having good teachers by training all medical students to be effective teachers since their careers will require teaching. Actually, one of the definitions of physician is teacher, and physicians are always involved in teaching their patients. Until better teachers are available, and even when they become available, students themselves should take a major role in educating themselves.

Students may overestimate the importance of teachers in their learning experience. By the time they have reached the status of medical students, they should recognize that it is the active process of learning, not the passive experience of being taught, that counts. Many teachers fall below that standard designated as the ideal teacher. Thus, many students are forced to take a major role in educating themselves. The development of such intellectual self-reliance is an essential aspect of becoming an effective physician.[10] Solving problems or clarifying issues that their teachers are unable to help them with proves to be salutary educational experiences for students. As Carl Lashley has said: "The students who are worth teaching don't need it."

THE GOOD TEACHER

Teachers have always had an honorable place in our society, and a measure of respect has been automatically given them. To some extent the profession of medicine has spelled out more clearly the position of the teacher than have other professional groups.

The responsibility of physicians to teach their art is set forth in the oath of Hippocrates, for almost 25 centuries the credo of the medical profession. It specifies the relationship of teacher and medical student and states in the following words the duty of the physician to teach the art of medicine:

> According to my ability and judgment, I will keep this oath and this stipulation—to reckon him who taught me this Art equally dear to me as my parents, to share my substance with him, and relieve his necessities if required; to look upon his offspring in the same footing as my own brothers, and to teach them this Art, if they shall wish to learn it, without fee or stipulation; and that by precept, lecture, and every other mode of instruction, I will impart a knowledge of the Art to my own sons, and those of my teachers, and to disciples bound by a stipulation and oath according to the law of medicine.

The physician-teacher can also derive comfort from these words spoken by Sir William Osler in 1911, at the opening of the new Pathological Institute of the Royal Infirmary in Glasgow:

> In the hurly-burly of today, when the competition is so keen, and there are so many seeking the bubble reputation at the eyepiece and the test-tube, it is well for young men to remember that no bubble is so iridescent or floats longer than that blown by the successful teacher. A man who is not fond of students and who does not suffer their foibles gladly, misses the greatest zest in life; and the teacher who wraps himself in the cloak of his researches, and lives apart from the bright spirits of the coming generation is very apt to find his garment the shirt of Nessus.[5]

The opportunity of teachers for influencing their students is immeasurably great. The teachers' own observation of students and their involvement with them become a valuable resource for the students in their growth toward maturity. Young persons are in need of face-to-face relationships with authorities who demonstrate their concern for them both by support and by judgment. Physician-teachers have as great an opportunity as that of any teachers to influence their students because of the tradition of teaching in medicine, as the words of Hippocrates and Osler testify.

Teachers must allow themselves to be used by students. Their obligation is to help students learn rather than to force students into their mold. They must accept the students' challenges if they expect their challenges to be accepted. They must be stoical in their reception of the students' attacks, and with them assume a detached attitude in examining the questions at issue. Both students and teachers must accept the basic precept that it is the students who must do the learning and that true learning begins with not knowing the answer.[17]

In his essay on the education of character, Buber describes the difficulty of creative resolution of conflict between teacher and student as illustrated in this passage:

> He must use his own insight wholeheartedly; he must not blunt the piercing impact of his knowledge; but he must at the same time have in readiness the healing ointment for the heart pierced by it. Not for a moment may he conduct a dialectical maneuver instead of the real battle for truth. But if he is the victor, he has to help the vanquished endure defeat; and if he cannot conquer the self-willed soul that faces him (for victories over souls are not so

easily won), then he has to find the word of love which alone can help to overcome so difficult a situation.[3]

Teachers' conviction that they have "made a difference," even with a few students, reassures them that medical education is something far more complex and fundamental than training students to know the classification of drugs, make differential diagnoses, or speak the language of medicine. Mere training can be done by machines, but education requires an attention to students' personal concerns that programmed courses cannot give.

THE TEACHER AS ADVISOR

Students probably turn more often for counsel to favorite and trusted teachers than to assigned advisors or deans. Good counseling requires time, talent, and understanding, and the teachers chosen by students are not always prepared to fulfill this responsibility. Psychiatrists are professionally prepared, but their relationship to students may be compromised if the dean has access to psychiatric records without the students' permission. Fortunately, the dean rarely has access to such records.

The institutional atmosphere may discourage some students from seeking counsel from anyone within the setting of the medical school. Students sense an attitude among certain faculty members that those who need aid are probably weaklings who should not be given help to carry them along in a rugged course of training. Fortunately, a larger percentage of faculty gives the impression that students who need help and seek it are sensible. This latter attitude helps create between students and faculty an atmosphere of confidence and respect, rather than one of suspicion and distrust.

Faculty members may enhance their acceptability as advisors to students by acknowledging that students are persons with names, homes, hopes, fears, aspirations, and troubles and by behaving in a manner which conveys the belief. Miller suggests that a concern for individuality may also relieve the passion for anonymity which characterizes medical students, a passion born of the belief that their progress toward the goal of graduation is less likely to be blocked if they remain essentially unidentified for four years.[14] The acknowledgment of students as individuals may relieve or at least temper the feeling that teachers are more concerned with judging students' qualifications than helping them as persons toward their goal. It is almost impossible to ask any kind of help, especially that of a personal nature, from a teacher who is perceived first as a judge.

The learning environment is created primarily by the faculty and student body. Students see as the best kind of teacher "one who is available, friendly, willing to give time to students, interested in them as individuals, prepared to admit one's own ignorance where ignorance exists, and able to combine practical and theoretical concepts in teaching."[14] The worst teachers may know and teach a great deal but have been identified by students as being uninterested in them. This type usually gives facetious answers to questions or indicates in other ways a distaste for the novice.

Perhaps the teacher-advisor should adopt an approach like that used by Socrates with his students:

> My art is like that of midwives but differs from theirs in that I . . . look after their minds when they are in labor and not after their bodies; and the triumph of my art is in thoroughly examining whether the thought which the mind of the young man brings forth is a phantom and a lie, or a fruitful and true birth. . . . The reproach often made against me, that I ask questions of others and have not the wit to answer them myself, is very just . . . but those who talk with me profit. Some of them appear dull enough at first, but afterwards, as our acquaintance ripens, if the gods are gracious to them, they all make astonishing progress; and this is the opinion of others, as well as their own. It is quite clear that they never learned anything from me; all that they master and discover comes from themselves. But to me and to the gods, they owe their delivery.

THE TEACHER AS EVALUATOR

The value climate of the educational program includes, at times, a generalized attitude toward students that emphasizes their probationary status. In other words, they are acceptable as medical students, but they must still prove their right to be accepted into the profession. As a consequence of such an attitude, Bloom identifies three responses on the part of students:[2]

1. A feeling of "being on trial" similar to and continuous with their status in premedical education.
2. An attitude that the experience is more a "trial by ordeal" than a justifiable test of the important abilities that will be required of them in their future professional role.
3. An awareness that "survival by playing it safe" and the inherent dependency of a clearly subordinate status are encouraged;

the feelings of freedom to explore and to develop individual interests are discouraged.

The evaluation of students is a valid endeavor of the faculty for a variety of reasons. Yet, even when done positively and supportively, it
can emphasize further students' probationary status rather than the
progress they are making in their professional maturation.

The Nature of Evaluation

The whole process of identifying, observing, measuring, and analyzing
various aspects of a learner's performance is what is called "evaluation." In fact, anything that the teacher does to determine the extent to
which the teaching-learning process is succeeding comes under the
heading of evaluation. Evaluation is the result of the teacher's concern
with the goals of education and does not have to be done in a way that
is punitive. Much of what is called "teaching ability" consists in the
ability to make valid and objective judgments about the progress made
by learners. The good teacher has learned what to notice and what to
ignore in the way of behavior and what interpretations and conclusions
to draw.

The teacher's role as evaluator of learning may appear to be somewhat at odds with his or her role as stimulator and promoter of learning. Lindgren writes that some of the confusion may be resolved if we
think of teachers as having two basic roles, that of the participant and
that of the observer:

> In his role as the participant, he plans educational programs, de-
> velops methods and uses materials in order to carry out the pro-
> grams, and participates in the social interaction in the classroom
> while performing his specialized functions as a teacher. In his role
> as an observer, he is more detached: he analyzes students' back-
> grounds, notes how students are reacting to his methods and ma-
> terials, and makes certain conclusions regarding the progress
> made by individual students, as well as by the class in general.
> There is a tendency for teachers to subordinate one of these roles
> to the other. Some teachers become immersed in the daily give-
> and-take of the teaching-learning process, whereas others play
> detached, judgmental roles, never fully committing themselves to
> active participation.[12]

Obviously, it is not easy to coordinate the warm and human role of
the participant in teaching-learning with that of the cool, detached,

and objective role of the observer, but this is a problem that every teacher must face and resolve. The best justification for evaluation is the desire to improve teaching and learning.

In the promotion of learning, an ongoing evaluation system is needed by which faculty and students can effectively measure the success or failure of their educational objectives. Such a system must comprehensively assess the potential and growth of the individual student in becoming a good physician. It must consider the student's ability to comprehend varied bodies of knowledge, to apply that knowledge in clinical and nonclinical situations, and to perform tasks requiring synthesis and conceptual thinking. Aside from these cognitive factors, there should also be a means of assessing those personal qualities and attitudes in students that would tend to make them effective medical practitioners, such as their ability to work with peers, professors, and others; their sense of responsibility; their proficiency in communication; their ability to function well in stressful situations; their adeptness at ethical decision making; and their demeanor in patient care.

Pellegrino has identified a profound moral issue which may be escaping us today: "I am worried about the paucity of discussion about competence and proficiency in current student demands. This very important professional value is also an important human value without which the physician's whole being is compromised. We must guard as carefully against the romanticism of service without knowledge as against proficiency without compassion."[15]

Defining Competence

Medical schools are often urged to shorten the period of training for physicians without lowering the quality of the graduates. This places a heavy burden on quality control. J. B. Carroll wrote in the *Teachers College Record*: "Our educational system is a somewhat mad world in which we hold time as a constant and allow achievement to be a variable."[4] Medical educators such as Hess and Levitt urge us to explore methods for permitting achievement or a comprehensive evaluation of competence to become the constant, and time in school and course requirements to become the variable.[8] In other words, the school may graduate groups of students after three, three and one-half, three and three quarters, or four and one-half years in medical school. With this kind of flexibility will come a new set of tasks for the medical school.

Has anyone yet defined, in an adequate and precise way, the minimum level of competence believed to be essential for entering the graduate phase of medical education? Schools are addressing themselves to identifying the minimum fund of knowledge students should possess; the kinds of illnesses they should be able to diagnose; the illnesses they should be able to treat; the types of diagnostic and therapeutic procedures they should have performed; the level of skill that should be demonstrated in relating to patients, keeping medical records, and working with others on the health team.

The development of medical school curricula has been made more difficult because the end product of the educational process has often not been properly delineated. As Kane and his associates have emphasized, once a clear concept of the desired end product is shared by all factions of the curricula planning body, the task of specific curricula building with learning objectives becomes possible.[9] Unfortunately, the statement of outcomes or objectives for instruction has rarely formed a basis for curricula building in medical education. Kane and associates emphasize further that failure to state explicitly the goals of the education process creates a double loss: (1) teachers cannot be sure they are presenting relevant materials and (2) students do not have important information available to facilitate independent learning.

After defining the level of competence essential for entering the graduate phase of medical education, schools must find ways for comprehensively assessing competence. Paper and pencil examinations are part of the process of evaluation because they provide a convenient method for measuring conceptual learning. The practice of medicine is much more than the understanding of concepts and includes that critical dimension of performance in which students are called upon to apply both their knowledge and their interpersonal and psychomotor skills to patients. Methods for practicing techniques and for measuring on-the-job performance in a scientifically acceptable way are evolving in many places.[9]

There are numerous approaches to evaluation, all of which contain both strengths and weaknesses. The large number of experimental modifications of grading systems and other forms of evaluation attest to the dissatisfaction with present practices and the continual search for better methods.

EVALUATING FACULTY EFFECTIVENESS

A comprehensive system for evaluating students should also provide a means for evaluating the faculty as effective teachers and models for the students to whom they are responsible. Evaluation of the faculty should include the measurement of such factors as teachers' attitude toward students, patients, and colleagues; their ability to teach well; the quality and quantity of relevant knowledge they are able to impart; and whether students have in fact learned what was supposed to have been learned.[16]

A number of schools are developing methods of evaluating the effectiveness of the faculty. As a requisite for passing any course, students are required to evaluate the course and the faculty teaching the course. Computerized forms are used, and every effort is made to maintain the confidentiality and frankness of students' responses. A summary of student evaluations of each faculty member is usually sent semiannually to that teacher's departmental chairman and personal file, to the curriculum committee, to the dean, and to the teacher.

Also, many schools are developing means whereby junior and senior students can assess the immediate relevance of freshman and sophomore basic science courses to their present clinical situations. Further, students through certain of their organizations evaluate faculty teaching and give a variety of awards in recognition of outstanding teaching.

Dr. Owen H. Wangenstein, distinguished surgeon and medical school professor, has stated that, since the responsibility of teachers to students far outweighs the obligation of students to teachers, teachers ought to recite before students each year the "Teacher's Oath." This oath would be a form of teacher evaluation in that it calls for an examination of teacher effectiveness by the teachers themselves. Dr. Wangenstein has written for us the "Teacher's Oath."[19]

Fellow students: Aesculapius, timeless physician of all ages and nations, we beseech you instill in this faculty's teachers a fervent desire to become spirited and effective preceptors of all our student progeny. Your teachers do recognize, appreciate, and solemnly declare to place the enviable privilege as teacher near the top of other demanding priorities: care for patients and research to improve our fellowman's lot. May we, by example and precept, awaken in each of you an eagerness to excel in all aspects of your accepted trusts. May all of us come to know the abundant rewards of shared opportunity, the finest of paymasters. May greed for money never cross the threshold of our minds. May each of us through prudent and thrifty living come to know the satisfaction and contentment of sharing our bounty with good causes and especially with institutions of learning that created for us the priceless opportunity of spending our lives in the service of our fellow men and women. With complete dedication and unremitting industry, some of you may come to stand with your work and discoveries before the courts of posterity and eternity. Fellow students, let us build together a friendly and quickened reciprocal student-teacher relationship that would have found acceptance in the eyes of our beloved Hippocrates.

EVALUATING ADMINISTRATIVE STRUCTURE AND EDUCATIONAL ATMOSPHERE

There should be a method by which the administrative structure and the educational atmosphere are continually under evaluation in order to insure that a school's objectives are resonant with the health needs of society. Also, since the impact of the medical school environment on students is a major factor in their professional maturation, failure to monitor this environment or atmosphere is a grievous disservice to students.

In all evaluation, there is a dimension of gamesmanship or one-up-manship on the part of the evaluator as well as the one being evaluated. Also, there is the hope on being evaluated that one will get a better break than one actually deserves. Such an idea is behind a famous toast: "May you already have arrived safely in heaven before the devil discovers that you are dead."

THE TEACHER AS SCIENTIST

Medical school teachers are usually scientists. If students are to understand their teachers, they must comprehend the three figures or archetypes into which the popular image of the scientist is split.[11]*

The first is the Benevolent Magician, whose ancestry derives from the rainmaking shamans. From there onward, every century created its own savant-shamans whom it could venerate. Among the most popular ones have been Pythagoras, Sylvester II, Maimonides, Venerable Bede, St. Thomas Aquinas, Paracelsus, Galileo, Newton, Franklin, Mesmer, Edison, Pasteur, Einstein, and Freud. The Benevolent Magician has certain features in common with the artist. Both are unselfishly devoted to lofty tasks. The Benevolent Magician symbolizes the self-transcending element in the scientist's motivational drive and emotional makeup—the quest for the harmony of the spheres and the origins of life. The conquering urge is derived from a sense of power, the

---

* I have drawn from Koestler's discussion of the three character types in science and have used his terms.

participatory urge from a sense of oceanic wonder. Koestler emphasizes strongly the sense of wonder:

> In all the great and generous minds from Nicolas of Cusa down to Einstein, we find the feeling of awe and wonder, an intellectual ecstasy of distinctly religious flavour. Even those who professed to be void of it based their labours on an act of faith: the belief that there is a harmony of the spheres—that the universe is not a tale told by an idiot, but governed by hidden laws waiting to be discovered and uttered.[11]

Whyte expresses the same idea in a similar vein: "The mystic believes in an unknown God; the thinker and scientist in an unknown order; it is hard to say which surpasses the other in nonrational devotion."[20]

The second archetype is the Mad Professor, whose work serves the quest for aggrandizement and power. The Mad Professor—either a sadist or obsessed with power—looms in popular fiction from Jules Verne's Captain Nemo, H. G. Wells's Dr. Moreau, and Mary Shelley's Dr. Frankenstein to the monsters of the horror comics. This type is a witty, sarcastic Mephistophelian character, a sinister jester plotting to commit some practical joke on humanity. If stripped of the gaudy adornments that folklore and fiction bestow, the Mad Professor will turn out to be an archetypal symbol of the self-assertive element in the scientist's aspirations. Koestler describes this type succinctly: "In mythology, this element is represented by the Promethean quest for omnipotence and immortality; in science-fiction it is caricatured as a monstrous lusting for power; in actual life, it appears as the unavoidable component of competitiveness, jealousy, and self-righteousness in the scientist's complex motivational drive."[11]

The Uninspired Pedant is the third figure into which the popular image of the scientist has been split—the dry, dull, diligent, pedantic, uninspired, scholarly bookworm who is petulant and jealous of anybody who dares to interfere with his or her crabbed little world. This imaginary type is similar to the religious scholars whom Erasmus lampooned: "They smother me beneath six hundred dogmas; they are surrounded with a bodyguard of definitions, conclusions, corollaries, propositions explicit and propositions implicit; they are looking in utter darkness for that which has no existence whatsoever." The Uninspired Pedant stands between the Benevolent Magician and the Mad Professor, is an indispensable stabilizing element, acting as a restraining influence on the self-asserting, vainglorious conquering urges on one side and as a skeptical critic of the inspired dreamer's on the other.

The student needs and seeks in each teacher a blending of the three archetypes of the scientist. Such a teacher, according to Koestler, will induce the student, with proper aid and guidance:

> ... to make some of the fundamental discoveries of science by himself, to experience in his own mind some of those flashes of insight which have lightened his path . . . the paradoxes, the "blocked matrices" which confronted Archimedes, Copernicus, Galileo, Newton, Harvey, Darwin, Einstein should be reconstructed in their historical setting and presented in the form of riddles—with appropriate hints—to eager young minds. The most productive form of learning is problem-solving. The traditional method of confronting the student not with the problem but with the finished solution means depriving him of all excitement, to shut off the creative impulse, to reduce the adventure of mankind to a dusty heap of theorems.[11]

CONCLUSION

The impact of the institutional atmosphere on students is a major factor in their successes and failures in learning the science and art of medicine.[13] The ideas and actions of the faculty and house staff (residents and interns) affect the students by setting the conditions under which problems arise and learning is enhanced or hampered. Faculty expectations of students, rules of the road, and the way the faculty interprets and defines the rules constitute facets of the environment in which students learn and act.

Medical schools are organized in an "authoritarian" manner. The faculty and administration have enormous power over the students. Students learn shortly after their enrollment that if they are dropped, their chance of being reinstated in that medical school or another one is slim. Until the M.D. degree is conferred, their budding medical careers could be permanently terminated. The faculty and administration, in principle, can control tightly a variety of student activities. If such control and power are exercised, students will have no opportunity to build their own perspectives and will simply take on ideas forced on them.

Students, moreover, face a series of school situations in which they are obliged to perform academically for the faculty. The faculty assess students' ability and the amount learned largely on the basis of these performances. The students realize that survival in medical school is dependent on making the right kind of impression on the faculty—to present them with either the substance or the appearance of learning.

The question arises immediately, however, as to what will impress the faculty as real learning, for students testify that faculty reactions cannot be predicted in any logical or uncomplicated way. Simple methods of making a good impression may not suffice. Thus, the students must be sensitive to faculty demands and modify their behavior accordingly, even when these demands seem unrelated to the real purposes of medical school.

While students must be sensitive to faculty demands, what kind of relationship to faculty do students really want or what kind of relationship do they think most helpful to them? Stritter and associates asked medical students to identify characteristics of teachers which they thought were most helpful in facilitating learning. In a factor analysis of these data they found that the most important factor was making students active participants in the learning process.[18] This included teacher behaviors such as encouraging students to raise questions, providing students the opportunities to practice both technical and problem-solving skills, and explaining to students the basis for the teachers' own actions and decisions. Thus, what the students want and see as important is different from what often happens, i.e., teachers do the preponderance of talking, provide mostly factual information, and rarely challenge students to think through a response.[6]

REFERENCES

1. Arrowsmith W: The future of teaching. Arion. Spring, 1967, p 9
2. Bloom SW: The medical school as a social system—a case study of faculty-student relations. Milbank Mem Fund Q 49:1 (part 2), 1971
3. Buber M: I and Thou. Edinburgh, Clark, 1937
4. Carroll JB: A model of school learning. Teachers College Record 64:723, 1963
5. Cushing H: The Life of Sir William Osler. Oxford, Clarendon Press, vol 2, 1925, pp 295–296
6. Foley R, Smilansky J, Yonke A: Teacher student interaction in a medical clerkship. J Med Educ 54:622, 1979
7. Harrison TR: Contemporaries. Modern Medicine 35:150, 1967
8. Hess JW, Levitt M: New philosophies in medical education—their effect on recognition of competence. JAMA 123:1009, 1970
9. Kane R, Woolley FR, Kane R: Toward defining the end product of medical education. J Med Educ 48:615, 1973
10. Knowles MS: Self-directed Learning. A Guide for Learners and Teachers. Chicago, Association Press/Follett, 1975
11. Koestler A: The Act of Creation. New York, Macmillan, 1964, pp 255–267
12. Lindgren HC: Educational Psychology in the Classroom, ed 3. New York, Wiley, 1971

13. Marshall RE: Measuring the medical school learning environment. J Med Educ 53:98, 1978
14. Miller GE, et al.: Teaching and Learning in Medical School. Cambridge, Harvard University Press, 1962, pp 34–35
15. Pellegrino ED: Human values and the medical curriculum. JAMA 209:1349, 1969
16. Rose C: Stalking the perfect teacher. Chronicle of Higher Education 13:24, 1976
17. Ryback D, Sanders JJ: Humanistic versus traditional styles and student satisfaction. J Humanistic Psychology 20:87, 1980
18. Stritter FT, Hain JD, Grimes DA: Clinical teaching re-examined. J Med Educ 50:876, 1979
19. Wangenstein OH: Teacher's oath. J Med Educ 53:524, 1978
20. Whyte LL: The Unconscious Before Freud. New York, Anchor Books, 1962, p 66

8

PROFILES OF DEANS
AND HELP FOR
THE STUDENT

I will teach you, and guide you in the way you should go. I will keep you under my eye.

—Psalms 32:8

Students must learn how to deal with deans and their numerous assistants. The administrative organization of a medical school may range from the complex to the ponderous. Where the final decision-making power rests may be hard to locate or identify. Through these entanglements, students must make their way. If knowledgeable about administrative structures, they will be able to devise better strategies for dealing with problems than if they remain ignorant of the dean's work and organization.* Their success may be determined by their insight and foresight concerning the governance of the medical school.

Recently, the deans' responsibilities have progressively broadened, while their authority and their own ability to influence the course of events have not expanded concomitantly. A new dean, in assessing his position and the resources available to him for performing his duties, described his task as similar to that of a hummingbird trying to hatch an ostrich egg. Judging by the short tenure of deans in other schools, he wondered how limited would be his stewardship and how threatened by dissatisfaction on the part of dissident faculty and student groups.

Students, aware of the complexities in the administrative structure of their school, are realistic in asking: "Who will guide or rescue us in a crisis?" Deans of the type that their physician parents knew when they were medical students are seen infrequently today. Thus, students may not find as easily as did their parents that concerned administrative official with the power and authority to lead as well as referee.

---

* In this chapter, my intention is not to deal with the dean's complicated job in a modern medical school, for Glaser and others have written lucidly on this topic.[2, 4, 8, 9] My concern is with the interaction between student and administration at those points where a student's professional growth may be hampered or enhanced.

THE SEARCH FOR AN OMBUDSMAN

Busy deans have seldom had the time in recent years to be an ombudsman* for the student. They have usually assigned this role to the subdean in charge of student matters related to promotion, discipline, and
similar activities. Some students today see and experience the work of
such a subdean in the light of an adversary rather than an ombudsman.
Sometimes certain faculty members seem to promote an adversary
structure. For example, in a faculty committee meeting, a professor
raised the question as to why we insist on applicants having excellent
academic qualifications before we admit them and then are hesitant to
drop them if they do poorly. "Why can't the faculty be consistent?" he
asked. He refused adamantly to accept the explanation that the two situations are different. Because only the qualified student with proved
ability is admitted, with each failure, the school must examine its
teaching program and learning environment to determine its part in
the student's failure. Rehabilitation of a student and correction of his
or her problems rather than hasty dismissal should be the primary
concern of the school. Faculty members and deans should always consider the possibility that a school may be partly responsible for a student's poor performance. At times, a student's professional fate is determined on the basis of his or her having made 69 in a course instead
of a 70. Can any grading instrument be that precise and valid? Probably
not, if one takes seriously the continual search for better grading
methods.

Observing the process of dismissing a student from medical school
can be a revealing experience. Seldom are the issues clear and free of
emotional biases. The student may become a scapegoat in the classical
sense. Some of those with the authority to decide the student's fate
may project their dark sides onto the student. After the dismissal, they
feel cleansed and reassured regarding their purity and that of the medical profession. On the other hand, there are faculty members and administrators who mourn the loss of a student as if their own son or
daughter had been dismissed.

---

* An ombudsman (Swedish for "representative") is one appointed to take the
side of the individual against the monolithic barriers and restraints that are a
part of modern bureaucracy. John Hunter, the great British surgeon and anatomist, should be declared the patron saint of medical students and ombudsmen. On October 16, 1793, Hunter attended a meeting of the St. George's Hospital staff and while defending the interests of several students, was
contradicted and thoroughly antagonized by his colleagues. The pains of an-
gina commenced. He started toward another room, gained it, and fell dying
into the arms of a physician colleague.[6]

As the subdeans have strengthened their identity with the school and its policies, students have sought for ombudsmen on the faculty and have found them in a variety of departments, especially psychiatry. Psychiatrists have usually had no difficulty maintaining their loyalty to the individual student and have had no need to prove how "useful" they could be to the school. At times, however, they have permitted themselves to be misused by the administrative officers in their work with students. They may be chosen to help carry out administrative policies, lending the weight of psychiatric theory and psychodynamics to illuminate or obscure the issue, whichever one is needed at the moment.

A psychiatrist told of his experience several years ago that may well be descriptive of what is happening today in some medical schools. He served for a few years as a member of the committee on promotions and discipline—a busy committee, reviewing student performance and behavior. He became a star performer at the meetings, helping the committee and especially its chairman package in psychodynamic terms the decisions made on students. Often when a student was fighting for his or her life—not to be thrown out of school—and appeared before the committee to plead his or her case, the psychiatrist assumed a central role in the meeting. In decisive situations the chairman would let him carry the main brunt of the interaction with the student because he could ask "the right questions." If the dean thought the student should be saved, the psychiatrist would conduct the session in that light. If it were felt in advance that the student should be dismissed, the psychiatrist could create an atmosphere where such an action became imperative. "In other words," said this psychiatrist, "I developed such skill in playing this game that I could take two similar students with similar problems and package the findings in such a manner that a totally different decision would be reached on each of the two students; and the decisions would be upheld without a whimper by the top authority of the school, namely, the executive faculty." The psychiatrist went on to say that he wanted recognition and power and saw himself replacing the chairman of the department of psychiatry before too long. Soon he realized that he was selling his birthright for a mess of porridge and was preoccupied with his own needs instead of the welfare and needs of the students. Feeling that he had violated a sacred trust, he moved out of that situation and into private practice but kept a clinical appointment on the faculty. In his new relationship with the students, he represented them in their quest for professional maturity whenever the opportunity presented itself and had no need to prove himself useful to the school.

Good doctors always put their patients' needs first. Good teachers and good administrators do likewise in all relationships with students. What is best for the medical school and what is best for the community are seldom in conflict with what is best for students.

Students are rightfully suspicious of committees that exercise arbitrary dominion over them in the name of benevolence. Students testify that when a devastating decision has been made against them, they are often told: "We think this is best for you," or "This hurts us more than you." Especially disturbing to today's students are arbitrary rules concerning promotion and dismissal. Some of these rules have existed at certain medical schools for years without review or modification and no longer fit today's student or learning environment. The humanistic groups in medical schools have struggled long, and not always successfully, to remove from their catalogs such immoral and unethical statements as: "We reserve the right to forbid any student's continued enrollment in the medical school without assignment of reason." Actually punitive actions against students help neither students nor school. George Bernard Shaw has given us sound counsel in these words: "To punish a man you must injure him; to reform a man you must improve him; and men are not improved by injuries."

Fortunately, students today have many organizations of their own that give them input in some aspects of the governance of the medical school. Often these organizations develop guidelines to help students in crisis situations as well as in anticipatory guidance. Further, students serve, with full voting powers, on many of the decision-making committees of the medical school and thereby represent their peers in areas that vitally concern them. This recognition of the rights and responsibilities of students to have a voice in all phases of the operation of the medical school has greatly improved medical education and has made the educational environment more humanistic.

PROFILE OF DEANS

Since a medical school has a number of deans, each at a different level or serving in a different area of the administrative hierarchy, students should learn the personality profile and psychodynamic configuration of some of the most common types. Described in everyday language, these types are (1) the good parent, (2) the older brother, (3) the favorite uncle or mother's brother, and (4) the Eden snake. Prototypes of the good parent and the older brother are found in the Biblical parable of the prodigal son (Luke 15:11-32). The third type is drawn from the common experience of one's favorite uncle, usually the mother's brother. The fourth type is taken from the Garden of Eden story, where a snake showed some remarkable skills in dialogue and leadership. The four types may refer to deans or to subdeans of any rank.

The Good Parent. "Good parent" deans function with responsibility and imagination in the pursuit of valuable goals for the school. They consider the needs and well-being of their students, staff, and faculty of paramount importance. They possess empathy and warmth and the ability to be firm without punitiveness and indulgence in moral judgment. They avoid coercive authority but seek to foster the students' and the staff's independence and self-determmination. They are committed to helping all associated with them find daily work satisfactions, ego support, and opportunities for career growth. The "good parent" dean has attained that level of maturity characteristic of an autonomous individual with capacities for awareness, spontaneity, and intimacy.

An excellent discussion, applicable to the position of a dean, is found in Francis Bacon's essay "Of Great Place." Bacon begins by emphasizing that the more one is the superior, the more one becomes a slave:

> Men in great place are thrice servants—servants of the sovereign or state, servants of fame, and servants of business; so as they have no freedom neither in their persons, nor in their actions, nor in their times. It is a strange desire to seek power and to lose liberty; or to seek power over others, and to lose power over a man's self. The rising unto place is laborious; and by pains men come to greater pains.[1]

"Good parent" deans see purpose and meaning in their work and bear with grace and dignity their enslavement, in the sense that Bacon used the term.

The "good parent" dean may at times inadvertently play the game of "father knows best." A conscientious person who desires only the best for those whom one serves may become too directive in critical situations. Leadership in the context of "father knows best" often elicits two types of behavior: that of the passive good child or the rebellious adolescent.

"Good parent" deans may also play the role of rescuer. In the classical situation, the doctor is a rescuer. Thus, deans include this role in the province of their office. And among medical students much rescuing needs to be done.

The Older Brother. Out of the well-known Bible story of the prodigal son (Luke 15:11-32) has come a familiar personality type called "the older brother." While this term will be used to describe a particular type of dean, this type can be inclusive of both male and female deans, for both sexes are found in this category in our medical schools. Thus, I ask the reader to bear with the masculine language of "older brother," for to substitute a term like "the older sibling" would lose the ancient roots of the term.

"Older brother" deans are the hard-working, obsessive-compulsive persons who, in the language of developmental psychology, are referred to as anal retentive characters. They are neat, orderly, and concerned with control and production on schedule according to impersonal rules. They like to play it safe and avoid involvement in those matters that could interfere with their rise to positions of greater power and prestige. Their forte is management, not leadership.[5]

They are highly competitive, especially with those at their level and below on the totem pole. They are watchful and obsessed with knowing in detail everything that is going on around them. Their greeting and parting words to their subordinates may be "Keep me informed." Delegating authority is difficult for them, for they feel strongly that deans must keep control over every facet of their so-called province. They fear losing control, and this characteristic keeps everything tight. Their approach to all issues is a moralistic and legalistic one. They are hesitant and slow in making decisions because they are "rigor mortised" by every jot and tittle.

Since "older brother" deans are highly ambitious, power oriented and seldom genuinely courageous, they may fiddle with minutiae and avoid coming to grips with knotty and urgent problems in the academic center, such as the abuse of a student by a sadistic or misguided faculty member; destructive actions by a departmental chairman against a staff member; and unproductive faculty members who have become parasitic on both school and student.

Their fear of expressing feelings and "coming alive" causes them to miss the joy of living. For example, if older brother deans were faced with an experience like that of Lady Chatterly and her lover, they would not focus on the act of love between Lady Chatterly and the gamekeeper, but they would be more concerned with the circumstances surrounding the act of love than with the act itself. While others would be interested in what Lady Chatterly and her gamekeeper did in the woods, this would be of only passing interest to older brother deans. They would be more interested in how Lady Chatterly and her lover got into the woods, what arrangements were made for a shelter in case of inclement weather and for refreshments, how they accounted for their absence, whether either party could recover incidental expenses, and, if so, how. In other words, they would find the administrative side of love more absorbing than its purely erotic aspects.

The "older brother" dean has some characteristics similar to the "counterfeit executive," a term used by Kurt Einstein in his business of locating and screening attractive candidates for high executive positions.[10] The counterfeits are persons who have maneuvered themselves into a high position that is beyond their capabilities. They are unproductive in many areas of their responsibility, unwise in their decisions, and destructive of the morale of the people around them. They conceal their identity to delude themselves and others by surrounding themselves with other counterfeits.

"Older brother" deans repeatedly play certain games that reveal their more prominent character traits. One involves a stalking method. They monitor carefully the behavior of certain students or faculty members who have aroused their suspicions or who represent a lifestyle different from theirs. Sooner or later, they catch the person or persons in something which they consider an indiscretion. Motivated by jealous rage, a smile of victory sweeps over the face: "Aha! Now I've got you, you son of Aesculapius." They raise immediately that question which chills students to the marrow of their bones: "Are you fit for the practice of medicine?" Although rarely said explicitly, they imply to the persons that they have been watching them, hoping they would make a slip: "And now that you have been caught, I am going to let you have the full force of my righteous indignation." Some of these actions by the dean have little or no justification in the behavior of the students or faculty.

A second type of game they pursue is "I play it by the book." They administer corrections, punishments, and even rewards always by the book. To substantiate their actions, they can always find a rule in an old catalog, a set of minutes, sanctioned by tradition, or from some rule book. They are never without a rule to support an authoritarian position. They need the rule book to protect themselves against retaliations and to justify their actions. When some of these rule book actions turn out to be destructive, they take comfort in the fact that they followed the book as carefully as a "legal eagle." Such a legalistic approach to life led Mark Twain to describe that kind of person as "a good man in the worst sense of the word."

A third favorite game is "It shall come to pass," which relates to the self-fulfilling prophecy. The dean likes to prophesy or predict certain future happenings. Almost invariably, these prophecies relate to happenings which he or she has the power and authority to bring to pass, at least in part. For example, Peter Simple flunked out of school this year. Next year, Joe Jones comes to the dean's attention, and the dean casually drops the remark that Joe Jones looks exactly like another Peter Simple. This casual statement sets in motion a complicated chain of events which may result in fulfilling the dean's prophecy.

Another game the "older brother" dean plays constantly is "Big Brother is watching." Students do not appreciate being too closely observed or spied upon. Such deans prize highest those students or faculty members who keep them informed and consider them the loyal ones. With certain students and faculty members serving as official "bird watchers," the result is the flaming of the students' already existing paranoia.

A reader of the first edition of this book mentioned that he saw in the "older brother" dean none other than Felix Unger of Felix and Oscar fame in the television show, "The Odd Couple." Yes, there are some deans around who could be Felix's twin.

The Favorite Uncle or Mother's Brother.   Possibly one could designate this type of dean as either the "favorite uncle" or the "favorite aunt," but favorite uncle carries a clearer picture of this classic type. Thus, again the masculine term will be used but with no intent to exclude women deans from this category.

Usually one's favorite uncle is mother's brother. Thus, "favorite uncle" deans possess maternal qualities. The justice they dispense is always tempered with mercy. They relate to students and faculty as colleagues and rejoice in their successes and are saddened by their defeats. They are sensitive, capable of deep feelings, and benevolent in that they wish only good for those whom they serve.

Students trust them completely, for they can be counted upon to stand with them in any crisis. When facing serious and seemingly insoluble problems in students, giving up on or abandoning a student is usually not an option considered. They think in terms of rehabilitation, not abandonment. Their unspoken philosophy is, "In working with a highly selected group of persons, such as medical students, we ought to be able to find a satisfactory solution to almost any problem encountered in such students." And as one would surmise, their accomplishments with students are great indeed.

In their leadership of the school, they are imaginative and innovative, open to change, and willing to experiment. Structure and direction characterize their leadership, and they follow a middle road between permissiveness and authoritarianism.

Administrators and managers are sometimes grouped in the following four types: (1) the hard nose, (2) the whipcracker, (3) the human relater, and (4) the situation manager. The "favorite uncle" dean is seen as a blend of the last two types—the human relater and the situation manager.

"Favorite uncle" deans run the risk of being placed in the role of patsy, at times, by students. Their maternal traits lead them to do for students what their mothers would do, for they understand them and accept them as do their mothers.

Also, "favorite uncle" deans may be encouraged too often to play the happy warrior role, taking on too readily and with too much relish those who desire anything less than the best for their students.

The Eden Snake as Dean.   Because the story of the snake's conversation with Eve in the Garden of Eden (Genesis 2 and 3) is so well known, it is not necessary to review it here. The Eden snake does represent a dean type not uncommon today. The masterful way in which the snake interacted with Eve sets forth some administrative and professorial qualities that merit attention.

The "Eden snake" deans, in subtle ways, foster independence and self-determination. They are able to see the veneer with which students often cover themselves and to expose the fears, faults, dreams, and hopes of the "real person inside." They point out new ways of gaining knowledge, ways that could be hazardous. They confront, they offer options, and, above all, they are able to bring out hidden things within their students— often strengths and great potential. Thus, "Eden snake" deans possess a unique quality for challenging students in both professional and personal maturation.

CONCLUSION

Medical school administration is complex and not easily understood. At times the complexity may obscure for the student the essential nature of the educational process.

The great medical schools of a few years ago were built around great faculties. Deans were the leaders of their faculties, and their leadership brought unity and significance to everything that the institution was and did. Administrative machinery was at a minimum, and the educational program centered on the student-professor concept. With the administrative hierarchy of the medical school patterned now after American business, the dean has become primarily the executive of the trustees, and his or her leadership of faculty and students is minimal. The group of subdeans handles the relationships with and commitments to students and faculty. A unified leadership and a sense of community are lacking, however, in many medical schools. Attention is being given to how the situation can be improved, and groups and individuals are studying the problems related to the governance of the academic medical center.[3, 7]

A final word for the student. In dealing with abrasive structures in

medical schools, generations of students have used the rallying cry, *illegitimi non carborundum* ("Don't let the bastards grind you down").*
It is to be hoped that this motto will mobilize sufficiently the inner resources of today's students to assure them of victory in the attainment of their goals.

REFERENCES

1. Bacon F: Of Great Place. Essays and New Atlantis. New York, Walter J Black, 1942, pp 42–46
2. Glaser RJ: The medical deanship: Its half-life and hard times. J Med Educ 44:1115, 1969
3. Ingersoll RW: The evaluation of administrative performance. J Med Educ 52:526, 1977
4. Levitt M: The medical school deanship: Facts and fancies. Pharos July 1968, pp 86–90
5. Menzies HD: The ten toughest bosses. Fortune, April 21, 1980, pp 62–72
6. Mettler CA: History of Medicine. Philadelphia, Blakiston, 1947, pp 84–85
7. Report of the Commission for the Study of the Governance of the Academic Medical Center. New York, Josiah Macy Jr. Foundation, 1970
8. Rhodes P: Who would be a dean? A light-hearted look at the impossibility of the task. Br Med J 1:953, 1977
9. Rogers DE: Reflections on a medical school deanship. Pharos 38:115, 1975
10. Welles C: Test by stress. Life, August 18, 1967, pp 69–74

---

* Some may ask about the derivation of this phrase. I asked Dr. William B. Bean about it, and he consulted his friend and colleague, Dr. Oscar Nybakken, retired head of the Classics Department, University of Iowa. Dr. Nybakken stated that he has heard the expression often, and that in Niagara Falls, home of the Carborundum Company, it is printed on ashtrays, and other objects. He said that the Latin is atrocious, neither grammatical nor idiomatic, and is a phrase of late contrivance. If a modern Latin version is desired, he would suggest *illegitimis atteri non patiundum,* but would guess that medical students will find best suited for their purposes *illegitimi non carborundum.*

9

DEVELOPING
TOLERANCE FOR
UNCERTAINTY

*The one mark of maturity, especially in a physician, and perhaps it is even
rarer in a scientist, is the capacity to deal with uncertainty.*
—William B. Bean[1]

Although our knowledge of health and disease is vast, little of this
knowledge is complete or certain. Possibly because of the nature of
their earlier education, students enter medical school with the expectation that medical science has developed a body of factual knowledge
that, if learned diligently, will enable a doctor to practice with confidence, competence, and certainty. Many students are ill-prepared intellectually or emotionally for the discovery that in the practice of
medicine major decisions must frequently be made from knowledge
that is fragmentary and open to question. The development of the ability to accept uncertainty and to deal with it effectively is for many students the most difficult adaptational task confronting them in medical
school. Some never develop this ability.[2]

Much of the teaching in the first year or two of medical school tends
to inculcate an expectation of certainty of knowledge and a phobic
aversion for and intolerance of uncertainty. This inculcation has been
particularly true in the teaching approach of certain professors of anatomy where their "patients," the cadavers, offer a much more stable situation than does the hospital ward. To suggest an expectation of the
certainty of knowledge is a serious betrayal of the essence of the scientific movement, according to Whitehorn, who emphasizes that science
is better symbolized by the question mark, signaling a doubt and a further look.[20] The questioning per se best represents science as a powerful instrument of progress in the medical profession.

The care of sick people is the unique contribution of doctors. Doctors' indispensable role with the sick relates to their function as decision makers in the face of uncertainty. The patient's welfare is the doctor's cause. Thus, the education of physicians is directed toward
acquiring the knowledge and skills needed for assessment of the patient's condition and for being the patient's advocate.[14]

Through their medical training, students are placed on a track where they acquire an extensive scientific knowledge, where they become adept at the interpretation of data, and where they become sensitive to the interaction between patients, physicians, and disease. With this kind of background, they continue to grow in competence and in concern for their patients. At the same time, knowing with certainty is something that physicians rarely achieve; thus, developing a tolerance for uncertainty is an urgent task. Yet, the warning of Francis Bacon contains an encouraging promise: "If a man will begin with certainties he shall end in doubts, but if he will be content to begin with doubts he shall end in certainties."

THEORETICAL CONSIDERATIONS

The immediate need of scientists is to prove, whereas that of practical persons is to understand or get the job done. Practical persons (practicing physicians) must be prepared to accept bigger risks. Scientific theorists know they will expose themselves to sharp criticisms from their colleagues if they put forward any conclusion that is not as near to demonstrable certainty as an empirical conclusion can be. Thus, they cut their initial assumptions to the barest minimum.

In making a decision about a patient, practitioners have to weigh the probabilities. However, it is not sufficient to play the statistics game without recognizing the gravity of the different issues that may be at stake. The probability of a particular mishap may be comparatively low, yet if the effects would be grave and irreparable (such as death for a patient), practitioners are ready to insure heavily against it. On the other hand, if the effects would be relatively trivial, then, even though the likelihood is much greater, physicians are willing to face the risk. When they work effectively and skillfully with such probabilities, they are tolerant of uncertainty and not rendered anxious by it.

One of the benefits of a broad education is help in escaping the tyranny of first impressions and of naive preconceptions. Such an education helps one learn to suspend judgment and action, not indefinitely and vaguely, but long enough and thoughtfully enough for the orderly review of evidence and the weighing of probabilities and values. It is difficult to weigh alternatives, or even to be aware of them without some ability to tolerate uncertainty. Frightened or anxious awareness of uncertainty hinders the operation of good judgment and the use of common sense. Whitehorn points out the shortcoming of the physician who is technically trained but not educated:

> The technically trained physician, as distinguished from the educated physician, will, of course, become aware in his own field of

the diagnostic risks of snap judgments and the risks of inadequate differential review, but if obsessed by the inner compulsive demand for certainty, he may lack the equanimity to face the uncertainties sensibly; he may try compulsively by the unwise and neurotic multiplication of tests and superfluous instrumentation to achieve the illusion of certainty; and such behavior may in actuality be only a manifestation of another type of superstition—a modernistic and expensive superstition, but still a superstition—the superstitious faith in the lab report.[20]

The technically overburdened physician who is inadequately educated in the broader human sense is often inwardly constrained to maintain, when facing patients and colleagues, a pose of certainty and a false attitude of omniscience, which are likely to evoke in both patients and colleagues an uneasy suspicion and distrust.

The Triad of Problems in Uncertainty

Problems relating to uncertainty, as they confront both medical student and physician, can be grouped into three categories: (1) uncertainty deriving from limitations in current medical knowledge; (2) uncertainty that results from personal limitations—one's own incomplete or imperfect mastery of available medical knowledge and skills; (3) uncertainty in distinguishing between personal ignorance or ineptitude and the limitations in current medical knowledge.

Limitations in Current Medical Knowledge. The student quickly recognizes that the different medical sciences vary with respect to the limitations of medical knowledge. In anatomy, most knowledge appears clear-cut and exact, standing in sharp contrast to the limitations seen in other basic science disciplines, such as pharmacology. There are similar differences among the clinical sciences. The gaps in psychiatric knowledge, for example, are much greater than those in the field of obstetrics and gynecology. It would not be difficult to arrange the fields of medicine according to the degree of uncertainty that characterizes them.

The question is raised as to whether those fields in which limitations of knowledge are particularly prominent offer more or fewer means of coming to terms with uncertainty. Psychiatry does a fairly good job in dealing directly and openly with uncertainties because of the considerable limitation of knowledge in the field and because much of the training in this field focuses on what is going on within the student in the patient-healer encounters. In other fields, wide variations are seen, depending as much on the concerns, insights, and personality types of the individual professors as on the limitations of knowledge in a particular field.

Another question relates to the influence of one's tolerance for uncertainty on the choice of a career. Do students who find it difficult to accept the uncertainties that they encounter elect to go into fields of medicine in which there is less likelihood of meeting these uncertainties? Even in choosing a highly specialized field, rather than general practice, one narrows the range of potential uncertainty with which he or she will have to deal as a doctor by narrowing the scope of practice. I have observed in numerous students this factor operating in the choice of a specialty. Individuals vary widely in their conscious awareness of the influence of the factor of uncertainty.

Renee Fox mentions that clinical investigators, with their research activities combined with patient care, become specialists in uncertainties related to the limits of present medical knowledge. She makes this observation in her sociological study of a Metabolic Group whose investigative and clinical activities centered in problems related to the functioning of the adrenal glands:

> Because they worked close to the growing edge of things in the capacity of researchers, the physicians of the Metabolic Group were confronted with uncertainties of the medically unknown in a variety of forms. These included uncertainties regarding fundamental biochemical and physiological mechanisms underlying the phenomena and conditions they studied; uncertainties connected with the experimental compounds and procedures with which they worked—their basic properties and potential clinical effects; methodological uncertainties, related to the laboratory techniques they were developing; and finally, clinical uncertainties that were nonexperimental in nature, which had to do with the diagnosis, treatment and prognosis of their patients' illnesses.[5]

Actually, clinical investigators may intentionally seek out problems of uncertainty, and, to some extent, deliberately induce them. Also, "chance" factors, which investigators do not plan or anticipate, play a considerable role in bringing various uncertainties to the attention of the investigators and in determining the direction of their experimental work. This type of involvement with uncertainty brings about an effective and productive working relationship with it.

Personal Limitations.   The second type of uncertainty results from imperfect mastery of what is currently known in the various fields of medicine. Obviously, no persons can have at their command all the information, lore, and skills of modern medicine, yet, there are significant individual differences in the mastery of available knowledge.

Students vary in the level of skill that they achieve at each stage of their training. Those who find it easy to memorize details and retain them may have in the study of anatomy an advantage over their classmates who lack such skills. Those with quantitative skills may handle data easily in their laboratory experiments where their less fortunate classmates may struggle. Students whose manual dexterity is highly developed may not experience the same degree of personal inadequacy as the less adroit students when they begin to perform surgical procedures. Also students who relate comfortably and with warmth to other people find it easier to get along with patients than do their introverted classmates. These variations in aptitudes, skill, knowledge, and personality traits lead to individual differences in the extent to which students experience the uncertainties which derive from limitations of skill and knowledge. Students also differ widely in the awareness of their own limitations and in response to these limitations. Some students are much more troubled than others by their real or imagined lack of skill.

The uncertainty factors linger on through one's student days and after graduation. An intern, during his first year out of medical school, after diagnosing correctly lupus erythematosus in a patient who had offered a difficult diagnostic challenge, shows in his ruminations a rather sophisticated approach to handling his uncertainty. He states:

> So I wasn't all that smart, but still I felt very good that I'd picked it up. Sometimes it seemed to me that diagnosis is about half pure chance and half magic. You take a history and do a physical examination with your eyes and ears constantly open for the red flags. So a red flag drops somewhere in the history, something that kicks off a signal, and you start poking around in that direction; or maybe the flag drops because something in the physical exam doesn't seem just right, and all through you are thinking of possibilities and discarding them a mile a minute. I tried later to remember the different things I had thought of while I was working up this case, and it was just fantastic. I'd bet I sifted through forty different diagnoses in ten minutes and had at least one solid reason for discarding every one of them. And some of these guys just seem to pick the right answer out of the air every time. How they do it I don't know.[4]

Personal Limitations Versus Limitations in Medical Knowledge. This third category begins to diminish in importance for students as they grow in competence and experience. As their medical knowledge and practical skills grow, some of this uncertainty gives way.* In all aspects of their training, cognitive learning and a greater sense of certainty go hand in hand.

Preclinical students go through a period in which they are inclined to regard their uncertainty as reflecting their personal inadequacy. Then with growth of their knowledge and the deepening of their experience, their perspective on their own uncertainty changes. Now that they know more and are surer of themselves, they realize that although some of their uncertainty is attributable to their ignorance, some of it is justified. In other words, they become better able and more confident in distinguishing between those aspects of their uncertainty that derive from their own lack of knowledge and those that are inherent in medicine. When they free themselves from thinking of their uncertainty as largely personal, they find it more appropriate to give voice to the doubts they feel.

Their more affirmative attitude toward doubting is not just a product of book knowledge and technical skill but also results from what they learn about the uncertainties of medicine through their daily contact with members of the faculty. They find many professors who acknowledge in a particular situation that they do not have the immediate command of the known medical facts, or that the problem at hand represents one of the big gaps in present medical knowledge. They also discover that when faculty members or students examine a patient, each person's findings may differ some in type and degree.

Thus, in observing their teachers in classroom and clinical situations, students discover that they are subject to the same uncertainty that students are experiencing and that they deal with these uncertainties in a forthright manner. During my student days, some comforting counsel came from the director of the hospital where I was an extern. He often reminisced about his earlier busy career as a family practitioner. He stated that in diagnosing a patient's problem, "I always left a hole in the fence big enough for me to back through if later I had to modify my diagnosis." I have never forgotten this positive and anticipatory approach to uncertainty.

The group relationships of a student should never be overlooked in training for uncertainty. Membership in the "little society" of medical students, namely one's class, has some of the characteristics of special-

---

* Students long for the time when they can take a good history and do a thorough physical examination quickly and be sure they have missed nothing. Until they learn what corners can safely be cut, they must follow the first commandment of the neophyte in medicine: "Thou shalt leave no stone unturned."

ized group training for a combat mission. Renee Fox states the issue clearly: "A medical school class is a closely-knit, self-regulating community, with its own method of 'tackling a big problem' like that of uncertainty."[6]

Action Clears the Air

Physicians deal in science, and science equals knowing. Implicit, however, in that "knowing" is skepticism, whereby physicians must always be ready to accept new information, even to the point of contradicting previous knowledge.

The primary definition of physicians' responsibility is to do everything possible to forward the complete and early recovery of their patients. Even with highly competent work, physicians cannot guarantee success. The existence of impossibilities and uncertainties imposes strain upon physicians and makes it difficult for them to have a "purely rational" orientation to their job. Nonrational mechanisms are noted as prominent in the reactions of sick people to their situations and those of their families. In spite of the discipline of their scientific training and competence, physicians are not altogether exempted from corresponding tendencies. The strains existing on both sides of the physician-patient relationship are such that one must expect to find, not merely institutionalization of the roles, but special mechanisms of social control in operation. Talcott Parsons in *The Social System* gives perhaps the first systematic sociological discussion of the "uncertainty factor" in medical practice and its significance for the physician, patient, and the patient's family.[13]

The borderline between impossibility and uncertainty is often indistinct. This lack of firm delineation places serious strains on a well-integrated balance of need, skill, effort, and expectation of result. Within this situation, Parsons points out, a variety of motivational factors operates to drive action in one direction, namely, success of the therapeutic enterprise.[13] Physicians are trained and expected to act and not to be passive observers. The patient and family are also under strong emotional pressures "to have something done."

An excellent illustration of this situation is where the decision to perform a surgical operation is in the balance and where, from a technical point of view, there is a strong element of uncertainty. The surgeon must weigh the risk of delaying further or deciding not to operate at all against the risk of an operation. There tends to be a bias in favor of operating. The surgeon is trained to operate and is usually a person of action. Also, inactivity and anxious waiting are hard to bear for both patient and family. The decision to operate "clears the air" and makes everybody feel better. The American culture predisposes more to this pattern of activity than most others and probably has had much to do with our tendency to glorify the surgeon, whom Parsons describes as indeed a kind of culture hero.[13]

The problem of the bias in favor of active intervention, of giving the benefit of the doubt to operating in surgical cases, underlies the problem of "unnecessary operations," about which there is considerable discussion. In the folklore of the subject, financial incentive is often mentioned as related to whatever tendency there may be to perform unnecessary operations. Other powerful motives operating in the same direction, however, overshadow financial incentive. In a surgical practice, the uncertainty factor is inevitably great and, therefore, predisposes to a bias in favor of active intervention. Patients and families share this bias and reinforce the bias of the action-oriented surgeon who is "happiest when operating."

Probability as a Guide

The sciences concerned with disease deal largely with probabilities. The probability varies in degree but almost always falls short of certainty. For example, even when a diagnostic category is well established, there may be facets of that disease in a particular patient that create new problems in treatment and prognosis.[9] Physicians learn to take probability as their guide. In dealing with patients, the habit of discerning and acting decisively is all important. Gowers, in 1905, cautioned his colleagues in internal medicine that decisive hesitation is far wiser than hesitating decision.[7]

In his advice to the young physician, Oliver Wendell Holmes wrote, "Let me recommend to you, as far as possible, to keep your doubts to yourself, and give the patient the benefit of your decision."[8] The patient benefits from faith in the outcome and faith that the physician knows for certain what to do and what will happen. On the other hand, a physician's education and practice suffer when a closed mind and too much certainty replace doubt.

Mumford, in a fascinating study of internship and residency training, points out that the balm of reassurance and certainty in treatment may be an enjoyment that patients receive more often at a community hospital than at a university teaching hospital: "It may be that some patients in teaching hospitals become socialized at least to an appearance of accepting uncertainty just as their physicians are socialized to admitting it."[11] This apparently accepting attitude toward uncertainty is expressed by some patients who have long histories of repeated admissions to a teaching center. These patients make such statements, with some pride, as: "They are going to try ... now." and "We don't know whether this will help, but ...."

Developing a Critical Attitude

If medical students have any sense of history, they soon become cognizant of the passing character of much that is presented to them as hard scientific truth.* In medical school they must develop an ability to examine conflicting data critically. They are helped to some extent, in the development of this ability, when divergent viewpoints are presented regarding clinical problems. In other words, from the beginning of their career, they learn of conflicts and uncertainties rather than being doled out "the straight facts."*

Four dangers may evolve from this suggested approach. Certain students become depressed and frustrated by an approach that leads them to conclude that *nothing* is reliably known. Second, there is the danger of inducing the hypercritical state. Lasagna emphasizes that to be a virtue, criticism must fall somewhere "between petulant querulousness and blind faith, and not deteriorate into cynical disenchantment and disengagement from life."[10] The third danger may be to introduce too much hesitation in one's decision-making ability. Fortunately, the very nature of medical practice forces the doctor's hand in making decisions regarding the care of patients. Every act of patient care requires a decision, for the physician is in the arena of action. The medical interests of the great philosopher John Locke probably contributed greatly to his empiricism. The scholarly philosopher can be a skeptic or agnostic in the confines of the study, but Locke could not afford a suspension of intellectual commitment at the bedside of the sick. Fourth, the student may seek for omnipotence as one aspect of his or her striving to achieve professional competence. The quest may reflect many nonrational fantasies, motives, and defenses that influence the more rational pursuit of professional skill.[16]

CONCLUSION

From the beginning of recorded history, humans have demonstrated intolerance for the unknown. When nature does not easily disclose her

---

* A fourth-grade pupil has unknowingly described the situation well: "Many things about medicine that were once thought to be science fiction now actually are."

secrets, humans may seek to satisfy themselves by establishing even for the physical universe "a law which they call *the uncertainty principle.*"[15] They find, however, that tolerance for uncertainty is a healthy necessity at every stage of development.[2]

Unfortunately, when students arrive in medical school, their past education seems to have given them the impression that for every question there is a single, definite answer. They soon learn in medical school that both the problems they encounter and their solutions have an indefinite character. Knowing with certainty is something that physicians can rarely, if ever, achieve; uncertainty is inherent in the nature of the work that physicians do. They must foster the ability to accept uncertainty and recognize that there is no one-dimensional, single answer, except perhaps in the mathematical and in the precise sciences. Thus, in developing a tolerance for uncertainty, they are becoming masters of their own uncertainties.[17, 18]

Medical students' professional maturity begins to take shape with the courage to live with doubt, to accept with humility the fact that the best they can do is to gather approximate evidence which points in the direction of approximate truths. William Osler has emphasized that "the physician's scientific training brings to his practice an incalculable gift, which leavens his whole life, giving exactness to habits of thought and tempering the mind with that judicious faculty of distrust which can alone, amid the uncertainties of practice, make him wise unto salvation."[12]

The scientist's first need is to doubt, while the first need of the therapist is to believe. The good physician combines the two. The "scientist aspect" helps one to challenge old treatment regimens and look for new approaches and answers in healing—testing, questing, doubting. The need to believe helps in relationships with the patient and enables the physician to inspire confidence in the midst of uncertainty.

A core part of physician identity is the sense of responsiveness and responsibility in the face of pain and helplessness. Physicians have the awareness that despite their inadequacy and ignorance, people place their lives in their care and entrust to them their bodies and minds. Physicians have often been called absurd healers—using absurd in the existential sense that Albert Camus would use it.* Probably it is absurd, yet the noblest of human effort, that physicians repeatedly find it necessary to exert all their will and strength to move ahead with their patients, whether the road be clouded by uncertainty or blocked by hopelessness.

---

* Albert Camus, in *The Myth of Sisyphus,* defines what is absurd as the confrontation of this irrational world with the wild longing for clarity whose call echoes in the human heart.

There is a story by that renowed Spanish writer and philosopher, Miguel de Unamuno, in which a priest, living in a small Spanish village, is adored by all the people for his piety, kindness, and the majesty with which he celebrates the mass.[3, 19] To them, he is already a saint, and they speak of him as Saint Don Emmanuel. He helps them with their plowing and planting, tends them when they are sick, hears their confessions, comforts them in death, and every Sunday, in his rich, thrilling voice, transports them to paradise with his chanting. Actually, Don Emmanuel is not so much a saint as he is a martyr. Long ago his own faith left him. He is an atheist, a good man doomed to suffer the life of a hypocrite, pretending to a faith he does not really have. As he raises the chalice of wine, his hands tremble. A cold sweat pours from him. He cannot stop, for he knows that the people need this of him, and that their need is greater than his sacrifice. Still ... still ... could it be that Don Emmanuel's whole life is a kind of prayer, a song of joy to God?[19] He preserved hope in those whom he served when there was no hope within himself. Probably, in the last analysis, the physician in caring for patients is more like Don Emmanuel than Hippocrates.

REFERENCES

1. Bean WB: On ambiguity. Arch Intern Med 112:3, 1963
2. Beres D: Certainty: A failed quest? Psychoanal Q 49:1, 1980
3. De Unamuno M: Abel Sanchez and Other Stories. Translated by Kerrigan A. Chicago, Regnery, 1956, pp 207–267
4. Doctor X: Intern. Greenwich, Connecticut, Fawcett, 1966, p 153
5. Fox RC: Experiment Perilous. Glencoe, Illinois, Free Press, 1959, p 28
6. Fox RC: Training for uncertainty. In Merton RK, et al. (eds): The Student-Physician. Cambridge, Harvard University Press, 1957, p 220
7. Gowers E: A metastatic mystery. Lancet 2:1593, 1905
8. Holmes OW: The young practitioner. In Davenport WH (ed): The Good Physician. New York, Macmillan, 1962, p 182
9. Knaggs SJ, Barnes AJ, Maclean CB: The decision tree for teaching management of uncertainty. J Med Educ 49:1184, 1974
10. Lasagna L: Life, Death, and the Doctor. New York, Knopf, 1968, p 15
11. Mumford E: Interns—from Students to Physicians. Cambridge, Harvard University Press, 1970, p 162
12. Osler W: The leaven of science. Univ Penn Med Mag, 1894
13. Parsons T: The Social System. Glencoe, Illinois, Free Press, 1951, pp 449–469
14. Schoolman HM: The role of the physician as a patient advocate. N Engl J Med 296:103, 1977
15. Schwartz EK, Wolf A: The quest for certainty. Arch Neurol Psychiatr 81:69, 1959

16. Sharaf MR, Levinson DJ: The quest for omnipotence in professional training. Psychiatry 27:135, 1964
17. Spooner MA: Dealing with uncertainty in family medicine. J Fam Prac 2:471, 1975
18. Spooner MA: The ability to live with ambiguity. Canadian Family Physician, March, 1974, pp 115–117
19. Selzer R: Mortal Lessons—Notes on the Art of Surgery. New York, Simon & Schuster, 1976, pp 18–19
20. Whitehorn JC: Education for uncertainty. Perspect Biol Med 7:118, 1963

10
THE WOMAN MEDICAL STUDENT

The reason firm, the temperate will,
Endurance, foresight, strength, and skill;
A perfect woman, nobly planned,
To warn, to comfort, and command.
                    —William Wordsworth

When Elizabeth Blackwell, the first woman to be accepted to a medical school in this country, entered Geneva Medical College in 1848, the editor of the *Boston Medical and Surgical Journal* wrote: "She has been induced to depart from the appropriate sphere of her sex and led to aspire to honors and duties which, by the order of nature and the common consent of the world, devolve upon men alone."

The concept of woman's role expressed in this editorial lingers on in many quarters, although it is often obscured by an egalitarian veneer. Regardless of what belief is professed, Americans of both sexes frequently act as if the possession of a uterus uniquely qualifies its owner for domestic service. Consider, for example, the 1968 student rebellion at Columbia University. Students from the radical left took over some buildings in the name of egalitarian principles that they accused Columbia of flouting. Yet, no sooner had they occupied the buildings than the male militants blandly assigned their sisters-in-arms the task of preparing food. They, the men, would plan further strategy. The reply these men received from the women was that domestic tasks behind the barricades were desegregated that day.[3]

The image of medicine as predominantly a masculine career is rapidly changing in this country. A woman told her female medical colleagues in a Detroit meeting: "Medicine is a woman's field usurped by men." A "man's world" image of medicine drastically restricted the medical talents of many women a century ago. With the restrictions came the guffaws as when, in 1852, a Philadelphia pharmacist refused to fill a prescription for Dr. Hannah Longshore, telling her to "go home and darn your husband's socks." Of course, today in many countries of the world, female physicians outnumber the male ones.

If the Philadelphia pharmacist who insulted Dr. Hannah Longshore in 1852 could return today to his native city, the special programs for women in medicine developed by the Medical College of Pennsylvania

(formerly the Woman's Medical College) would hopefully have a salutary effect on his soul. He would be illuminated particularly by the ar-
chives and special collections related to medicine, the women in medicine oral history project, and the bibliography of the literature on
women physicians—a bibliography that presents published literature
on the lives of women physicians and healers dating as far back as
1750.[5, 38]

In the preparation of the present edition of this book, the question
was raised whether a chapter on the woman medical student was still
needed. A majority of women consulted about the matter felt that the
chapter is needed, for many of the issues addressed in the first edition
of the book are still with us and deserve attention. Today, the women
who come to medical school bring with them their unique biological
makeup and some cultural conditioning for the feminine role.[29] Their
increased numbers in medical school are bringing to the profession a
balance that is badly needed in this country.

This balance will be beneficial in many important areas. One can
argue that the women medical students that now comprise a sizable minority (and sometimes not a minority) of their medical school classes
increasingly will be subject to the pressures of their professional group
culture and will, simultaneously, modify the content of that culture. In
other words, one would expect women to become more like men in
career plans and in attitudes and values about the practice of medicine
and the men to become more like women with respect to these same
variables.[37] As Shapiro and Jones emphasize, it is probable that the
physician identity shared by men and women will increasingly reflect
some of the values and attitudes traditionally associated with women
in our culture.[37]

IDENTIFYING THE OBSTACLES

Many women in medicine first went into nursing, medical technology,
or a similar field before entering medical school. In part, they were
steered toward careers considered to be "female" and compatible with
their "abilities." They soon discovered that medicine was what they
wanted, that their ability for such a career was not lacking, and that
medicine was as "female" as "male." Thus, a potential obstacle to be
aware of may be the tendency still existing in many segments of our
society to associate medicine with maleness.

Women physicians at a recent conference emphasized that the practice of medicine is particularly compatible with a number of characteristics associated with our culture's concept of femininity. They men-

tioned that the earliest healer in the life of the child is usually the mother. It is she who applies the antiseptic and bandage and sits protectively by throughout the sleepless night.[40] These women considered many specialties particularly suited to the biological and emotional makeup of women. Yet, they stressed, when a child grows up in our culture, whether boy or girl, that child tends to look to a male as a healer rather than to a female. Why? The answer lies in the differences in the acculturation of boys and girls. From earliest life and throughout their growth and development, many are confronted with differing expectations. These significant differences in cultural expectations inevitably lead to prejudices that may become deterrents to the aspirations of women to become physicians.

Further, it is often argued that many men in our society avoid courting assertive and intelligent women. This, in turn, places a ceiling on the ambitions of certain young women who are guided by what they think men will tolerate. Such women tend to downplay their own abilities lest they become too successful in the eyes of men. As Margaret Mead has said, in our culture boys are unsexed by failure, girls by success. Hopefully, this is changing.

Psychological and sociological studies show that American girls are often dissuaded from showing independence and intellectual originality and are instead encouraged to become homemakers, living through the achievements of their husbands and children. "Altering the traditional male and female roles so that the members of both sexes can achieve their fullest potential will necessitate change on all levels, from rewriting children's books to include the working mommy as well as daddy, to a shift in the educational curriculum away from home arts for girls. An emphasis in the mass media on the contributions of women professionals is another of the host of steps to be taken that may seem minor at first, but are actually indispensable in changing a child's approach to life."[20]

A girl's image of what she can accomplish while remaining "feminine" has something to do with the educational and professional attainments of her mother. If she grows up with a mother who achieved a life of her own in addition to caring for the family, she will be more likely to accept a demanding career and not to feel that her total commitment must be with her own future family. Hutchins has shown in his study that where a good model exists for the resolution of conflict between home and career, it is much easier for a girl to endeavor to do both.[15] In Ginzberg's study of women receiving graduate degrees at Columbia University in medicine and academic fields, three-fourths had mothers who had worked at some point in their lives.[11]

The lack of a female model for combining a professional life with marriage may be an obstacle when a girl tries to combine the two in her own life. The AAMC survey of women dropouts from medical school revealed that more than two-thirds had mothers who were housewives, while among the group of women who made regular progress in medical school only half had mothers who were housewives.[16] This obstacle will diminish for an increasing number of young women because a larger percentage will have mothers who are working outside of the home in a job or profession.

Hutchins has compared the educational level of the mothers of women medical students with the educational level of the mothers of male medical students in the same year. Over 15 percent of the women had mothers who were professionals, as compared to 5 percent of the men, and on the average the mothers of the women were better educated.[15]

What may make the prospect of becoming a physician worthwhile for the young woman is the enrichment of her life—the full use of her gifts and the need for self-growth which cannot be easily dismissed. Even young girls have some awareness of how easy it is to evade the responsibility of their own development, to neglect their own individuation, to use Carl Jung's term. They are often able to project ahead to their fortieth year and visualize the prospect of many empty years when their services to humankind can no longer repeat themselves in the form of duties rendered to their growing children. They seem to be insistent on transcending that aspect of feminine psychology so clearly described by D.H. Lawrence in his novel *The White Peacock:* "This peculiar abnegation of self is the resource of a woman for escaping the responsibilities of her own development. Like a nun, she puts over her living face a veil as a sign that the woman no longer exists for herself. She is the servant of God, of some man, of her children, or maybe of some good cause. As a servant, she is no longer responsible for her self which would make her terrified and lonely. To be responsible for the good progress of one's life is terrifying."[19] In spite of its terrifying dimension, an increasing number of women are assuming responsibility for their own development.

The desire for personal independence is emerging as a significant factor in a woman's choice of medicine as a career.* In the AAMC questionnaire, which offered 20 reasons for choosing medicine as a career, women ranked "desire for independence" fourth in importance. An "interest in science" and an "interest in people" were tied for first

---

* This is in line with the findings of an extensive report on the life styles of educated women. The majority of these women were described as placing a high value on self-determination and the exercise of autonomy.[2]

place. "Curiosity about the body" was listed second, and the "service motive" was given third place.[16] Interviews with women applicants and medical students support this ranking. Many women state directly or imply that they want to retain their socioeconomic status through their own merits rather than through dependence on their husbands. The need for involvement in an engrossing professional activity often co-exists with the desire for independence. Although some women in med-icine may average less time in practice than men, their combined home-and-practice commitments generally give them fuller schedules. (This is discussed further in this chapter.)

FINDING THE WAY TO MEDICAL SCHOOL

Women are finding it easier today to learn about a career in medicine and to take those steps that lead to medical school. Medical schools and the medical profession are beginning to take the initiative in in-forming school counselors of the wide spectrum of opportunities avail-able for women doctors.

Working in a hospital or volunteering may be a helpful step toward a medical career. There is a general agreement that no finer approach exists for clarifying and strengthening one's motivation for the study of medicine than work in a hospital. In the hospital, also, a girl may have an opportunity to come in contact with women physicians. Jobs for students in hospitals are not plentiful. Today, more such hospital op-portunities are needed where potential medical students can be ex-posed to medical practice, to the kind of people who are doctors, and to the kind of life they would have to lead if they were to become doctors.

The number of women students in medical school has increased rap-idly during the past few years. The entering classes of some medical schools are 50 percent female. Yet, the question continues to be asked if certain medical schools are discriminatory toward women in admis-sion policies. Probably the answer is "yes" and in ways that may be hidden or on the surface do not appear immediately as discriminatory. The old belief lingers on that a female applicant has to possess the quality of gold to pass as silver. Anyway, large numbers of women are applying to medical school, and many are being accepted. Thus, some of the former obstacles are being removed.

In the past, counseling during the school years was frequently a de-terrent to women entering medicine. Beginning in grammar school and continuing into college, women were generally not encouraged to take up the study of medicine.[31] This is changing, and young women are seeking a different set of goals for their adult lives. Also, the national climate of opinion concerning sexual roles is changing, and more women of high intellectual caliber are of their own choice deciding to become doctors.

Age is not as much a factor as it once was in the selection process. In fact, there has recently been a substantial increase in the number of applicants admitted to medical school who are older than the typical student of age 21. In part, this reflects a response to the greater openness on the part of medical schools to accept women on an equal basis with men. It also reflects women's growing dissatisfaction with traditional role assignments in our society. Some women have had their fill of certain of these roles and are now seeking other options. Many of the older women applicants speak quite frankly of having neglected their own individuation or maturation and of having given everything to husband or growing children, if they were married. Now they want to assume a greater responsibility for their own growth and to prepare themselves for a life that they can live rather than living life through someone else. These women seem to be insistent on transcending that aspect of feminine psychology so clearly described by D.H. Lawrence in his novel *The White Peacock* and mentioned earlier in this chapter.

The question is often asked, "What does an admissions committee look for in a woman applicant to medical school?" Academic and intellectual qualifications are identified, along with strong motivation for the study of medicine, emotional maturity, the capacity to relate with warmth to others, stamina, and a clear sense of identity.

THE PATH THROUGH MEDICAL SCHOOL

Medical schools in our country are still a predominantly male world, containing both hidden and open prejudices toward women medical students. Although this is changing, the female influence is far from equal at this time. Some of the prejudice *supposedly* grows out of an inability to accept a woman who will possibly be a "part-time" doctor and who has taken a place that could have been filled by a male who would be a "full-time" doctor. The situation is much more complex than such a statement implies. The statement is mentioned, however, because one hears it from a variety of sources. Studies by both Patricia Williams and Marilyn Heins show that not only are the workweeks of the female and male physicians converging, but also the percentage of active physicians in the two groups are converging as well.[12, 43] Actually, the productivity of women physicians is increasing while that of male physicians is decreasing. In spite of such career inhibiting factors as marriage, children, and the decreasing availability of household help, a higher percentage of women physicians are practicing longer hours for more years than in the past. In other words, their productivity is high and converging with the shorter workweek of male physicians.

Advantages and Disadvantages

A woman entering medical school, the supposedly man's world, may feel self-conscious, because she is unsure of how she will be received. She may overreact to conceal or inhibit "womanly attributes" and overconform or overproduce in an attempt to make up for her perceived downgraded status. She may try to be as unobtrusive as possible and not create "trouble" or attract attention by holding back in class discussions or by accepting assignments that keep her in "invisible" positions. But by bowing to pressure to make herself unobtrusive or adopting one of the other mechanisms mentioned, a woman student is inadvertently asking about the appropriateness of her presence in the field in which she has chosen to work. Similarly, the teacher may also try to compensate by being overly solicitous, congenial, courtly, or undemanding in the professional interaction. The woman medical student has a dual task: She must learn the dynamics of handling inappropriate responses to herself, and she must learn the skills of the profession. And she must accomplish this with fewer role models than the male student has. Fortunately, today she is doing a good job handling the situation.

Male students frequently allude to female students as having unfair advantages in relationships with male professors, although they are hesitant to identify the nature of these advantages. Possibly Sally Kempton has identified one of the potential advantages: "My father taught me some tricks. From him I learned that it is pleasant and useful to get information from men, pleasant because it is easier than getting it for yourself, and useful because it is seductive: men like to give information and sometimes love the inquirer, if she is pretty and asks intelligently."[17]

Many women students feel that it is an advantage to be a woman in medical school. They claim that because of their sex they enjoy more pleasant treatment by both fellow students and faculty than they feel is accorded men students. The opportunity for male-female interaction in a community where males are in the majority is cited as a source of pleasure, particularly where they feel that they have maintained a clearly feminine role. Women students today emphasize that an advantage is theirs only when they maintain the dependent role of student; they are not looked upon equally in matters of judgment and decision making.

Along with testimonies of positive treatment in medical school come strong complaints. Some women feel that they are singled out by their teachers, that their errors are more easily noticed and remembered, and that every failure on their part is ascribed to their sex. Others feel that their work is not taken seriously by their instructors and that the faculty expects less of them than of the men. A substantial number feel that the faculty expects more of women—harder work and better performance.[20] There is then a wide diversity of opinions on how women are treated in medical school and the meaning of this treatment. Also, the women students may be treated differently by teachers and peers in the classroom and in the hospital.

A comparison of the scores of women and men medical students on the Edwards Personal Preference Schedule shows several differences in the two sexes, which may account for the ability of some women to get along in and adjust smoothly to the difficult medical school situation. As measured by the heterosexuality scale, women medical students have less need for participation in activities with the opposite sex than do their female colleagues in the general college group.[15] The low "heterosexuality" score among women medical students may be a reflection of their capacity for sublimating sexual desire as long as the situation is difficult and demanding. The long hours of classroom, laboratory, and library work leave little time for seeing men outside of medical school. Although male medical students, usually after a cocktail or two, may ask their women classmates if they came to medical school to land a husband, it is absurd to believe that anyone would follow such an arduous path in order to achieve marital goals. Yet it is an old and inappropriate question that still haunts the halls of medical schools. Women who want to meet eligible bachelor doctors could much more easily enter nursing or work in a medical school or teaching hospital, thus sparing themselves the difficult premedical preparation and the demands of medical school.

Search for Identity

The woman's search for identity in the male world of a medical school is a formidable task. She has fewer role models whom she can emulate, for the number of women faculty members is small. Yet, her need for role models, especially at the beginning of medical school, is acute.[34] Some women students deny their femininity and assume a more mas-

culine role, perhaps hoping thereby to open the door to the male world.
Other women seek to clarify their identity by becoming superfeminine.
Some gain entrance and acceptance in the male world by marriage to a
medical student. Others become part of a group of women medical students and do almost everything with the group.

The threat to a woman student's identity may be intensified by the
nature of the work she does. The long hours of close and tedious work
in classroom, laboratory, and hospital soon lead her male classmates to
view her as "one of the fellows." This attitude is quite acceptable to
some women, while others consider it as assaulting the core of their
identity and the essence of their being. A similar but reverse situation
would probably occur, however, if the majority of students were female. A year after Woman's Medical College* admitted for the first
time a few male students, I asked a woman in that initial class what had
been the reaction of the women to their male classmates. She replied
without hesitation that each was treated "as one of the girls."

The matter of femininity may loom large in a setting where one must
excel and compete with male colleagues. The crisis in female identity is
a serious problem for certain women medical students.[10] A common
testimony by many is, "I have been made to feel that I am of neuter
gender." Some have an easier time excelling when they minimize sexual differences. Others appear to function better by creating a girls' en-
clave within the larger student body. Some women students have no
trouble whatsoever being intellectually productive while remaining
feminine and accomplish the needed balance without strain. They
seem to have become experienced from childhood in handling contra-
dictory signals and goals.

Men students play a major part in enhancing some of the identity
concerns of women medical students. One beautiful and intelligent girl
asked me one day: "Why do so many of my classmates insult us by
wanting to go to bed without courting us?" One could reply, "Is this not
the way some medical students relate to women?" Other girls are asked
by their male classmates: "Do you want us to treat you as a woman or
as an associate?" At coffee breaks, the men seem to take delight in discussing in the presence of women classmates their dating activities or
plans with others. In such conversations, no indication may be given
the women students that they have ever been considered as potential
dates. Again, one could reply, "Usually they have not, because their
male classmates are generally looking for a more home-oriented type."

Fortunately, identity problems of both female and male students
may be fewer as a better balance is reached in male-female representa-

---

* Now the Medical College of Pennsylvania.

tion in each class. The "good ole boy" attitude will be softened in the male students, for the influence of women will relieve the "good ole boy" of the burden of being so macho.

Special Counseling

Medical school presents a group of special problems for women, many of them culturally determined. Other problems experienced by women are the same as those discussed in the chapter, "Psychological Problems of Medical Students."

Often the woman experiences role conflicts within herself. She may try to reject her femininity in favor of a nonsexual "professional" orientation, but she is rarely able to abolish all desires for a conventional family role. If a woman experiences this conflict, she may fail to find satisfaction as a physician until she is able to integrate her role as a woman with her career achievement need.

Because of her own set of priorities and the heavy demands of her studies, the woman student generally feels that she would like to postpone marriage. Yet, the pressure to marry may be difficult to resist. The general pattern of early marriage in this country has particular significance for the woman medical student. Many women in the United States are married before the age of 21. Perhaps this imposes pressures on most women, medical students not excepted, to seek and find husbands. Nevertheless, it seems that medical school is beginning to attract women who are resisting these pressures.

Ten or 15 years ago, it was rare for a woman applicant to medical school to mention that she might not marry or that if she did marry, she planned not to have children. When such a statement was made, she hastened to explain why she had made such a decision and to assure the interviewer that she was sexually normal and healthy. Today, a woman applicant can make such a statement and feel no compulsion to explain the motives behind it. She may have established her priorities and be able to resist society's subtle or open pressures for early marriage.

Usually toward the end of their second year in medical school, a number of students lose interest in school and become quite depressed, a condition sometimes called the "sophomore syndrome." Although this syndrome is seen in women and men, it is more common in women. This muted cry for help appears to be a kind of declaration of dependence and of helplessness. The clinical years of training are beckoning with heavy responsibilities for the care of patients. The approaching requirement for greater independence and self-assertion brings to the surface unresolved dependency needs and fear of separation from those who have sustained them in a more supportive environment. It is difficult for these students to achieve a true separation and resolution of their neurotic dependency needs. While they want opportunities to function independently, they are not yet psychologically prepared for them.

In spite of approaching the clinical years with anxiety and depression, the female medical student generally finds the situation on the wards much more to her liking than she had expected. Competition is lessened, and she feels comfortable in the role of the caretaker. The nurturing ability that is often a feminine characteristic gives her a special insight into her patients' needs, to which the patients respond with gratitude. It is rare for patients to be rejecting once they have gotten to know their doctor, despite the fact that she is female. Actually, it may be a relief for many patients because they may look upon a woman as a person with whom they can feel less threatened or with whom they can regress as they can with a mother figure.

Medical educators are coming to feel that counseling has not been adequate or tailored to meet the specific needs of women in medical school.[7] When counseling is given, it frequently comes too late to be of use. A somewhat higher percentage of women than men seek counseling or psychiatric help in medical school.[40] Early anxieties and motivational questions appear to be greater among women, although they are commonplace but more concealed, among men. Women seem to be the victims of "abrasiveness" in medical school more frequently than men. (The experience of "abrasiveness" results from those factors which make medical school an ordeal but which do not necessarily contribute toward making a good physician.)

One effective approach to counseling has been support groups for women medical students. The students meet in small groups at weekly intervals throughout the academic year with women faculty members. The groups may be formed from a single class or mixed with representatives from all the classes. The University of North Carolina School of Medicine, in support groups for women students, describes their program as being of great assistance to women in helping them with the acquisition of satisfactory professional and female identities, as well as functioning as an important preventive health measure.[13]

Many educators emphasize the importance of providing the female students with a counselor of their own sex. As members of a minority group in medical school, women have special problems of adaptation in addition to practical difficulties such as housing (particularly in cities where schools are located in high-crime neighborhoods). A sensitive woman, trained as a physician, can act as a role model, help greatly with specific advice, and give emotional support.[7, 34]

Ability and Outlook Related to Sex

A study by Walton reveals that women are more competent than men in their medical studies.[41] The study, done at the University of Edinburgh on senior medical students, included 59 women and 182 men. Walton obtained information from psychological testing, interviews, questionnaires, and data available in the dean's student files. In personality, the women students were more anxious and more introverted than men students. Measurable differences according to sex occurred in the attitudes of students toward teachers. More women than men considered the amount of personal contact they had with teachers as adequate. A smaller percentage of women than men felt that their teachers gave them insufficient guidance. As for examinations, the women showed a greater readiness to have their knowledge and skill tested. The author concluded from this readiness that women students take their training more seriously.

Although only a few students felt that they were given enough direct clinical responsibility in the wards, those content with the amount of responsibility given for patient care were almost all men. To explore how moralistic students were at the beginning of a clinical clerkship, a question was designed to discover whether they would expose their own beliefs in a clinical context. They were asked how appropriate it is for doctors to convey their own ethical and moral values to patients. The women were found to begin their study of psychiatry, for example, with a much less moralistic orientation, two-thirds regarding doctors' concepts of right and wrong as irrelevant in the management of patients. Men, in contrast, were more moralistic, the larger number regarding it as useful and proper that physicians should express their ethical standards to patients.

While only a few students were technically oriented rather than patient-oriented, among the technicians men tended to predominate. Women students had a greater desire for personal involvement with patients and were more concerned than were the men about becoming excessively attached to some of their patients.

Although the Walton study just described is helpful in pointing out many of the critical factors in evaluation and comparison of male and female medical students, one will probably find today that the similarities are so great that the few differences are obscured or of little significance. For example, a recent study shows that gender has no relationship to medical school performance in clinical clerkships.[14]

Attrition

In the past, the attrition rate of women medical students has been higher than that of men. Nonacademic reasons have been as responsible as academic ones for the difference in rates. Although current figures are not available, many medical educators believe that the difference in dropout rates for both academic and nonacademic reasons may soon be negligible. Others believe that the difference in dropout rates will remain significant in spite of the changes in society involving the status of women.

An AAMC study lists the factors that the women dropouts for nonacademic reasons emphasized as causing them difficulty in medical school: (1) academic and psychological pressures of medical school; (2) emotional problems; (3) loneliness and unhappiness; (4) social and dating problems; (5) lack of time for studies; (6) poor study habits; (7) lack of confidence in ability to become a doctor.[16] Of course, many of these factors overlap and some have academic overtones.

Because some of the traits associated with attrition are traditionally feminine (less need for achievement, dominance, and aggression and more of a deference need), women stand a greater chance of dropping out than men—irrespective of the difficulty of absorbing the curriculum or of combining marriage and medicine. Aggression and dominance, frequently associated with intellectual performance, are often frowned upon in women, and the need to achieve has not been developed to as great an extent in women as in men.[21] Also, the fact that women can obtain achievement gratification by bearing and rearing children may occasionally dissipate the need for achievement in intellectual areas. At the same time, the changes in society involving women will surely influence their life and work in medical school and in the practice of medicine.

SPECIAL QUALITIES THAT WOMEN BRING
TO MEDICINE

The question is often asked if women bring to medicine some special qualities or characteristics that men may lack. I believe the answer is "yes." At the same time, it does not concern us here as to what blend of inheritance and cultural conditioning enters into the formation of these specific qualities. Only a few of these qualities are discussed.

Sensitivity.   A woman brings to medicine an indispensable quality—sensitivity. Sensitivity is part of a woman's charisma. Men are often wary of the sensitivity a woman brings to her work. Instead of utilizing it, men may try to smother it. This need to smother sensitivity has found its greatest emphasis in training students for "detached concern" in the doctor–patient relationship.

Psychiatrist Natalie Shainess states that because of woman's sensitivity, reverence for life takes on the profound meaning of the fostering of life and concern with well-being—the well-being of others as well as one's own. Shainess goes on to say that "while this is a matter for all humans, it is more so a matter for women, who are, in a sense, the caretakers of humanity."[35]

"The female," writes Ashley Montagu, "acquires . . . a competence in social understanding which is usually denied the male." Montagu goes on to say that this is "one of the reasons why women are usually so much more able to perceive the nuances and pick up the subliminal signs in human behavior which almost invariably pass men by. . . . Men tend to think in terms of the all-or-none principle, in terms of black or white."[28]

Closely related to sensitivity, and possibly a part of it, is woman's capacity for intuitive awareness of personal and social phenomena. This includes the aptitude for picking up subliminal clues that, when they are put together, can produce a diagnostic assessment of individuals or situations with more penetrating insight than the usual processes of conscious thought can achieve. This characteristic is neither universally nor exclusively feminine, but it is likely to be developed to a higher degree in women.

More Compassion and Less Rationality.   Women physicians, especially when their numbers are increased, will bring to medicine the matriarchal principle and partly neutralize or soften the present patriarchal-authoritarian structure. Medicine is in need of more blending of these two principles. The matriarchal principle is that of unconditional love, intuition, natural equality, compassion, and mercy. (Writers such as Erich Fromm de-emphasize female dominance which is often included in the matriarchal principle and is also excluded from the definition here.) The patriarchal principle is that of conditional love, hierarchical structure, abstract thought, man-made laws, and justice. In other words, mercy and justice represent, to a great extent, the two principles.

The purely matriarchal principle may stand in the way of the full development of the individual. On the other hand, the purely patriarchal principle may interfere with love and equality and be overly concerned with man-made laws and obedience. When the matriarchal and patriarchal principles are combined, however, each is colored by the other: motherly love by justice and rationality and fatherly love by mercy and equality.[9]

Female Doctors and Adequate Interpretation.   In their treatment of human sexual inadequacy, William Masters and Virginia Johnson emphasize that the key to successful treatment is the dual-sex team. They have found that it takes both a man and a woman therapist to treat a couple effectively.[22] I wrote to Masters and Johnson and asked them if they felt that other aspects of medicine required the woman for effective delivery of health care. Their reply was strongly in the affirmative:

> Insofar as any comments on woman's place in medicine are concerned, these are indeed purely a prejudiced version of our strong feelings relevant to the theoretical value of equal sex representation. From our prejudiced point of view, there is no field of medicine that to at least a marginal degree does not reflect orientation to, or even confrontation with, material of sex connotation. We are irrevocably committed to the concept that each sex needs interpretation. When comprehension of the psychophysiology of sexual orientation is a consequence, we simply do not believe the male capable of fair interpretation or nonprejudiced representation of the female and vice versa. So long as the Lord has willed that we are not to experience the opposite sex's response patterns, we must always acknowledge the rational values of impact and rapport.
>
> If someone states "I don't like carrots," one's mental imagery of said vegetable and its taste doesn't need personal interpretation, but when a woman attempts to describe her feelings in response to sexual relations, a man is lost. Honestly, we are not trying to be simplistic but simply don't have the words to describe the inevitable feeling of psychosocial support that comes from adequate interpretation.
>
> Since male physicians must inevitably deal with the female sex, it would be tragic if they didn't have adequate resources for effective interpretation. Not only must the resources be adequate from an interpretative point of view, but adequate educationally so that the interpreter can speak our professional language effectively. Our fear is that we don't have sufficient female representa-

tion in many areas of medicine. It seems extremely arbitrary to re-
strict the female physicians essentially to pediatrics, internal
medicine, psychiatry, or general practice. All areas of medicine
need contrasex interpretation.[23]

An Integrative Watchfulness.   In general, there has been a persistent
division of labor between men and women that assigns what Elaine
Cumming calls instrumental roles to men and socioemotional, or integrative, roles to women.[6] Instrumental roles are defined here as those
requiring focused, specific goal-directed skills. Those who hold these
instrumental roles pursue the major goals of their social system by
adapting it to the demands of other systems and to the outside world in
general. Integrative roles require diffuse, general skills, and those who
hold them pursue the goals of the system by adapting its members to
one another and to their common value system. If the roles in the social
system of a factory are used as an illustration, the sales manager and
the production manager would be playing instrumental roles and the
personnel manager an integrative one.

The traditional family is a small social system. The husband ensures
the family's continued independent existence by playing an instrumental role in the occupational system. The wife, on the other hand, main-
tains the integrity of the family by controlling internal tensions with
interpersonal skills. Of course, both husband and wife can fill both roles
but usually when labor is divided between them, the woman in the family will assume the more integrative function and the man the more instrumental. Women tend to carry their integrative roles from the family in which they were learned over into larger systems.

Uesugi and Vinacke used competitive games in which men and
women participated to throw light on power strategies.[6] They found
that in any given situation men could be classified according to the
strategies they used for winning. Women did not seem much interested
in winning at all, except to amend the rules so that no one could win or
to decide that the prize should be divided evenly—that is, that everyone should win. Women were, however, interested in accommodating
themselves to the situation and preventing strain among the players.

In general, the core of the feminine role is a kind of diffuse, integrative watchfulness—a monitoring operation that identifies sources of
tension as fast as they appear. In contrast, the core of the masculine
role is the ability to strive toward a distant goal in spite of interruptions
and tensions.

Flexibility of Operation.   Flexibility of operation is an attribute peculiar to women that will have an increasingly important place in today's
society.[1] Many women have had to develop flexibility in order to sur-

vive limiting circumstances without being paralyzed by frustration. Because their skills and creative energies have been expressed mainly through promoting the successful growth and functioning of others, women have developed remarkable versatility concerning their own preferences and goals and unlimited competence in making things over—food, clothes, furniture, the home itself, or the social situation within which they operate. In a period of rapid and major changes in medical training and practice, flexibility in thought and action is an extremely valuable quality.

LOOKING BEYOND MEDICAL SCHOOL

Residency training programs are modifying their scheduling requirements to permit young physician-wives to take care of a family and also complete their training. The normally long hours of physicians in such programs are reduced by one-fourth to one-half, and the training periods are lengthened accordingly. This type of flexibility permits a woman to combine her advanced training with family responsibilities.[30, 36] Later, in the same way, she may divide her time between her family and the practice of her profession, with the time allotted differently at various periods in her own life cycle.

Flexibility is not present in all training programs but is increasing. Margaret Mead has written, "The academic world is fundamentally hostile, by tradition, to those acts of femininity which involve childbearing."[26] Even where the hostility may not be an emotional factor, the institutionalized requirements of many medical centers remain at odds with those of wifehood and motherhood. Gradually, however, requirements are being changed, and the changes are bringing widespread benefits.

Although women doctors do not achieve as many firsts in their field as do their male colleagues, they usually express themselves in a wider range of abilities and interests. David McClelland points out that the phrase "part-time" catches a lot of the essence of the feminine style of life in a very practical sense.[24] The woman doctor may work part-time in a variety of capacities. She may spend part of her life being wholly a wife and mother and another part being a physician. Her psychological makeup permits this degree of alternation more easily than for a man who will often blindly follow a single course. A woman's success is often less visible because it consists of the sum of a group of activities rather than the result of a single-minded pursuit of one. This is not to imply, however, that some women will not follow with great success a single pursuit, such as the total commitment of time and energy to the practice of medicine.

It is relevant and important to mention at this point that the increasing number of women in medicine along with the influence of the women's movement are factors in changing practice patterns, with new benefits accruing to both male and female physicians. Patricia Williams has listed some of these benefits:[43] "Appreciation of family life and of the right and obligation of both parents to participate has increased. Tolerance of different life styles has become more accepted with diminishing rigidity and separation of the traditional masculine and feminine roles. An increasing number of male physicians are no longer apologetic about limiting their practice to play the major role in their family life or to pursue other interests. Women physicians, while still bearing heavy responsibilities for household management and child care, are benefiting from these expanding roles."

Finding a Compatible Specialty

A woman is not limited in the type of specialty practice she can enter, and reasons for selecting a specialty may vary from woman to woman within any one field. The choice of work hours can be an incentive, and such fields as pathology, radiology, anesthesiology, dermatology, and ophthalmology provide excellent scheduling opportunities. The sheer attraction of a field, however, may convince a woman to make sacrifices in favor of her interest and override her more practical considerations. In a recent study, women medical students identified their three top specialty choices as family practice, pediatrics, and internal medicine.[25]

A look at women in graduate medical education permits us to see what residencies women have recently chosen. The latest report of residents on duty as of September 1, 1978 is in the March 7, 1980 issue of the *Journal of the American Medical Association*.[44] Of all residents on duty, the number of women residents was 11,839, or 18.7 percent. The highest proportions of women residents were in internal medicine (22.5 percent) and pediatrics (18.6 percent). Psychiatry had 10.8 percent of women residents and obstetrics-gynecology had 8.8 percent. Other proportions were: family practice, 7.9 percent; pathology, 7.0 percent; surgery, 5.5 percent; and anesthesiology, 3.8 percent.

Many women entering the specialty of obstetrics and gynecology express the desire to bring a "female" approach to the profession. Their capacity to empathize more deeply with the problems of other women may lead them to a different view of hysterectomies or oophorectomies. In spite of irregular hours and inflexible scheduling, women will continue to be attracted to this specialty because of their natural attraction to the birth process.

Women physicians have a unique role to play in psychiatry. Maternal feelings can be of great value in treating the emotionally disturbed. The field of child psychiatry has been dominated from its beginning by the contributions of outstanding women.

Testimony by some women physicians suggests that problems which arise in some specialties are not found in others. Radiology, pathology, and anesthesiology are listed as suitable specialties by one woman physician because "the public often doesn't see the M.D., so whether male or female makes no difference to them." A pathologist notes, "My microscope doesn't care if I'm pregnant—and my hours are much more flexible."

Numerically, more women are in general practice than in any specialty. One general practitioner, some years ago, took on the duties of medical attendant to the Watford Soccer Team, which made her the only female medical officer in Britain's "big league" soccer. What did she think about having to check the players in their dressing room before each game, during half time, and at the end of each game? "It's all in the line of duty," she said, "and no different from taking care of little boys and grown-up men in the normal way." The soccer players liked having her as their physician, although her presence did tone down some of the locker room horseplay.[27]

How comfortable a woman feels practicing her specialty depends largely on the resolution of any conflict that might exist between her female and professional roles. She usually resolves the conflict by finding a specialty that is least likely to be incompatible with the female role. Kosa and Cocker, in a study of women in specialities, outline the sources of role conflict and common means of resolution:

> If we consider the problem of females as the minority sex in medicine, we may theoretically outline three main areas of role conflict as well as professional procedure to cope with those conflicts. It is reasonable to assume that: (1) the professional role tends to impose limitations upon the full realization of the female role; (2) the female role tends to limit the full realization of the professional role; and, in addition, (3) female practitioners face particular difficulties in assuming those professional duties which are more or less incompatible with female tasks. While the three areas of conflict are, to a great extent, overlapping and make it difficult, or impossible, to restrict the role conflict to one area only, women doctors tend to manage their professional careers by selecting for work those fields of medicine and that type of practice which are least likely to offer work duties incompatible with the female task.[18]

Dr. Alexandra Symonds discusses similar problems in her insightful article on the wife as the professional. She states that women, especially in the past, have paid an excessively high price when they combine identity work, such as a profession, with marriage.[39] Although some women, she states, have done this successfully, a sizeable number have developed depression, constriction of their own needs, and partial participation in their profession. Changes, however, are taking place, and young women are now growing up with a healthy sense of entitlement to all that life can offer and are avoiding some of the struggles and conflicts of the past.

Prejudice

The woman physician must expect to meet some prejudice in her personal and professional relationships. While most of it will be discouraging and frustrating, some of it will be humorous. Dr. Dorothy V. Whipple tells the story of making a house call to see a small sick boy during World War II, when there was a great shortage of doctors. As she entered the room, the child whined, "I don't want no skirt looking at me." The father soothed the child, saying, "Never mind, sonny, these days you gotta take what you can get."[40]

All specialties are open to women, although some—such as surgery—are accused of discouraging women. Women have pointed out that surgeons have rejected them in both overt and subtle ways. For example, we might ask why surgeons remove so few testicles and so many ovaries. During a recent cancer conference, the surgeons present discussed their attitudes toward orchiectomy versus oophorectomy, and it was agreed that surgeons rarely hesitate to remove an ovary but think twice about removing a testicle. The doctors readily admitted that such a sex-oriented viewpoint can and does arise from the fact that most surgeons are male. Said one of them, wryly: "No ovary is good enough to leave in, and no testicle is bad enough to take out."[45]

Democratization of Career Opportunities

There are a number of changing trends which should lead to democratization of career opportunities for women in medicine, as well as in other fields. Cynthia Epstein has identified these trends, a few of which are given here because of their special relevance to medicine:

1. Schools are recruiting from a wider social base. The experience of studying with fellow students from varied backgrounds will

prevent the future professional from expecting everybody to be like himself.
2. Most educational institutions are coeducational or becoming so. Having studied with women should make these men less resistant to working with them.
3. The population explosion and the rising need for specialized personnel create pressures on the professions to recruit from a broad base.
4. Ideological changes have upset the mandatory quality of traditional modes of education and work. The older patterns of the "establishment" are being called into question by vociferous and gifted challengers.[8]

Marrying a Doctor

The majority of women in medicine are marrying other physicians.[32] Although it is difficult to get an accurate and current figure, nationwide, more than 60 percent of female doctors are believed to be married to doctors. Many of these doctor couples are arranging for both spouses to combine family and career interests and tasks.

Like most couples, dual-career marriages face many stresses and strains.[4, 33] Psychiatry professor David G. Rice has studied and treated many dual-career couples. He has identified some positive characteristics in the marital interaction of dual-career couples who are able to improve their marriages:[33]

1. Freedom from rigidly prescribed gender role behaviors and constraints.
2. Flexibility and willingness to try new behaviors.
3. A willingness to share power or influence in the relationship and an appreciation of how competition may have both facilitative and destructive effects.
4. An openness to one's own and one's spouse's feelings, as well as a valuing of effective communication.
5. Appreciation of each spouse's right to self-fulfillment and a willingness to make sacrifices in this regard.

CONCLUSION

This chapter has discussed the woman medical student's road to professional maturation. After admission to medical school is achieved, today's woman student, cognizant of obstacles to achieving fulfillment both during and after medical school, must be prepared to examine herself continually in order to keep her balance in what is still largely a medical world of men. Increasingly more urgent and relevant for her is the question she and others ask: "What special and unique talents does the woman bring to medicine?" The twentieth-century American financier and public servant Bernard Baruch, himself the son of a physician, probably foresaw the true potential: "Women are a natural in the field of medicine. Give them technique and training and you will furnish mankind with better doctors than ever before."

Tolstoy once said, "When I have one foot in the grave I will tell the truth about women. I shall tell it, jump into my coffin, pull the lid over me and say 'Do what you like now.' " That woman is essentially mysterious, eluding rational analysis and explanation, has been a popular article of faith in most periods of history. In recent decades, this quality has been referred to as "feminine mystique." Illustrative of this are the forms of the woman archetype or of the symbol of femininity that still today assume a confusing variety of blendings and transformations in our society: (1) the Mother, the Magna Mater, somehow identified with earth, from whose womb all life germinates and comes to birth; (2) the Virgin, the feminine ideal, for whose sake the hero in every man bestirs himself to confront dangers and attain the prized goal; (3) the Siren, the temptress, the symbol of sensual allurement and ecstasy which distracts man from his essential task; and (4) the Harpy, which represents femininity in its repellent and frightening aspect, whether as witch, vampire, Erinys, lamia, Medusa, or any other configuration of female horror.[42] Today's male medical student, working beside his female classmate, will be influenced in his reactions to her by these four archetypes of femininity.

Greater awareness is needed of how man and woman have viewed and presently view each other, at both conscious and unconscious levels of their thinking. It is to be hoped that their attitudes toward each other will foster only constructive relationships in the complex medical enterprise.

REFERENCES

1. Adams M: The compassion trap—women only. Psychology Today 5:71, 1971
2. Bachtold LM: Personality characteristics of women of distinction. Psychology of Women Quarterly, Fall, 1976
3. Bem SL, Bem DJ: We're all nonconscious sexists. Psychology Today 4:22, 1970

4. Bryson JB, Bryson R: Dual-career Couples. New York, Human Sciences Press, 1978
5. Chaff SL, Haimbach R, Fenichel C, Woodside NB: Women in Medicine: A Bibliography of the Literature on Women Physicians. Metuchen, New Jersey, The Scarecrow Press, 1977
6. Cumming E: Notes on the changing role of women. Panel discussion, Cleveland, Flora Stone Mather College, March, 1966
7. Davidson VM: Coping styles of women medical students. J Med Educ 53:902, 1978
8. Epstein CF: Woman's Place. Berkeley, University of California Press, 1970
9. Fromm E: Mother. Psychology Today 4:74, 1971
10. Gaensbauer TJ, Mizner GL: Developmental stresses in medical education. Psychiatry 43:60, 1980
11. Ginzberg E, et al.: Life Styles of Educated Women. New York, Columbia University Press, 1966
12. Heins M: Career and life patterns of women and men physicians. In Shapiro EC, Lowenstein LM (eds): Becoming a Physician—Development of Values and Attitudes in Medicine. Cambridge, Massachusetts, Ballinger, 1979, pp 217–235
13. Hilberman E, et al.: Support groups for women in medical school: A first-year program. J Med Educ 50:867, 1979
14. Holmes FF, Holmes GE, Hassanein R: Performance of male and female medical students in a medicine clerkship. JAMA 239:2259, 1978
15. Hutchins EB: Minorities, manpower and medicine. Washington, DC, Assoc Amer Med Colleges, Technical Report No. S-663, 1966
16. Johnson DG, Hutchins EB: Doctor or dropout? A study of medical student attrition. J Med Educ 41:1097, 1966
17. Kempton S: Cutting loose. Esquire, July, 1970, pp 54–55
18. Kosa J, Cocker RE: The female physician in public health, and reconciliation of the sex and professional roles. Sociol Soc Res 49:295, 1965
19. Lawrence DH: The White Peacock. Carbondale, Southern Illinois University Press, 1966
20. Lopate C: Women in Medicine. Baltimore, Johns Hopkins Press, 1968
21. Maccoby E: Women's intellect. In Farber S, Wilson RHL (eds): The Potential of Woman. New York, McGraw-Hill, 1963
22. Masters WH, Johnson VE: Human Sexual Inadequacy. Boston, Little, Brown, 1970
23. Masters WH, Johnson VE: Personal communication, May 18, 1971
24. McClelland D: Wanted: A new self-image for women. In Lifton RJ (ed): The Woman in America. New York, Houghton Mifflin, 1964, pp 187–188
25. McGrath E, Zimet CN: Female and male medical students: Differences in specialty choice selection and personality. J Med Educ 52:293, 1977
26. Mead M: Gender in the honors program. Newsletter of the Inter-University Committee on the Superior Student, May, 1961, pp 4–5
27. Medical World News, December 15, 1967, p 77
28. Montagu A: The Natural Superiority of Women. New York, Macmillan, 1953

29. Mount E: The feminine factor. Soundings 53:379, 1970
30. Muller C, Jussim J: Medical education for women: How good an investment? J Med Educ 50:571, 1975
31. Nemir RL: Women in medicine during the last half century. JAMWA 33:201, 1978
32. New York Times, October 12, 1979, p A18
33. Rice DG: Dual-career Couples—Conflict and Treatment. New York, Free Press, 1979
34. Roeske NA, Lake K: Role models for women medical students. J Med Educ 52:459, 1977
35. Shainess N: The eternal woman. Marriage, November, 1968
36. Shapiro EC, Driscoll SG: Training for commitment: Effects of the time-intensive nature of graduate medical education. In Shapiro EC, Lowenstein LM (eds): Becoming a Physician—Development of Values and Attitudes in Medicine. Cambridge, Massachusetts, Ballinger, 1979, pp 187–198
37. Shapiro EC, Jones AB: Women physicians and the exercise of power and authority in health care. In Shapiro EC, Lowenstein LM (eds): Becoming a Physician—Development of Values and Attitudes in Medicine. Cambridge, Massachusetts, Ballinger, 1979, pp 237–245
38. Sutnick AI, McLeer SV: Programs developed from concerns for women in medicine. J Med Educ 54:627, 1979
39. Symonds A: The wife as the professional. Am J Psychoanal 39:55, 1979
40. The Fuller Utilization of the Woman Physician. Report on a conference on meeting medical manpower needs, Jan 12–13, 1968. Washington, DC, Women's Bureau, Dept of Labor, 1968
41. Walton HJ: Sex differences in ability and outlook of senior medical students. Br J Med Educ 2:152, 1968
42. Wheelwright P: The archetypal symbol. In Strelka J (ed): Perspectives in Literary Symbolism. University Park, The Pennsylvania State University Press, 1968, pp 214–243
43. Williams PB: Recent trends in the productivity of women and men physicians. J Med Educ 53:420, 1978
44. Women in graduate medical education. 79th annual report— medical education in the United States, 1978–1979. JAMA 243:870, 1980
45. Women M.D.'s join the fight. Medical World News, October 23, 1970, p 22

11
MINORITY AND DISADVANTAGED STUDENTS

*In planning and pursuing a career in medicine, you should make a firm commitment to success, and remember how far you have come and how close you are to realizing your goals.**

—Dr. Anna Cherrie Epps

During the 1960s, medical educators, students, and many others, responding to the forces for change in our society, began to recognize our country's need for more minority and disadvantaged individuals in the study and practice of medicine. While great progress has been made, we have yet a long way to go before these groups are represented in the medical profession in proportion to their representation in the general population.

Since the access to good health care is a right and not a privilege, all our citizens are needed to create an equitable health care system. As Andrew Young has said, "We need more minority physicians and biomedical scientists, not only to improve the health care status of their own communities but to enhance the health of this nation through the infusion of our citizen genius."[25]

Of course, it is not reasonable to believe that because one is a member of a minority, one will automatically serve in a minority community.[5] At the same time, it is reasonable to believe that health services within inner-city and rural areas can be increased by a substantial increase in the number of minority physicians. While race and ethnicity are not sole determinants of practice site, they are important considerations.

The minority groups in our country with serious under-representation in medicine are blacks, Mexican-Americans, American Indians, and mainland Puerto Ricans. Disadvantaged students may or may not

I am indebted to Dr. Anna Cherrie Epps, Director, Medical Education Reinforcement and Enrichment Program (MEdREP), and Assistant Dean for Student Services, Tulane University School of Medicine, for her guidance and generous help in the development of this chapter.
* From a statement to the 1980 summer program participants, Medical Education Reinforcement and Enrichment Program, Tulane University School of Medicine, August 15, 1980.

be members of a minority group. Medical schools differ somewhat in whom they classify as disadvantaged, but usually students are so classified who meet one or more of the following criteria: poverty-level socioeconomic status, parents' lack of formal education, education in a small rural school or an isolated school with a predominantly minority enrollment, and membership in a large family.

It should be noted that terms such as "minority" or "disadvantaged students" do carry for some a negative bias or even a derogatory connotation.[7] Other terms have been suggested such as "nontraditional" or "new" students,* but such terms have lacked the clarity and precision needed for general use. Usually, in this chapter, the term "minority" or "disadvantaged" will be used to encompass both minority and disadvantaged students.

COMMITMENT TO GETTING INTO MEDICAL SCHOOL

Minority and disadvantaged students face some special challenges and obstacles related to their commitment and motivation for a career in medicine. Although the dream to become a doctor may have entered the mind early, more discouragement than encouragement has usually been offered by others in the student's environment. It is well established that much negative counseling has come from teachers who may see the student as aspiring to something beyond what the teachers themselves attained or as beyond the realistic reach of the student.

Negative counseling is only one of the potential obstacles in the student's path. Other obstacles relate to finding appropriate career guidance, a lack of contact with professionals who can be identified as role models, a lack of necessary financial resources, and the over-all competitive machinations involved in gaining entrance to medical school. Competing for admission to medical school has been and still is for many minority and disadvantaged students "like trekking toward an infinitely receding horizon."[24] Although their MCAT scores and GPA's have improved steadily, other candidates have shown similar improvements in their records. Among the other problems may be reading deficiencies, poor study habits, difficulty with standardized tests, lack of moral support and encouragement, as well as the detrimental effects of social and cultural isolation.

In spite of these obstacles, the dream of becoming a physician can be

---

* For example, at Oakes College of the University of California at Santa Cruz, where innovative programs have been developed to strengthen the basic skills of students who need help, these students are referred to as "new students," in an effort to avoid any hint of a derogatory reference.[7]

realized. Dr. Walter Leavell summarizes in a few words what it takes: "To convert your dream into a reality will require diligence, preparedness, and perseverance."[14] One needs not only to develop the personal and intellectual skills required but also to become informed about and understand the admissions process for gaining entry into medical school.

Early decisions relate to the selection and number of schools to apply to. Some applicants do not get accepted to medical school because their choices of schools are inappropriate. Further, some students submit too few applications. It is generally recommended that each student apply to a minimum of ten schools. If a student qualifies for the AMCAS fee waiver, then he or she should apply to the maximum number of schools allowable under that program. One's personality and life-style should be given some consideration in the choice of a school. Would you be more comfortable in a small community or in a large city? Would the number of minority or disadvantaged students at a particular school be an important factor in influencing you to choose or reject the school? Check with minority students at any school being considered to learn how these students perceive their school and what is happening to them. Factors that could adversely affect your life at a medical school should be closely scrutinized.

Apply to all medical schools in your home state, both public and private. State schools give preference to students who live within the state, and the tuition is usually low. Also, travel expense as an interviewee and later as a medical student will be reduced because of the proximity of the school. Special financial aid programs are sometimes available to in-state residents. Private schools are more costly, and sometimes the competition is keener. They do have some scholarships and may choose a substantial number of students from the state in which they are located.

In applying to public and private schools located outside of your state, remember that both types of schools consider minority students from out-of-state, although usually your best chances are in your home state. Because of travel expenses and other factors, the cost of your education will almost always be greater at an out-of-state school.

Each medical school has some distinct and unique characteristics, its own set of goals and objectives, and its standards for accepting applicants to each year's entering class. Request from each school its bulletin and inquire about any special minority programs that may be offered. Also, you may wish to purchase a book entitled *Medical School Admission Requirements, USA and Canada* from the AAMC, One Dupont Circle, N.W., Washington, D.C., 20036. This book, revised annually, offers composite information on each school's admission requirements, as well as other valuable information pertaining to the history and philosophy of the school. Also available for purchase from the AAMC is the publication *Minority Student Opportunities in United States Medical Schools.*

Often when a medical school brings together its data on a minority or disadvantaged student, significant information in the student's application folder is meager. Sedlacek and Brooks address this situation.[21] Either the applicant has no experiences of the type he or she is asked about or does not remember or consider them as significant. Further, in the regular admissions situation, the use of GPA and MCAT scores to prescreen applicants before interviewing them may be a reasonable approach. With the minority applicants, however, a more productive approach is feasible, that of using the interview early to look for certain characteristics and other information not elicited in the application. Because of the small number of minority applicants, this type of interviewing would be quite manageable. After the interview, the GPA and MCAT, as well as other data, then could be used appropriately. The following questions have been suggested for use in the interview.[21]

- How strong is the positive self-concept or confidence of the student? Are determination, strength of character, and independence present?
- Has the student made a realistic self-appraisal, especially academic? Are deficiencies recognized and accepted? Are genuine efforts being made to overcome these, to develop the self, and to broaden individuality?
- How well does the person understand and deal with racism? Can the person handle institutional racism without becoming blindly angry or permissive and submissive? Is the person committed to fighting to improve the system?
- Are long-range objectives preferred over more immediate goals, and is the person able to respond to deferred gratification?
- Is there a strong support person available for them to turn to in crises?
- Has the person had successful leadership experience in any area pertinent to his or her background?
- Has there been any demonstrated community service, any involvement in his or her cultural community?
- Are there demonstrated medical interests in any area pertinent to the person's background?

Some further comments about the interview are indicated. Although an opportunity for an interview at a medical school is eagerly sought by students, the interview is usually approached with apprehension as well as misinformation about its nature and purpose. Since minority students may have had little experience in the past with being interviewed, they may not make use of this opportunity to the fullest extent. Thus, if students can get an opportunity for simulated interviews through summer enrichment programs, their premedical advisors, or a minority student office at a medical school, they are more likely to use their interviews to maximum advantage in the admissions process. Interviews are discussed further in the chapter in this book titled "The Search for the Ideal Medical Student."

It must be stressed, as Judith Krupka points out, that interviews provide a useful means by which nontraditional or minority applicants can be more fairly and adequately assessed and bring a human dimension into the admissions process that tends at times to be dehumanizing to applicants.[13]

Any applicant may enhance the value of his or her application by careful attention to detail so that the maximum amount of pertinent information is given to the admissions committee. An underutilized part of the application form is the space provided for "Personal Comments." This space can be used to give some insight about one's hopes and aspirations for a career in medicine. It offers an opportunity to let your personality and individuality be recognized. You may outline the development of your interest in the study of medicine and the type of experiences that influenced or strengthened your motivation. Further, any unique or outstanding accomplishments or extenuating circumstances in your life may be mentioned. Although some applicants leave the space for "Personal Comments" blank, it should be used creatively as another opportunity for strengthening your hand in getting into medical school.

In considering motivation and commitment in a broader context, refer to Chapter 1.

RETENTION

The Report of the Task Force on Minority Student Opportunities in Medicine stressed the retention of minority students in medical school as one of its seven goals: "Strengthen programs which support the normal progress and successful graduation of racial minority students enrolled in medical school."[20]

Failure of a student to graduate from medical school after occupying a place in the school is a great loss to the student, to the medical school, and to society. Thus, it is the responsibility of schools to develop a supportive and humanistic environment for all students and particularly those from racial minority groups. Geertsma has noted that the educational environment as well as related counseling must facilitate the development of trust and self-esteem among minority students.[10] Attempts to nurture these qualities should begin during the prematriculation period and continue after the students begin their professional training.

The medical school environment is a crucial factor in the professional development of minority and disavantaged students. Support services including academic and administrative advising, individual and group counseling, and crisis intervention are essential. The atmosphere must be supportive and humanistic and communicate to students that *all* are welcome and *all* are given the opportunity to succeed and expected to do so.

The evaluation of student needs is an important and ongoing part of all retention programs. Appropriate identification of personal or academic difficulties aids the student and the medical school in determining the underlying factors and in seeking effective solutions. This evaluative process can be incorporated easily in the routine systems utilized in most medical schools for monitoring student performance.

Tutorial programs are available in many medical schools, and tutorial assistance is provided when it is requested. Tutorial programs that are successful are the ones that eliminate the negative bias against students who seek academic help. Minority students, as well as others, find beneficial the note-taking services, test files, weekly review or pre-examination sessions, and study skills programs that many medical schools provide.

Personal counseling services represent an important area of student support. Matters of confidentiality, however, must be highly respected, and students must know that there will be no betrayals of confidence. Unfortunately, there is usually in medical schools a paucity of counselors with a minority background. Students are quicker to seek out, trust, and confide in counselors with backgrounds similar to their own. When the "right kinds" of counselors are not available, students rely heavily on one another for emotional support and in some cases develop emotional support systems outside of the medical school.

A substantial number of medical schools now offer summer programs for minority students who have been accepted for admission. These programs have a worthy set of goals: (1) to reinforce the student's academic knowledge base; (2) to strengthen the student's study, test-taking, and reading skills; and (3) to familiarize the student with the medical school environment. Many students find these programs particularly helpful in the review of their science knowledge and in allowing them the opportunity to become acquainted with the medical school environment.[1, 12]

Whereas special support services are important for the retention of racial minority students, they do not take the place of the support given routinely by minority role models. The presence of minority faculty members and administrators with whom students can identify is essential to a comprehensive medical school retention program. Medical schools that lack minority faculty in the basic or clinical sciences, as well as in administration, are not convincing to students about providing a suitable environment for the education and socialization of minority students. It is hoped that all medical schools are now embracing faculty development programs to correct their imbalance. In the meantime, medical schools are being encouraged to identify and use minority practicing physicians and basic scientists as guest lecturers, volunteer faculty, and preceptors.

In general, the success of retention programs for minority students depends to a large extent on a positive institutional environment, the presence of minority staff, accessibility of support services to all students, effective use of the faculty, and institutional financial support. *The AAMC Task Force on Minority Student Opportunities in Medicine* makes four recommendations to medical schools for assuring the success of racial minority students:[20]

1. All medical schools should have individuals or an office with clear responsibility for representing the interests of racial minority medical students. These individuals or the staff of the office should be sensitive to minority needs and have an understanding of minority group values and culture.
2. Medical schools should support organizations among racial minority students that serve vital social functions and enable these students to contribute collectively to the cultural, political, and academic life of the medical school.
3. Medical schools should improve their academic support programs and provide academic evaluation on a regular and frequent basis.
4. Medical schools should improve their personal support programs. Specific programs should be developed to increase the emotional support base provided to racial minority students.

RECRUITMENT AND IDENTIFICATION

Recruitment is an active endeavor, not a passive one. Since the applicant pool for medical school is close to three times the number of available places, most medical schools exert little effort toward recruitment. Yet, when we consider minority students, we are confronted with the stark fact that these students are seriously under-represented in both the applicant pool and the accepted student group. Thus, it is imperative that medical schools cooperate with and expand recruitment endeavors aimed at minorities.

Recruitment should begin early, especially at the high school level. It must be a multifaceted endeavor. It may involve changing a person's mind about a previously formed career choice, changing mistaken attitudes concerning the preparation required for particular careers, and informing a person accurately about what is really involved in the education for, and pursuit of, a particular career such as medicine. In describing the efforts of 16 institutions in directing black students into careers in health fields, J. Henry Sayles lists the major features of the recruitment program: (1) distributing recruiting material directed at minority students to high school counselors who are in a position to influence these students in their career choices; (2) searching out students with academic potential instead of concentrating only on the "super" minority student; (3) focusing on changing mistaken ideas about preparing for health careers; (4) promoting an "I-can-cope" attitude; (5) organizing health career awareness activities; (6) keeping students informed of all developments in the health field that could be of interest to a potential health professional; and (7) providing counseling—personal and academic—to students who are committed to or considering a career in medicine or a related field.[22]

Although many people offer explanations for the inadequate number of minority students who seek or attain a health career, black students themselves give their reasons as:[2] inadequate financial assistance, length of preparation and schooling to become a health professional, lack of information regarding health careers, lack of preparation in grade and high school, lack of preparation in college, inadequate counseling in high school and college, lack of education of parents due to past discrimination, fear of discrimination in professional schools and in the health professions, family pressure to follow occupations similar to those of other members of one's family, and pressure from friends to follow careers not too different from their own.

In the list given above, inadequate financial assistance is mentioned at the top. Some believe that the biggest problem in recruiting is money.[11] As funds for undergraduate and graduate programs are cut back, minority students are often the hardest hit. Unable to pay their way through medical school, minority students turn away from medicine or go where financial aid is available. As the funds dry up, discouragement and hardships increase for those who cannot bear the cost. It is hoped that since this problem has been clearly identified, schools and government agencies will eliminate this formidable barrier for minority and disadvantaged students getting a medical education. To do otherwise would confirm a fear that there is today a diminishing concern for minorities in American society.

We must continue and increase our recruitment efforts at all levels, creating awareness in secondary schools and colleges. Summer programs are an indispensable part of carrying out this mission. All working in recruitment must seek to create or identify avenues for encouraging and informing students of not only the need for more minorities in the health fields but also of the requirements for achieving this goal. These and similar issues are explored in depth in the Cadbury-Epps book *Medical Education: Responses to a Challenge— Minorities and the Disadvantaged: Development and Representation in the Health Professions.*[3]

Summer Enrichment Programs for Undergraduates

The weak preparation for the rigors of medical education on the part of many minority students reflects the inadequacy of secondary and higher education, both in terms of course work and career counseling.[16] A long-range solution to the problem of maintaining minority students in the educational enterprise is to make early identification of able students and provide enriched educational programs during these years. Many such programs are available now both at undergraduate schools and at medical centers, especially during the summer months but with a few continuing their activities throughout the academic years.[17, 18] After participating in enrichment programs, many students are able to handle the rigorous medical school curriculum without undue difficulty.[4, 16]

In a broader context, recognition of the scarcity of minority health professionals and the overall uneven distribution of health personnel throughout the country prompted the development of reinforcement and enrichment summer programs. These were implemented initially in minority health professional training institutions. They are at present in operation at many medical centers throughout our country, particularly where there is commitment to eradication of inequality of opportunity in education for under-represented groups, such as minorities and the socioeconomically disadvantaged. These programs are goal-oriented: to identify, inform, recruit, retain, and ultimately graduate an increased number of minority and socioeconomically disadvantaged youths in the fields of health care throughout the nation.

Today, these enrichment programs are well established in some of our institutions of higher education, particularly in some medical centers. An excellent example of such a program is the Medical Education Reinforcement and Enrichment Program (MEdREP) of Tulane Medical Center, directed by Dr. Anna Cherrie Epps. Programs similar in format to Tulane's are found at the University of Southern Illinois, Harvard University, The University of Texas Medical Branch at Galveston, Barnard College, Baylor College of Medicine, University of New Mexico, Temple University, College of Medicine and Dentistry of New Jersey, Cornell University, Howard University, and many others. For a more definitive listing of summer programs for undergraduates in a professional medical education environment, see the table of listings in the Pisano and Epps' chapter in *Medical Education: Responses to a Challenge.*[18]

It is not my purpose to describe here the details of these programs, for they are described well elsewhere.[17, 18] It is appropriate, however, to emphasize the objectives of these programs. They serve to identify and recruit into the health professions and other related fields the socioeconomically, culturally, and educationally disadvantaged students, especially from among minorities, whose background and interests make them candidates for engaging in the delivery of health care to underserved groups. In addition, the summer programs inform and introduce these students to the practical and simulated experiences associated with the pursuit of a health career, thus providing them with a more realistic approach to the requirements for entrance into the health professional fields.

The summer programs are directed at the development of the academic prerequisites and personal qualities that are essential characteristics of those who seek a health career. Through these programs, there is a reinforcement of interest in the health professions, enhancement of motivation, and candid discussion of academic performance expectations in the participating students. These objectives are attained through the use of education skills, academic reinforcement and enrichment activities, exposure to and experiences in the medical center academic and clinical environment, as well as an introduction to health care delivery. These programs greatly expand the horizons of those aspiring to serve in the health care enterprise.

In summary, enrichment programs that are broad in scope offer students a rewarding educational experience and a comprehensive view of health professional school life.[18] Participating students gain a realistic understanding of what it means to pursue a health professional education and career. This understanding is often accompanied by a personal reaffirmation of interest and increased motivation for pursuing a health career. Further, adjustment to a health professions institutional environment should be easier because the program experience enhances the student's self-esteem and increases his or her self-confidence.

Premedical Advising

In properly guiding and counseling minority and disadvantaged students, advisors have a special set of opportunities and responsibilities. Non-minority and inexperienced advisors must become aware of these opportunities and responsibilities. A first step is to identify the students who are interested, or potentially interested, in a medical career. This identification may not be easy, for minority students tend to be cautious about setting their goals too high, and as freshmen and sophomores frequently declare majors in an allied health or pure science field. After gaining confidence through success in early courses, particularly science courses, they will begin to admit to career goals as demanding as medicine. Unfortunately, a great deal of this self-evaluation is carried out in isolation, and the result is that many students counsel themselves out of a career in medicine. This problem is prevalent at predominantly white colleges where there are few role models, little peer support, and sometimes negative counseling.

A different problem for the premedical advisor is the minority student who enters college with unrealistic goals of becoming a physician and must be guided toward a different career. This problem exists at all schools, whether or not the student body consists predominantly of minorities. In any school the problem becomes a delicate one when the counselor's advice can be interpreted as an expression of prejudice or failure to understand the true talents of the student.

Because of past educational deficiencies, many minority and disadvantaged students are late in demonstrating their academic capabilities. Advisors should not make the mistake of discouraging such students solely on the basis of poor early records. At the same time, advisors should look for clear indicators of potential. Positive indicators of potential may include an improvement in performance when courseload is reduced, evidence that a student's time and energies are divided between studies and a job, marked improvement as a result of participation in academic support programs, and perhaps better performance in courses where reading skills do not interfere.

It would be helpful if effective counseling or advising began for students in high school. As Leavell has mentioned, for some professional endeavors a lack of advisor contact and continuity of advice presents relatively few problems for the student, since subsequent stages of education are not strongly related to the preceding stages.[15] This is *not* the case for the minority student interested in medicine, for the basic education that is a prerequisite for the study of medicine should begin minimally at the high school level. Leavell pinponts the issue succinctly: "The minority student who enters college without having taken a course in high school biology, chemistry, or physics is academically behind his peer group on the first day of class in these comparable subjects at college irrespective of the level of the individual's intellectual ability. Herein lies the dilemma of the minority student which necessitates costly and after-the-fact educational reinforcement programs at the medical school level to bridge the educational deficits."[15]

Since the successful pursuit of a career in medicine requires some long-range planning, it is generally difficult for minority students to aspire to this goal when they have little information about the profession or contact with individuals in the profession. Sedlacek and Brooks note that in the absence of available role models and because the reinforcement system has been relatively random for them, minority students may have difficulty perceiving the relationship between current work and the ultimate practice of their profession.[21] All who are interested in increasing the number of minority physicians must provide grade school and high school advisors and students with more information about a career in medicine. Minority medical students and minority physicians in the community should be asked to participate in student advising, for they serve as role models and are challenging examples of accomplishment and service. Further, other positive steps include science fairs sponsored by medical schools, as well as weekend and summer programs that permit interested students to gain experience and insight into the medical profession.

Any person in a position to advise minority students should be aware of the following programs: precollege preparatory programs for minority students; summer enrichment programs in which students may participate while they are in college; postbaccalaureate programs and other academic arrangements for minority students who decide late or otherwise do not have the necessary premedical courses; the AAMC Medical Minority Applicant Registry (Med-Mar) that provides the channel for any minority applicant to have basic biographical information sent to the admissions offices of all medical schools in the United States; and the Simulated Minority Admissions Exercises (SMAE), a program in which advisors can participate to gain firsthand knowledge into the practical aspects of medical school admission processes, particularly as these relate to minority students.[6] Further, since the Medical College Admissions Test (MCAT) looms as a frightening obstacle for many students, advisors and students should be aware of special information about the MCAT. Helpful information can be obtained from publications such as the AAMC's *The New MCAT Student Manual*[23] and *A Complete Preparation for the New MCAT*.[8]

In other sections of this book, work in a hospital or health-related facility has been mentioned as a way of clarifying or demonstrating a person's motivation for the study of medicine. To require or suggest this type of work may be poor counseling for a minority student with minimal financial resources. A better course of action for such a student may be to take a summer job that offers maximum income potential and do volunteer work in a hospital during his or her spare time, since the major purpose of work in a hospital is for the student to have a realistic perspective of what being a physician entails, rather than for the experience itself. If a student is unable to get some kind of hospital experience, for financial or other reasons, he or she should call this to the attention of the admissions committee so that it does not appear as a lack of motivation.

FINANCIAL AID TO STUDENTS

Financing a medical education continues to be a major barrier for minority students who wish to pursue a career in medicine. Once admitted, students must grapple with how they will finance their medical education. There is a paucity of grants-in-aid monies available today, in comparison to 10 or 15 years ago, and students must rely more heavily on loans. At the same time, there is a substantial increase in tuition, living expenses, and the cost of books and supplies. Debts of enormous proportion can accrue before the student graduates.

In spite of limited funds, medical schools strive to soften the financial burdens of students. Minority Affairs deans maintain a close day-to-day working relationship with the school's financial aid officer and keep abreast of the relative needs of each student. Efforts are made to insure that all grant monies are used appropriately. Further, students are helped toward securing low-interest, long-term loans. Also, medical schools are active in seeking grant and loan funds from alumni, private donors, and foundations.

The federal government is phasing out need-based scholarship and loan programs in favor of federally guaranteed loan programs (utilizing funds from commercial lenders) and scholarships requiring service commitments. Most of the scholarship dollars provided by the federal government now require repayment by the recipient after graduation through service in a health care shortage area.

An analysis of all the sources of financial assistance to minority students is not appropriate here. Most medical schools publish a bulletin showing the amount and source of their scholarship and loan funds, and these publications are available to students on request. Students are encouraged to discuss the options available to them with medical school financial aid officers.

There are two service programs that some students find attractive: the National Health Service Corps Scholarship Program and the Armed Services Scholarship Programs. Each pays a monthly stipend, all tuition and fees, as well as the cost of books and equipment. In accepting one of these scholarships, students obligate themselves to serve one year for each year of scholarship support, with a minimum service period of two years.

In its financial aid to students, the federal government is focusing primarily on the legislation geared to support the National Health Service Corps as a viable solution to the problem of maldistribution of doctors. Many contend that the federal government has made loan programs and other potential aid sources less attractive in order to enhance recruitment for the Corps.[9] Of course, such an approach does not give adequate consideration to financing medical education for students unable to secure a place in the National Health Service Corps or those who cannot, for personal or family reasons, serve in the Corps. Anyway, it is hoped that new federal legislation will be enacted soon to make available more need-based scholarship funds without service commitment. Such funds are necessary to encourage financially disadvantaged and racial minority students to choose medicine as a career and to assist financially those racial minority students desiring careers in academic medicine or research.

Obviously the financial barriers to a medical education must be surmounted for those students who are economically disadvantaged. We all have a responsibility in helping to achieve this goal, and we must accept the challenge.

MEETING SOCIETAL RESPONSIBILITIES

Medical school admissions committee members speak of some of the agonizing decisions they have to make regarding the selection of students—both minority and non-minority. Only a portion of qualified applicants is accepted. The students left behind often ask: "What do the students selected have that we don't have?" At times there is little difference between the two groups, when all factors in evaluation are considered.

Not infrequently a non-minority student confronts an admissions committee and asks a straightforward question: "Why did you not accept me when some of the minority students you accepted do not have grades and MCAT scores as good as mine?" The student's question is an expected one and has been around for a number of years. It has all kinds of implications related to justice, fairness, correcting societal wrongs, equal representation of groups in our society, privilege, and accountability.

What admissions committees seek to measure in students is motivation and potential, for in many students these parameters give information that grades or MCAT scores do not give. Supreme Court Justice William O. Douglas spoke to this issue when he said that an admissions committee is fully justified in looking at a black applicant who pulled himself or herself out of the ghetto into a junior college and may thereby demonstrate a level of motivation, perseverance, and ability that would lead a fair-minded admissions committee to conclude that this student shows more promise for the profession than the son or daughter of an affluent alumnus who received better grades at a top university. Justice Douglas was stating that potential, motivation, and how far one has come in one's struggle may characterize the superior student better than the criteria frequently used.

In 1976, the Association of American Medical Colleges filed an *amicus curiae* brief with the California Supreme Court in the case of *Bakke v. Regents of the University of California.* The brief argues that medical schools should be permitted to tailor their policies to meet perceived educational and societal needs. The following statement from the brief pinponts the task facing admissions committees:

> The primary purpose of the medical school admissions process is to select from among applicants deemed qualified to study medicine those who, in the judgment of a duly constituted admissions committee, will become physicians most likely to contribute to the needs of the country or the state for medical care. This purpose necessarily implies that some subjective judgments must be made in assessing the needs of the state and the likelihood that one individual, more than another also qualified for medical study, will tend to serve those needs. Many criteria should be applied to aid in this difficult evaluation process, including relevant personal characteristics. When the institution's goals include training professionals to serve a presently underserved minority population, the consideration of race as one of many measuring tools is relevant, "rationally related" to the enunciated purposes, and in pursuit of a "compelling state interest."

CONCLUSION

Although much has been accomplished in the recruitment and education of minority students, much remains to be done. It had been hoped that by 1975 medical schools would have achieved an enrollment of racial and ethnic groups that would reflect the demographic character of the population in the United States. The goal was not reached then and is far from being reached now. For example, the percentage of black students accepted today in medical school is a little less than it was in 1975 and a little over half of the percentage of blacks in our population. Further, only one out of every 11 students entering medical school is an American Indian, a black American, a Mexican-American, or a Puerto Rican from the mainland.

Nevertheless, progress has been made, and recognition must be given to the many medical schools, organizations, and individuals that have contributed to increasing the participation of under-represented minorities in medical education during the past 15 years.

Some of the special affirmative action programs that have come into existence over the past 15 years are being challenged as discriminatory. As Dario Prieto, director, AAMC Office of Minority Affairs, emphasizes: "If the progress thus far achieved in increasing the disproportionate numbers of minorities in medical school is to continue, a long-term commitment is required of all institutions, individuals, organizations, and the federal government."[19] Moreover, this will require a revitalization of energies, attitudes, and strategies, especially in the light of the legal confrontations and societal pressures that threaten this progress.

Our country needs to have minority students enter the medical profession, and in greater numbers if we are to solve the health needs of medically underserved populations. Our nation's health care problems are easier solved when minority students are recruited to medical school and effective methods used to assure their success in obtaining the M.D. degree. This is a worthy goal, and at some level, all in our nation should strive to meet this challenge. In doing so, we take another step in affirming our commitment to an ancient dream that "earth can be fair and all God's children one."

REFERENCES

1. Atencio AC: Pre-entry summer course for minority medical students. In Cadbury WE Jr, Cadbury CM, Epps AC, Pisano JC (eds): Medical Education: Responses to a Challenge. Mount Kisco, New York, Futura Publishing Company, 1979, pp 235–252

2. Bruhn JG, Hrachovy RA: Black college students' attitudes toward opportunities in the health professions. J Med Educ 52: 847, 1977
3. Cadbury WE Jr, Cadbury CM, Epps AC, Pisano JC (eds): Medical Education: Responses to a Challenge. Mount Kisco, New York, Futura Publishing Company, 1979
4. Clemendor AA, Moore ON: A premedical program for disadvantaged students. J Med Educ 53:658, 1978
5. Curtis JL: Blacks, Medical Schools, and Society. Ann Arbor, University of Michigan Press, 1971, pp 147-163
6. D'Costa A, Baghook P, Elliott P, et al.: Simulated Minority Admissions Exercises Workbook. Washington, DC, Association of American Medical Colleges, 1975
7. Dreyfuss J: Ethnic studies: A springboard, not a trap. Change 11:13, 1979
8. Flowers JL, Wallace WD: A Complete Preparation for the New MCAT: Health Careers Summer Program. Washington, DC, Howard University, 1978
9. French FD: Problems and perspectives of financing medical education. In Cadbury WE Jr, Cadbury CE, Epps AC, Pisano JC (eds): Medical Education: Responses to a Challenge. Mount Kisco, Futura Publishing Company, 1979, pp 217-232
10. Geertsma RH: A special tutorial for minority medical students: An account of a year's experience. J Med Educ 52:396, 1977
11. Henig RM: Minority admissions: An idea whose time has gone? The New Physician 25:28, 1976
12. Ireland CS Jr: Orientation of incoming medical students. In Cadbury WE Jr, Cadbury CM, Epps AC, Pisano JC (eds): Medical Education: Responses to a Challenge. Mount Kisco, New York, Futura Publishing Company, 1979, pp 253-275
13. Krupka JW: Admissions interviews. In Cadbury WE Jr, Cadbury CM, Epps AC, Pisano JC (eds): Medical Education: Responses to a Challenge. Mount Kisco, New York, Futura Publishing Company, 1979, pp 185-195
14. Leavell WF: Medical School Admission Guide for Minority Applicants. Cincinnati, Ohio, University of Cincinnati, 1979 (Copyrighted by the author)
15. Leavell WF: Premedical advising: Principles and practice. In Cadbury WE Jr, Cadbury CM, Epps AC, Pisano JC (eds): Medical Education: Responses to a Challenge. Mount Kisco, New York, Futura Publishing Company, 1979, pp 59-76
16. Levine HG, Williams LB Jr, Bruhn JG: Six Years of Experience with a Summer Program for Minority Students. J Med Educ 51:735, 1976
17. McGinnis RP: Special undergraduate programs for minority medical aspirants. In Cadbury WE Jr, Cadbury CM, Epps AC, Pisano JC (eds): Medical Education: Responses to a Challenge. Mount Kisco, New York, Futura Publishing Company, 1979, pp 77-95
18. Pisano JC, Epps AC: Summer programs for undergraduates in a professional medical education environment. In Cadbury WE Jr, Cadbury CM, Epps AC, Pisano JC (eds): Medical Education: Responses to a Challenge. Mount Kisco, New York, Futura Publishing Company, 1979, pp 97-119

19. Prieto D: Minorities in medical school, 1968–78. J Med Educ 53:694, 1978
20. Report of the Task Force on Minority Student Opportunities in Medicine. Washington, DC, Association of American Medical Colleges, June 1978
21. Sedlacek WE, Brooks GC Jr: Racism in American Education: A Model for Change. Chicago, Nelson Hall, 1976
22. Sayles JH: Minority students—letter to the editor. J Med Educ 50:1146, 1975
23. The New MCAT Student Manual, New Medical College Admission Test. Washington, DC, Association of American Medical Colleges, 1977
24. Walsh J: Minorities in Medicine—Report of a Conference. New York, Macy Foundation, 1977
25. Young A: Foreword. In Melnick VL, Hamilton FD: Minorities in Science—the Challenge for Change in Biomedicine. New York, Plenum Press, 1977

12
SPECIALTY CHOICE IN MEDICINE

To my sons: Whatever specialty they follow, may they never forget to be doctors.[27]

—Harry E. Mock

A major task in medical students' education is their choice of a particular career in the wide spectrum of possibilities within the profession. The high degree of specialization and the variation in career activities force medical students to make two difficult decisions. The first choice is between general practice and specialty training. Those who choose the latter must decide on a particular specialty and then give some thought to how their time will be divided within the specialty among activities such as teaching, research, and patient care. In 1930, about 75 percent of all physicians were primary care providers, mainly general practitioners. A half century later, more than 80 percent are specialists; and in another decade, the projection is 94 percent in specialty practice.[14, 17]

Students' decisions to specialize and their choice of a specialty may be determined by a number of influences. Among these are personality configuration; the approval and encouragement or disapproval and discouragement from senior colleagues, peers, family, teachers, and school; financial motives; and considerations of eventual status in the profession and in the community. Also, the aspirations of the prospective specialist must relate to his or her academic performance as a medical student. Further, the married student's spouse may exert an influence.

In deciding whether to specialize or enter general practice,* a student may be influenced by two social and environmental factors often overlooked. The first of these is pressure from patients. When patients have serious medical problems, they want "the best," and, lacking other bases on which to judge the qualifications of a physician, they will look for credentials from a specialty board as testimony to the practitioner's excellence. The second factor relates to the influence of

---

* Today many students are choosing the relatively new specialty of family medicine rather than entering general practice. The practice, or patient population, is similar, but specialty board certification is available in family medicine.

the federal government. As federal money and involvement increase in the delivery of health care, the government will strengthen its efforts to set up standards for such care. Governmental agencies already use board certification as a convenient criterion to establish standards for such care. The influence of this pressure from the federal government on the trend toward specialization seems obvious, although extensive research is needed to determine its full impact.

Federal actions, other than the one mentioned in the paragraph above, may also influence specialty choice both directly and indirectly. For example, the federal government has subsidized residency training in fields determined to be in short supply and has established individual and collective goals as admission to medical school and/or residency training as a condition for financial support.[13, 15] Further, the government claims a legitimate interest in the matter of residencies and has some leverage at its disposal via the methods of reimbursement for the care of hospitalized Medicaid patients.

Whereas some students come to medical school with their minds firmly fixed on a particular choice, most come with open minds and during the next three or four years examine carefully a number of specialties in the hope of finding the one that best meets their vocational aspirations. The majority of students who enter school with a fixed choice usually change their minds. In fact, nearly three of every four students make career changes between the freshman and senior years.[16]

Switching from one career choice to another in medicine may not be as great a change as one initially thinks. The fact that a significant proportion of specialists have worked in other medical fields before they enter the one in which they practice permanently perhaps attests to the fact that there is not a high degree of difference among the various types of practice. Sixty percent of public health physicians, 25 percent of internists, 32 percent of pathologists, 35 percent of psychiatrists, and 25 percent of surgeons practiced in one or more medical fields before they made their ultimate specialty choice.[6]

FACTORS IN SPECIALTY CHOICE

A number of factors are important in determining the ultimate career or specialty choice of medical students. The factors can be grouped in many ways, such as Funkenstein's division into intrinsic and extrinsic factors,[12] or better, four major categories: (1) personality makeup of the student; (2) student aspirations and life situation; (3) student perceptions of a specialty; and (4) medical school exposure.

Personality Makeup of the Student

The vocation of medicine draws many kinds of people, and each student's personality profoundly affects his or her choice of a specialty. Also, each specialty puts human beings under different stresses and those best suited to withstand the stresses of a particular field of medicine are more likely to enter that field. The relationship between personality factors and the choice of a specialty has been the subject of a number of studies.[7, 12, 26, 28, 32, 41]

In a study done by Livingstone and Zimet, students who planned to enter the specialties of surgery, internal medicine, and pediatrics were found to be significantly more authoritarian than those planning to enter psychiatry.[23] Students planning to become surgeons were at the high end of the authoritarian scale. This should be expected since surgery is the specialty most characterized by protocol, privilege, and hierarchy through the long progression of its training to the intricate rituals of the operating room. A recent study gives pediatrics, as well as psychiatry, a low ranking for authoritarian traits.[24] Actually, authoritarianism is a personality trait common to most physicians.[31]

Extremes of authoritarianism or nonauthoritarianism are potentially crippling for physicians, whatever their specialty. Too much authoritarianism distorts physicians' sense of reality and renders them incapable of a beneficial relationship with their patients; too little authoritarianism makes physicians liable to doubts, to extreme introspectiveness, and to a sensitivity so intense that they are unable to retain any kind of detachment necessary for useful service to a suffering human being.

The personality structure of some students is such that they prefer working with acute problems that lend themselves to immediate, clear-cut treatments resulting in rapid recovery. In the choice of a specialty and the choice of patients, they avoid the chronic. There are few who can tolerate well the burden of chronic illness. The interest in acute problems has been a major factor in the development of new specialties such as emergency medicine and intensive care.

Students' tolerance for uncertainty or ambiguity may strongly influence their choice of a specialty, as mentioned in a previous chapter on this topic.[3, 25, 49] Students who find it difficult to accept uncertainties often elect the fields of medicine where there is less likelihood of uncertainty. Persons vary widely as to their conscious awareness of the influence of uncertainty. Choosing a subspecialty narrows the range of potential uncertainty with which the doctor will have to deal.

Correlating personality attributes and specialty choice is not easy, but certain attributes can be identified as being consistent with clusters of homogeneous medical specialties.[40] In a study by Yufit and associates, specialties were divided into "people-oriented" and "technique-oriented" (less involvement with patients).[41] The clustering of people-oriented medical specialties revealed that groups of students selecting these specialties had some similarities in their personality structures. Also, these similar personality traits were meaningfully related to the activities characterizing these specialties. There was a more concise homogeneity of personality attributes of students selecting technique-oriented specialties than of those selecting people-oriented specialties where involvement with patients was more intense. Thus, differing personal attributes or needs are thought to influence specialty choice, leading to the conclusion that personality influences occupational choice.

Funkenstein divides students into "bioscientific" and "biosocial" types and labels careers in the same way.[12] Bioscientific careers include careers in basic sciences and in subspecialty practice. These careers attract physicians with scientific education of a high order and research skills. Although adeptness in interpersonal relations and ability to use knowledge of human behavior would be desirable, they are not obligatory. "Bioscientific" medical students have aptitudes, interests, and preparation consistent with being scientists and have a strong interest in intellectual achievement. Their scientific preparation is extensive, particularly in research and in the quantitative aspects of science. Biosocial careers encompass two major subcategories—"biointerpersonal" and "biobehavioral." Biointerpersonal careers require good skills in interpersonal relations, a strong service orientation, and an ability to apply science pragmatically to patients' problems. The general practitioner or family physician is the best example of this type of physician. Biobehavioral careers demand knowledge of human behavior and the ability to apply this knowledge in patient care. Psychiatry is the best example of a specialty under this classification. Many specialties combine different degrees of skills and interests, in varying combinations. This is especially true of primary care specialties. For example, the physician in the new specialty of family medicine needs interpersonal skills, the ability to apply science pragmatically, and an interest in the social and behavioral sciences.

What is noteworthy in any discussion of the effect of underlying personality traits, values, and attitudes in a particular specialty choice is that these traits, values, and attitudes are not formed to any significant extent during medical training but are present before medical school as part of the intricate weave of personality. Livingstone and Zimet state the situation well: "The medical student discovers the surgeon or psychiatrist or other specialist within himself and the hand of his values and attitudes slips into the glove of his future vocation."[23]

Student Aspirations and Life Situation

From images of the different specialties—images based more on hearsay and preconception than on precise knowledge—the student chooses a specialty. What image or specialty best fits the needs and self-image of the student? Factors operating within the individual and related to one's needs and self-image may be both conscious and unconscious.

There is the likelihood that a student's specialty choice is strongly influenced by financial and other commitments. For example, a student may want to become a surgeon but is compelled, in a sense, to enter general practice because of age or lack of financial resources or because of a fellowship which requires him or her to practice general medicine in a rural area.

Studies have shown a relationship between choice of specialty and parents' socioeconomic background.[20] The student's choice of a particular specialty may relate not only to current interests but also to past life situations.

There have been discussions about the influence of one's family name on the choice of a specialty. One may ask, if in a proper whimsical state, if certain names suggest a relationship. For example, among practicing physicians today, one finds Dr. Belcher and Dr. Rumble in gastroenterology, Dr. Brain in neurology, Dr. Hyman and Dr. Love in obstetrics-gynecology, Dr. Eye in ophthalmology, Dr. Finger and Dr. Hipp in orthopedics, Dr. Child and Dr. Little in pediatrics, Dr. Prettyman in plastic surgery, Dr. Comfort and Dr. Looney in psychiatry, Dr. Butcher and Dr. Cutter in surgery, and Dr. Semens and Dr. Waters in urology.

Student Perceptions of a Specialty

Medical students have definite ideas about the types of people who enter the various specialties. Whereas these ideas may change somewhat during the years in medical school, they remain noticeably stable during the preclinical and clinical years.* Korman and Stubblefield found a striking amount of fixation in medical students' categorizations

---

* Preclinical refers here to the first two years of medical school and clinical to the third and fourth years. The sharp division between the preclinical and clinical years is disappearing in medical schools today, however, because correlations of basic science and clinical topics as well as introductory courses in clinical medicine begin in the first year of medical school.

of physicians despite experiences over four years of medical education.[19] Also, in two studies done by Bruhn and Parsons dealing with student attitudes toward medical specialties, it was discovered that preclinical and clinical students showed considerable agreement in ascribing traits to the various specialties. Clinical students' characterizations of these specialties differed from those of preclinical students only in the former's changes in emphasis on certain traits. Furthermore, while students planning to enter a particular specialty emphasized the positive traits of their specialty, their stereotype did not differ greatly from students not choosing this specialty. Students saw themselves as possessing many of the traits that they ascribed to specialists in their chosen field.[4, 5]

Exactly how a student perceives a particular specialty is not as important for this discussion as the criteria the student uses in assessing the various specialties. Students speak freely of the kind of practice they hope eventually to have. They debate with each other the good and bad points of the many specialties. Becker and his associates, in *Boys in White*, have evolved 12 basic themes for classifying the various criteria used by students to assess the specialties.[2] I have put these basic themes in the form of questions without amplification, for each is self-explanatory.

1. Does this specialty have sufficient intellectual depth and breadth to keep one challenged and interested?
2. Are the medical problems encompassed by this specialty manageable in the light of our present state of knowledge?
3. What kinds of special skills or personality characteristics are required for success in this particular specialty?
4. What amount of heavy medical responsibility, of serious decision making regarding life and death is thrust constantly upon the specialist in this field?
5. In this specialty is one able to have a close relationship with patients of a kind one likes—a relationship that has no depressing or unpleasant aspects.
6. What types of nonspecific feelings, either positive or negative, are aroused by this specialty?
7. How long a period of residency training is required for this specialty?
8. Do students have a good experience while working in this specialty in medical school?
9. Are those practicing this specialty required to live in a large city in order to have a sufficient pool of potential patients?

10. Does this specialty have great prestige with the public and with one's medical colleagues?
11. Are convenient working hours and work that is not too hard possible in this specialty?
12. Does this specialty allow one to make an adequate amount of money?

Students do not use all of these criteria equally regarding specialty choice. They use some more than others and apply some more frequently to one specialty than another. Not surprisingly, many students give less attention to such criteria as money, hours, and prestige and pay more attention to the criterion of intellectual breadth, to the notion that their future work either must make use of all they know or must not be so broad as to preclude their knowing enough to do a good job.[2] The other criteria which rank high show a similar concern with the medical characteristics of the work—what the specialty offers for helping patients who need a doctor's care, the level of responsibility demanded, and one's adequacy in assuming this responsibility. In other words, students' concerns as reflected in these criteria are the concerns contained in their idealistic long-range perspective.

Factors other than economic rewards appear to play major roles in specialty selection. Many in medicine are fearful that this will change because of the astounding differences between the lowest paid and the highest paid specialists in medicine. For example, pediatricians and psychiatrists hold down the low side of the pay scale while surgeons, pathologists and radiologists are among the group on the high side. As Eaton has pointed out, clearly the social hierarchy envisioned by Plato—the greatest rewards going to those professions dealing with abstractions and concepts, the smallest rewards to those who use manual skills and techniques—does not hold for the specialists in medicine.[10]

Medical School Exposure

Every specialty attempts to attract the best and most suitable students. Faculty influence on specialty choice is a multifaceted phenomenon. Certain specialty choices, such as psychiatry and surgery, for example, may owe less to medical school faculty influence than do pathology and obstetrics. In other words, many of the students choosing the first two specialties may have had a long-standing interest in or at least knowledge of the fields in question, whereas those interested in the last two are possibly more open to influence. One can conclude from observation that faculty influence on specialty choice is greatest usually in the case of specialties that are less familiar before the student enters medical school. At the same time, one must remember that a strong negative influence regarding a well-known specialty such as surgery or psychiatry may result in a student changing his or her commitment to that specialty. For example, the student comes to medical school planning to be a surgeon but has unhappy experiences on the surgical service and is repelled by surgeon teachers. Surgery may be eliminated from that student's list of specialty considerations.

Dr. Theodore Drapanas, while chairman of the Tulane Medical School's department of surgery, concluded from personal observations that many medical students going into the specialty of surgery are attracted to it by great models whom they have had as teachers in medical school. Thus, strong professors with strong programs at a medical school attract students into the specialties represented by these professors and programs. Dr. Thorpe Ray, distinguished medical educator, shares Dr. Drapanas's view. In interviewing students applying for postgraduate medical training, Dr. Ray has for years asked them about the most significant factor entering into their choice of a particular specialty. Almost invariably, Dr. Ray emphasizes, the student's choice of a specialty is related to a strong model who has appealed to the student. One can ask Dr. Drapanas and Dr. Ray if these strong models did not serve to strengthen or confirm an earlier interest of many students.

A medical school faculty needs strong persons in every specialty. Using direct experience as the basic teaching method, each student can observe the nature of the discipline, the limits of competence of its professional members, how they contribute to patient care, what each specialty means to the patient, and how each student can work with the specialty.

Funkenstein's studies at Harvard differ from the observations of Drapanas and Ray. Funkenstein's data, collected over two decades, do not support the belief that the influence of faculty as role models is a strong determinant in specialty choice of students. "In none of the years of studying Harvard medical students, alumni/ae or our national sample of students," according to Funkenstein, "did more than 18 percent of the students feel that anyone on the faculty had influenced their choice of a career."[12] Funkenstein's 18 percent seems much too low when all specialty choices are considered.

A facet of role modeling must be mentioned here: "trait-modeling" versus "person-modeling." One generally assumes that trainees pick particular individuals as total or global models of a "good" professional and adjust their own behavior accordingly. A study by Stelling and

Bucher reveals that the process is not that simple.[39] They describe the most common kind of modeling as "trait-modeling," as opposed to "person-modeling." Trainees pick and choose from among the traits or characteristics they observe in the professionals around them, building their own version of the kind of professional they want to become. For example, a student might emulate the bedside manner of one, the teaching skills of another, and the work efficiency of a third. In other words, in the Stelling and Bucher study, students rarely reported taking one person as a complete role model. Thus, a composite of several may become the student's model.

Probably strong faculty members in a particular specialty reflect a strong program, and the strong program becomes a significant influence in that medical school. Anyway, a strong program is an important influence in specialty choice. For example, Nielsen found the quality of psychiatric educational programs in medical school, as measured by the peer review ratings of National Institute of Mental Health Grants, to correlate significantly with the percentage of graduates of each school who entered psychiatry.[29]

Factors other than strong models and strong programs, however, may be key influences in certain choices. For example, some of the new specialties do not have many strong models or programs around to influence students. When a graduating senior was asked recently about his specialty interest, he replied, "Intensive care." He went on to say that he and a few of his peers were intending to specialize in the treatment of "critical care" patients. Of course, there are models and programs available in this developing specialty, but not in abundance. At the same time, one can think of cardiologist Paul Dudley White, whose professional lifetime spanned the evolution of cardiology. He became a great pioneer and model but did not have in his early professional years the type of model or program to follow that he furnished for others in subsequent years.

Faculty members in medical school can play a more active role in specialty recruitment than simply that of serving as role models by their presence in the environment. Mature physicians who have devoted their careers to a particular field in medicine want to enlist the most promising young candidates as their junior colleagues. A top-ranking student at Cornell University Medical College reported an incident illustrative of a subtle recruitment approach: "After we had seen the patient and decided on his disposition, Dr. F. lowered his voice and said to me, 'What do you intend to do after medical school?' I told him internal medicine, and he said 'Good!' So far as I am concerned, this is a big fat pat on the back, and I don't know whom I'd rather have it come from. . . . It is nice to know that Dr. F. approves of me."[18]

COMING TO A DECISION

When a person is confronted by a complicated situation which arouses both approach and avoidance tendencies, one must resolve the conflict before one can reach a goal. The medical student usually experiences such conflict in the selection of a specialty. Often the conflict may be great and produce disturbing symptoms. Since finding a suitable specialty is a process of fitting one's personality (including needs, attitudes, values, and traits) to a given area of medicine, increased knowledge of oneself and the occupational role requirements should reduce the conflict and thus facilitate the process of choosing. Fortunately, medical school provides the student with opportunities for acquiring both self-knowledge and career role knowledge.

Most students begin to think seriously about specialization in their first or second year of medical school. Those who enter medical school with a specialty choice already in mind begin early to reexamine their choice. Without direct experience with clinical role requirements, students are seriously handicapped in choosing among specialties. Formerly, students had no experience with clinical role requirements until their junior year clinical clerkships. This has changed considerably today. Prior to coming to medical school, many students work in hospitals in a variety of clinical situations and learn an astonishing amount concerning the work of the different specialties. Furthermore, many medical schools are ensuring that students have some exposure to patients commensurate with their level of preparation from the beginning of their medical education. The motivating value of being able to work with live patients from one's entrance in medical school may be expected to pay high dividends in other areas, such as improved morale. Many medical educators hypothesize that students whose clerkship experiences are spread over three or four years instead of two will arrive at specific occupational goals sooner and that after a goal is chosen fewer of these individuals will shift to another career.

Seegal points out that students handicap themselves in reaching sound decisions regarding career opportunities by failing to undertake a rigorous personal inventory.[36] Most of these medical students have avoided the discipline of subjecting themselves to a searching inquiry. Seegal observed that while students will involve themselves in endless "bull sessions" regarding the prestige of one training program over another, they skillfully avoid the more important questions that only they can answer: "What kind of person am I? How do my personal qualities, assets, and liabilities compare with those of my classmates? What are the professional and nonprofessional opportunities in life which give me satisfaction, a sense of purpose, and fulfillment? Have I the stuff to realize my goals?" Seegal recommends for students, before seeking counsel from preceptors about career choices, a form of spiritual retreat similar to that practiced by religious groups over the centuries. The retreat for contemplation may be an abbreviated one, such as visiting a chapel for several hours, a long solitary walk, or a sojourn by the sea. In their exploration, during such a retreat, they must take a realistic look at themselves—past, present, and future. Such an opportunity may implement Emerson's statement: "Nothing can bring you peace but yourself." After the retreat and diligent efforts at self-appraisal, students are better prepared for a meaningful encounter with their advisors for reviewing assets, liabilities, and hopes. Effective communication and rational decisions then become possible between the students and advisors. And fortunately, most medical schools have developed faculty-student advisory systems to help in residency decision making.[43]

Self-evaluation can also be facilitated by discussions with advisors. Moreover, such tests as the Edwards Personal Preference Schedule (EPPS) and the Allport-Vernon-Lindzey Study of Values (AVL) may be used by the advisor to help in certain areas. For example, these tests differentiate the academically-oriented individual from the practice-oriented one.[34] Other tests may also be useful in gathering important information in an analysis of the individual's resources, weaknesses, and aspirations.

PSYCHOLOGICAL THOUGHTS ON DIFFERENT SPECIALTIES

Both the public and the medical profession tend to do some stereotyping of the people who are attracted to certain specialties. Also "myths" or "images" are perpetuated about particular specialists. Some take such observations seriously, while others view them with amused indifference. It seems appropriate, however, to look psychologically behind the stereotypes, myths, humor, and dynamics in specialty practice or choice. Such an endeavor may be self-revealing about where we fit in the myths or the myth-making.

Hans Zinsser has quoted his Uncle Fritz as saying: "Doctors may be roughly divided into physicians who know a lot but can't do anything and surgeons who can do a great deal but don't know very much."[43]

Nolen in his book *The Making of a Surgeon* describes a surgeon's key motives as impatience: "The guy that goes into surgery is the fellow who doesn't want to sit around waiting for results . . . he wants the quick cure of the scalpel, not the slow cure of the pill."[30] Doctor X, in *Intern*, describes this characteristic of the surgeon even more pointedly: "The surgeon regards himself as the one who cures with the stroke of the knife, scorning the internist's pills, promises, prayers, and postmortems."[8] Nolen identifies another trait a surgeon needs: conceit. He needs conceit to sustain him in trying moments when "he's battered by the doubts and uncertainties that are part of the practice of medicine."

Surgery is often spoken of as a sublimated form of sadism. There is no reason to think that surgeons are more sadistic than other people. The opposite may well be true. It is possible that surgeons have less unconscious guilt about their sadistic proclivities than most people and hence do not need to repress them but are able to use them constructively. They can sublimate sadistic impulses in a highly approved form of behavior. Strong public appeal is obvious in the dramatic interest which attaches to the surgical operation and the romantic interest which attaches to the surgeon. Surgeon and writer Richard Selzer characterizes well both the surgeon and surgical practice in answer to a question, why a surgeon would write: "It is to search for some meaning in the ritual of surgery, which is at once murderous, painful, healing, and full of love."[37] It is commonly believed that surgeons are most at home when operating. Selzer supports that belief in eloquent language: "One enters the body in surgery, as in love, as though one were in exile returning at last to his hearth, daring uncharted darkness in order to reach home."[37]

The surgeon's work is predominantly in the hands, with little use of the voice. Albert Schweitzer, the theologian, musician and philosopher, was asked why he turned to medicine and surgery when he was already well established in other fields. He replied: "I wanted to be a doctor that I might be able to work without having to talk. For years I had been giving myself out in words, and it was with joy that I had followed the calling of theological teacher and of preacher. But this new form of activity I could not represent to myself as being talking about the religion of love, but only as an actual putting of it into practice."[35]

The surgeon is perceived, especially by medical students, as being domineering and arrogant, aggressive, full of energy, and mainly concerned with his or her own prestige.[5]

Among specialists, surgeons have probably seen their specialty keep its "identity" more clearly than others and suffer from fewer "invasions" from outsiders. Favazza has stated the situation well:

> There is something comforting about the company of surgeons. Many other physicians who were once proud of their highly refined sensory diagnostic skills are now often beholden to labora-

tory technicians. Psychiatrists are busy defending themselves against the assaults of libertarian lawyers and against the masses of self-proclaimed "therapists" who offer a smorgasbord of psychic delights ranging from levitation to salvation. But surgeons stand secure. Neither nurses nor barbers nor butchers nor ministers are making claims about their own surgical proficiency. Confident and audacious, today's surgeons hold much of medicine's glamour.[11]

The jokes and speculations regarding the motivation for specializing in psychiatry exceed those related to most specialties. The psychiatrist has a professional interest in lonely, eccentric, and unloved people, and such an interest is likely to be a projection of the psychiatrist's own problems. The psychiatrist also has a deep interest in how the mind works, how it is controlled, or how it is healed. This interest may be a concern about the maintenance of one's own mental health. The psychiatrist indulges at times in feelings of arrogance and omnipotence. Since the things of the mind transcend those of the body, the psychiatrist may feel that he or she is operating on a higher plane than colleagues who deal with more mundane matters. The following bit of humor may contain more than a grain of truth: "The psychiatrist thinks he is God. The psychologist would like to be God. And the social worker is content just to be the mother of God." While the surgeon hides behind a mask, the psychiatrist has an even more protective shield—nomenclature.

A more realistic and less fanciful picture of the psychiatrist may be drawn from the following report. According to a recent study by Eagle and Marcos, medical students who choose psychiatry as a specialty are likely to be single, from big cities, politically liberal, interested in humanitarian ideas but not formal religion.[9] The authors' review of the literature indicates that students who decide to become psychiatrists are more people-oriented, nurturing, reflective, and open-minded. Also, these students are less concerned with power and status than most of their classmates. Further, those who select psychiatry tend to have a high capacity for tolerating ambiguity, tend to have considerable general anxiety, fear of death, and low self-esteem, as well as score low on authoritarianism.

In obstetrics, possibly, the childhood longing to know where babies come from is repeatedly and directly gratified. Karl Menninger goes a step further and points out that perhaps even more significant than curiosity is the factor of identification with the mother.[26] Hostility toward the mother is also mentioned often in psychoanalytic discussions. The Women's Movement may find it revealing to inquire why so many normal ovaries are removed and virtually no normal testicles.

The urologist had been kidded probably as much as any other specialist regarding motivation. This has helped the urologist to be more open-minded and at the same time more immune to speculations regarding motivation. During the phallic stage of child development, the child thinks that the penis is the most important organ of the body. Can it be that the urologist never surrenders that childhood assessment of the penis as the body's number one organ? Further, regarding childhood development, someone has mentioned facetiously that the urologist is the little kid peeping through the keyhole into the master bedroom, watching attentively special activities of the mother and father.

In the spirit of Freud, it can be said that proctologists have their preoccupation with the anal stage of development. They work with patients who share their interest in anal pursuits such as money making, plumbing, and bathroom activities while being highly fastidious regarding smells, cleanliness, and excretion. The patients of proctologists are usually ashamed to admit that they need them.

Internal medicine is one of the more scholarly specialties in medicine and in many ways the foundation of most other specialties. Internists are often spoken of as diagnosticians since the complicated problems of diagnosis are sent to them. They view themselves as the true physicians and healers. Among the attributes of the internist must be a liking for and aptitude for problem solving. Also the internist has become the family physician and participates in a doctor-patient relationship not unlike that of the family or general practitioner. Further, the internist bears a heavy responsibility in caring for the chronically ill and aged.[22] In the medical school setting, internists are not averse to overestimating the importance of their specialty in medical student teaching. They often feel that medical students should begin and end their clinical rotations in internal medicine. Someone has paraphrased Jesus' statement and applied it to the internist: "Verily I say unto you, no student cometh unto Hippocrates but by me."

Many doctors tend to mother their patients. In pediatrics, however, the maternal role is truly conspicuous. Pediatricians are highly respected because their young patients are very special people with special problems that frighten other specialists. All are happy to have pediatricians around with the know-how, the guts, and the patience to care for the troubles of these cherished, protected, but highly vulnerable patients. Also, pediatricians have probably done the best job of all doctors in high-level preventive medicine by orienting their major efforts toward keeping their patients healthy.

Kubie feels that considerable attention should be paid to unconscious determinants of behavior in physicians, for widely varying forms of scientific interest can serve as an acceptable cover for some of the forbidden concerns of childhood.* In other words, the scientific activities of adults can be distorted by the same unconscious childhood conflicts out of which their original interest in science may have arisen. This results whenever adult activities continue to represent earlier conflicts, and projections of unconscious personal conflicts can often be recognized through their adult scientific disguises.

As an example of the role of unconscious residues of childhood battles, Kubie cites the gynecologist whose ancient and infantile curiosities were not satisfied by the justified activities of his profession and who was plagued by an insatiable compulsion to visit burlesque shows. "One could hardly ask for a better experimental demonstration of the fact that unconscious needs cannot be gratified by conscious fulfillment. A comparable example is found in the x-ray man whose choice of career was determined predominantly by his unconscious curiosity about the internal structure of his mother's body. In all innocence, both men dedicated their lives to the service of childhood cravings which were buried in guilt and fear."[21] Most psychiatrists can pull from their files the case histories of numerous gifted persons who have built their lives on such psychological quicksand.

CONCLUSION

Although many factors can be identified as significant determinants in the choice of a specialty, other factors remain hidden or unidentified. The interaction of the many influences or factors is difficult to determine.[1] Further studies are needed to obtain a greater insight into how the medical educational environment affects the final decision-making process. It is obvious that the medical school environment will readily affect some values, but other values may be so deeply rooted in students' personal background as to withstand powerful influences for change. Entering medical students' decisions about a specialty are based on images of themselves and of medicine. During medical school, their own experiences and their observation of doctors operate to bring their self-image as trainees and the doctor-image of the all-knowing healer to the realistic focus of the scientific physician.[33]

In summary, among the factors entering into the choice of a specialty may be the prestige of a specialty, past life situation of the student, personality makeup, medical school experiences (both clinical and preclinical), patient contact, anticipated income, and faculty influences. Probably an important determinant of specialty choice is the influence

---

* Simmel discussed views similar to those of Kubie.[38]

of great teacher practitioners whom students have as teachers in medical school. Today, this influence may actually precede medical school since many college students work in hospitals and have considerable contact with the physicians practicing there. Later, experiences in medical school will couple with these earlier experiences in either a positive or negative fashion in the student's evaluation of the different specialties.

REFERENCES

1. Anderson RBW: Choosing a medical specialty: A critique of literature in light of curious findings. J Health Soc Behav 16:152, 1975
2. Becker HS, et al.: Boys in White. Chicago, University of Chicago Press, 1961, pp 401–418
3. Brudner S: Intolerance of ambiguity as a personality variable. J Per 30:29, 1962
4. Bruhn JG, Parsons OA: Attitudes toward medical specialties: Two follow-up studies. J Med Educ 40:273, 1965
5. Bruhn JG, Parsons OA: Medical student attitudes toward four specialties. J Med Educ 35:40, 1964
6. Coker RE Jr, et al.: Medical careers in public health. Milbank Mem Fund Q 44:239, 1966
7. Coker RE Jr, et al.: Patterns of influence: Medical school faculty members and the values and specialty interests of medical students. J Med Educ 35:518, 1960
8. Doctor X: Intern. Greenwich, Connecticut, Fawcett, 1966, p 16
9. Eagle PF, Marcos LR: Factors in medical students' choice of psychiatry. Am J Psychiatry 137:423, 1980
10. Eaton JS: The psychiatrist and psychiatric education. In Freedman AM, Kaplan HE, Sadock BJ (eds): Comprehensive Textbook of Psychiatry, ed 3. Baltimore, Williams & Wilkins, 1980, pp 2926–2946
11. Favazza AR: Willie of Guy's. MD Magazine 24:17, 1980
12. Funkenstein DH: Factors affecting career choices of medical students, 1958–1976. In Shapiro EC, Lowenstein LM (eds): Becoming a Physician—Development of Values and Attitudes in Medicine. Cambridge, Massachusetts, Ballinger, 1979, pp 187–201
13. Ginzberg E: The federal government's physician manpower policies. In Shapiro EC, Lowenstein LM (eds): Becoming a Physician—Development of Values and Attitudes in Medicine. Cambridge, Massachusetts, Ballinger, 1979, pp 261–272
14. Gough HG: Specialty choice of physicians and medical students. J Med Educ 50:581, 1975
15. Hanft, RS: Effect of federal policy on career decisions and practice patterns. In Shapiro EC, Lowenstein LM (eds): Becoming a Physician—De-

velopment of Values and Attitudes in Medicine. Cambridge, Massachusetts, Ballinger 1979, pp 249–260

16. Held ML, Zimet CN: A longitudinal study of medical specialty choice and certainty level. J Med Educ 50:1044, 1975
17. Jonas S: Medical Mystery—the Training of Doctors in the United States. New York, Norton, 1978
18. Kendall PL: Medical specialization: Trends and contributing factors. In Coombs RH, Vincent CE (eds): Psychosocial Aspects of Medical Training. Springfield, Illinois, Thomas, 1971, pp 449–497
19. Korman M, Stubblefield RL: Role perceptions in freshmen and senior students. JAMA 184:287, 1963
20. Kritzer H, Zimet CN: A retrospective view of medical specialty choice. J Med Educ 42:47, 1967
21. Kubie LS: Some unsolved problems of the scientific career. Am Sci 41:597, 1953
22. Kutner NG: Medical students' orientation toward the chronically ill. J Med Educ 53:111, 1978
23. Livingstone PB, Zimet CN: Death anxiety, authoritarianism and choice of specialty in medical students. J Nerv Ment Dis 140:222, 1965
24. Light D Jr: Becoming psychiatrists. New York, Norton, 1980
25. Matteson MT, Smith SV: Selection of medical specialties: Preferences versus choices. J Med Educ 52:548, 1977
26. Menninger K: Psychological factors in the choice of medicine as a profession. Bull Menninger Clin 21:51, 1957
27. Mock HE: Skull Fractures and Brain Injuries. Philadelphia, Williams & Wilkins, 1950, Dedication
28. Mowbray RM, Davies B: Personality factors in choice of medical specialty. Br J Med Educ 5:110, 1971
29. Nielsen AC: Choosing psychiatry: The importance of psychiatric education in medical school. Am J Psychiatry 137:428, 1980
30. Nolen WA: The Making of a Surgeon. New York, Random House, 1970
31. Oaken D: The doctor's job: An update. Psychosom Med 40:449, 1978
32. Paiva RE, Haley HB: Intellectual, personality, and environmental factors in career specialty choices. J Med Educ 46:281, 1971
33. Rezler AG: Vocational choice in medicine. J Med Educ 44:285, 1969
34. Schumacher CF: Interest and personality factors as related to choice of a medical career. J Med Educ 38:932, 1963
35. Schweitzer A: Out of My Life and Thought. New York, Holt, 1949
36. Seegal D: The retreat: A time and place for self-examination. J Med Educ 39:410, 1964
37. Selzer R: Mortal Lessons: Notes on the Art of Surgery. New York, Simon & Schuster, 1974, pp 15, 25
38. Simmel E: The doctor-game, illness and the profession of medicine. Int J Psychoanal 7:470, 1926
39. Stelling JG, Bucher R: Professional Cloning: The patterning of physicians. In Shapiro EC, Lowenstein LM (eds): Becoming a Physician—Develop-

ment of Values and Attitudes in Medicine. Cambridge, Massachusetts, Ballinger, 1979, pp 139–162

40. Walton HJ, Last JM: Young doctors aiming to enter different specialties. Br Med J 2:752, 1969
41. Yufit RI, Pollock GH, Wassermann E: Medical specialty choice and personality—initial results and predictions. Arch Gen Psychiatry 20:89, 1969
42. Zimny GH, Senturia AG: Medical specialty counseling: A survey. J Med Educ 48:336, 1973
43. Zinsser H: Hospital days. In Davenport WH (ed): The Good Physician. New York, Macmillan, 1962

13

SENSE AND SENSITIVITY IN MEDICAL ETHICS

Man is a reed, but a thinking reed; all our dignity consists in thought. Endeavor then to think well; it is the only morality.

—Blaise Pascal

With progress in medicine, technical decisions become easier, while moral problems and ethical decision making become increasingly significant and often difficult. Today's medical students find themselves in the midst of more revolutionary changes than have ever taken place before in their profession. These changes bring a continuous confrontation with decisions that must be made on an ethical or a moral basis.* With the advent of transplantation surgery, artificial organs, new methods of birth control, genetic manipulation, changing attitudes about abortion, and a host of other issues, the students and their physician teachers are having to rethink the old standards and guidelines of medical ethics. How should they feel, think, and act about these new practices and their consequences?

The rapid advance of technology is making the questions more relevant, urgent, and challenging. The theoretical has become or is rapidly becoming the actual. The technical advances in medicine have greatly increased the power of physicians. Formerly there were only a few things physicians could do for their patients, but now they have the power and skill to do many things. This power is growing daily—power with dimensions that are sometimes frightening.

In movies and literature, side by side with the glorification of science is expressed the age-old fear of peering too deeply into the secrets of nature, lest one desire to master powers beyond one's skill and, by tampering with forbidden secrets, bring down disaster upon oneself.[24] The same fear is implied in the title of Augenstein's book *Come, Let Us Play God,* although the book itself is a very realistic and interesting

---

* Often "ethics" and "morality" tend to be interchanged as though they were synonymous terms; however, the word "morality" is usually reserved for behavior according to custom, and the word "ethics" for behavior according to reason or reflection upon the foundations and principles of behavior.

appraisal of the applications and implications of the new scientific developments in medicine.[4] The public, in all good will, is afraid that medical scientists who push too far in their search for new knowledge may find themselves in a situation similar to Faust's. Faust, while fastening his eyes on the highest and noblest objects, suffered shipwreck in consequence of his bold, ambitious plans, and in the strife with the conditions which surrounded him lost all, including himself.*

ETHICAL AMBIGUITIES AND
SCIENTIFIC DEVELOPMENTS

Critical philosophical and moral issues related to the new technologies in the health field are discussed widely today. Along with our skills to manipulate the physical environment have come enormous skills to manipulate the brain as well as every other organ system of the body.

Writers such as Albert Rosenfeld, in *The Second Genesis,* group the new developments related to life and death into three categories: (1) the refurbishing of the individual or prolongation of life through gadgetry (transplantable and implantable organs and other body manipulations); (2) prenativity explorations (biomedical manipulations of the fetus, asexual reproduction, and genetic manipulations); (3) control of brain and behavior (surface and deep brain electrodes, pharmacological agents, and psychological manipulation through stress and other techniques).[56]

The transplantation of real organs, as well as the development of artificial ones, raises questions as to the nature of life itself and what is contributed to or taken away from the quality of life. Will the current advances in organ transplantation give rise to what has been described by Nobel Prize winner Joshua Lederberg as "the potential dehumanizing abuses of a market in human flesh"? Does human identity pose a limit on the repairing and replacing that can be done? " 'There's nothing anyone can do,' the old man whispered. 'Even without your gadgets, medic, you know what's wrong with me. You can't mend a whole body, not with all your skills and all your fancy instruments. The body wears out.... And even if you gave me a new body, you still couldn't

---

* It should be noted that it is the Marlowe or Christian Faust, not Goethe's, who is damned.[22] The latter will be saved as long as he strives. In a sense, this hubris was part of post-Christian humanism—the hope of modern man that Promethean intentions themselves secure salvation. Some of the disaffection with modern technology is perhaps the realization that such hubris can result in ill-considered technological advance and perhaps in tragedy.

help me, because down deep, where your knives can't reach and your instruments can't measure, is the me that is old beyond repair.' "[25] This passage from a science fiction novel raises a question about a dimension of life that cannot be overlooked by physicians today with their splendid array of technical equipment.

Both the patient and the physician may see that death is imminent. Yet the patient's death can be held at bay almost indefinitely with techniques and a technology that can feed, breathe for, and fashion artificial organs for the patient or, as in the case of kidney or heart transplants, replace organs with those of a donor. Such a patient may not be *living* in any acceptable human sense, and the triumphs of modern science may be interfering with one's right to die. Actually, many of the mechanical procedures now in use ought perhaps to be regarded in their proper function as temporary. Their purpose is to win time for the restorative measures to take place. If, after these mechanical measures have been given a fair trial, it becomes evident that the patient can never be restored to functioning on his or her own, it may be said that these mechanical procedures have failed in their purpose. All they are accomplishing is keeping the patient in a condition of artificially arrested death, and they should therefore be discontinued.

Other new developments have given increasing importance to the necessity of determining precisely the onset of death. For example, since the success of a transplant may depend on the prompt transfer of a viable organ, the physician has to determine precisely the onset of death in the donor. The widespread discussion of the issue of death is focused in part on eliminating legal barriers to the granting and procuring of human organs. A new definition of death has been developed since the traditional concept—cessation of heartbeat and respiration—is obviously inadequate in an age when these once final signs often can be reversed and the patient can be kept alive on mechanical respirators and pacemakers.

The American Bar Association House of Delegates has voted to define death legally as the total cessation of brain function rather than the cessation of the heartbeat. In passing the measure, the American Bar Association indicated that the traditional heart-stoppage definition relied on by the courts has become obsolete with the advent of the heart-lung machine and other medical equipment that can keep a patient alive in a limited sense with no brain function. This position is based on the concept of brain death delineated by the Ad Hoc Committee of the Harvard Medical School, in 1968.[1] Under guidelines developed by the Harvard Committee, a physician can pronounce a patient dead if the patient shows the absence of brain waves on the electroencephalogram for 24 hours, together with a lack of spontaneous breathing, fixed and dilated pupils, and no response to external stimulation. The Harvard criteria were adopted principally to enable surgeons to remove organs for transplantation while the donor's heart was still beating and the organs remained viable. Further, these criteria can also be used by physicians as acceptable evidence that life supports can be withdrawn with impunity.

Maintaining a clear sense of moral priorities can become extremely difficult, of course, when dealing with a potential donor who is being kept alive by mechanical means. At such a time, the surgeon, knowing that a patient is waiting in the wings for a kidney or a heart, may feel the pressure to stop resuscitation measures. One approach for meeting such an untenable situation has been to trust the vital decision to an independent medical team that has no professional or emotional investment in the potential donor or recipient. There is, however, no simple formula for finding the solution to this or similar problems in the doctor-patient relationship.

Recent biochemical and genetic developments have brought new methods of influencing conception, genetic potential, and fetal growth and development. Also, potential for corrective intervention at every stage of embryonic development is rapidly becoming a reality. Humorist Max Shulman once reported the touching case of a man who had been conceived in a laboratory, entirely by artificial techniques. Although orphaned before birth by science, the man developed a normal human craving for communication with his parents. Finally, after years of disappointment and frustration, he worked out a way to express his pent-up filial affection: "Every Father's Day he sent a tie to a test-tube in Kansas City." Two decades ago, when that heartwarming but zany tale appeared, asexual reproduction was only a vision. No longer is this the case. The terms "genetic engineering" and "genetic manipulation" have come into common parlance, and the knowledge represented by these terms raises possibilities that are sometimes frightening, sometimes heartbreaking—but seldom funny.

A number of hereditary diseases can already be diagnosed in utero by amniocentesis and then prevented by abortion. With further advances in genetics our concept of human rights and our concern with the quality of life will be enriched with a new right, that of being born without the handicap of a readily preventable serious genetic defect.

Two recent medical breakthroughs using gene transplants involve insulin and interferon. Scientists have gotten bacteria to produce insulin identical to that produced by the human body. Many diabetics now take animal insulin, which is in short supply and sometimes leads to allergic reactions in patients. The bacteria-produced insulin has a good chance of overcoming both the supply and the allergic problems. Biological researchers have used gene transplants to produce interferon, a protein found naturally in the human body in minute amounts. It is suspected that interferon could be a potent weapon in fighting viral infections, ranging from infectious hepatitis to the common cold. If some alarmists had had their way a few years ago, the research never could have been conducted.

Back in the mid-1970s, a group of politicians and scientists wanted to put severe restrictions on research in recombinant DNA. There was concern that infectious new organisms would escape from laboratories and contaminate surrounding neighborhoods. In part, to forestall local movements to ban recombinant research, the National Institutes of Health instituted some fairly stringent guidelines, one which prevented the use of human materials in gene transplants. These guidelines have since been relaxed, as NIH recognized that the fears of dangerous new bacteria were greatly exaggerated. Although laboratory researchers have now been working with recombinants for years, not a single illness has resulted. At the same time, this is not to suggest that risks don't remain. It is impossible to live in a risk-free world, and we must be careful not to try to legislate away all medical dangers and in turn deny ourselves some wondrous benefits.[61]

Abortion remains an issue. Some contend that the real issue is not abortion but compulsory pregnancy. Should a woman be compelled to carry a pregnancy to term against her will? Today, many persons believe that prohibitions against abortion rest on grounds of a private, personal religious conviction and hence are an interference with one's rights under the First Amendment. Actually, the issue is more complex than these statements indicate. The decisive question is whether there is a person in utero whom the law must defend. Such a question arose independently of the Judeo-Christian ethical tradition. Aristotle, for example, examined the matter in *Politics*. Medicine and law, if they are to remain humanizing endeavors, must be acutely sensitive to such issues as the one touched by the question of abortion: "Is there a defenseless person in utero in need of a champion?" As for compulsory pregnancy, this phrase suggests a reformulation of the question of natural law. One must consider the woman's relationship to her own biology. Human nature is perhaps best understood as a process of being rational and endeavoring to be self-determining. That which serves rational ends can be seen as that which is truly natural. For a woman to be compelled by her biology to be a mother is in an important sense unnatural. One's singular enterprise is rendering one's world rational. Compulsory pregnancy would be counter to this central human project. At the same time, the question of compulsory pregnancy does not preempt the question of abortion. The question of abortion must still be answered in its own right in order to avoid a dilemma in which there would be the conflict of the rights of possibly two persons (mother and fetus).[17]

New technologies in the control of brain and behavior are a source of growing concern in many segments of our society. Humankind's experiences with thought reform, both past and present, call for a reassessment of our techniques of teaching, influencing, motivating, and changing. Certain approaches today in advertising represent assaults upon both privacy and freedom. Especially needed is a clear understanding of what it takes to thwart coercive manipulation of human behavior.[38]

B. F. Skinner in his book *Beyond Freedom and Dignity* explores many positive dimensions of control.[59] Skinner points out that numerous kinds of control do not have adverse consequences at any time. Countless social practices essential to the welfare of the species involve the control of one person by another, and no one who has any concern for human achievement can suppress them. In order to maintain the position that all control is wrong, it has been necessary, says Skinner, to disguise or conceal the nature of useful practices, to prefer weak practices just because they can be disguised or concealed, and—a most extraordinary result indeed—to perpetuate punitive measures. The problem is to free people, not from control, but from certain kinds of control. A great achievement of physical and biological technology has been the freeing of people from aversive stimulation—from dangerous extremes of temperature, shortages of food, exhausting labor, and disease. People have not freed themselves from the environment; they have simply made the control exercised by the environment less malevolent. In the same way, Skinner contends, to make the social environment as free as possible of aversive stimuli, one does not need to destroy that environment or escape from it but redesign it.

Many prominent professionals, from behavioral scientists to theologians, take sharp issue with Skinner and declare his techniques philosophically distasteful and morally wrong.[60] Human beings have such difficulty with control, and with the limits of their ability to give meaningful direction to their lives, that they stand in too much awe of one who can teach pigeons to play ping-pong. Our contemporary social climate provides a ready mood for embracing dangerous remedies.

The medical profession must keep a sharp eye on all of its activities related to the manipulation of the psyches and somas of patients. The basic trust which characterizes the doctor-patient relationship should never be threatened by even a hint of the improper use of any pharmacological agent, procedure, or technique by the physician. Seymour Halleck identifies the problems facing doctors, especially psychiatrists:

"While there are many people in our country who are wary of the psychiatrists' power to control behavior, there are also many who would encourage psychiatrists to use their power to shape citizens in such a way that they are more conforming. I predict psychiatrists will soon experience an increase in pressure from both groups. If we are to respond to these pressures rationally and humanistically, we must familiarize ourselves with the legal and ethical implications of behavior control. And we must develop a system of internal regulations of our activities that will satisfy the needs of our patients, ourselves, and the general public."[32, 46]

The capability and knowledge of biomedical science in its quest for and discovery of truth has been anxiety provoking at times for the general public (which includes the physician and scientist). Part of the anxiety is related to the necessity to adjust, emotionally and intellectually, to the changes wrought by the new technologies. Sir William Osler, in a period of revolutionary medical changes, sought to console his troubled colleagues by quoting to them some lines from Keats' poem "Hyperion," showing the poet's faith in progress:

> So on our heels a fresh perfection treads,
> . . . born of us
> And fated to excel us.[48]

Obviously special philosophical, moral, and legal problems arise as dimensions of most of these new developments. Some of the frontiers extend far beyond medical treatment and rehabilitation. Thus, the usual codes which guide the doctor in relationship to patients are inadequate. Laws and public policies, as well as legal and religious precedents, may be anachronistic or grossly inadequate in coping with these scientific breakthroughs.*

The new developments are contributing greatly to our liberation. At the same time, we must recognize and avoid the new dangers that liberation brings. Discussions have been endless about the value of human life, the sanctity of the human body, and the advisability of sustaining the life of a patient who may remain bedridden or incapacitated. A

---

* Bishop Francis Simons, in elaborating on an intervention he made at the Second Vatican Council, says quite directly, "Whenever the good of mankind demands that the general rule or commandment should not apply, it does not apply. This evident consequence gives us an easy solution of certain moral problems which have bedeviled moral theologians who believe in the absoluteness of the commandments." He goes on to stipulate as elastic and changeable eight once-supposed precepts of the natural law (mirabile dictu): "Truth-telling, killing, abortion, suicide, sterilization, masturbation, divorce and marriage, and artificial insemination."[58]

physician's duties are humanitarian and humanistic and involve participation in the curing of disease, the relieving of suffering, and the preserving of life. Fulfillment of these duties requires reverence for human
life and human dignity. As Dr. Michael E. DeBakey points out, a decision related to whether a particular life will be useful and productive is
not the physician's to make, and "the physician who assumes this and
other divine prerogatives regarding human life is guilty of the sin
known to the ancient Greeks as hubris."[16]

I believe with Reinhold Niebuhr that our capacity for doing evil is as
unlimited as our capacity for doing good. C. S. Lewis has given us a
somewhat similar observation that each new power won by us is a
power over us as well. We need therefore to be alert to both the promise and the threat of our science and technology if we are to exercise
control responsibly over them for good rather than evil ends. We function as humans in the measure to which we control our techniques and
are not controlled by them, and that science and technology function
best when they serve human need and purpose rather than vice versa.

While not discounting the attendant problems, I am convinced that
the new scientific discoveries and capabilities offer a rich potential for
increasing the dignity and integrity of humans. Thus, I view with dynamic expectancy the positive increase in fulfillment that can come
with each new scientific development. The quality of our lives from
now on will depend considerably on science and the uses we make of it.
Its advances will alter our concepts of life, identity, human relationships, and death. Although the potential for evil is always present, I
believe that good predominantly will come from the discoveries of science. When humans can choose, they usually do not prefer to do evil.
They prefer love over hate, self-esteem over shame, and self-mastery
over impotence.

Scientific Investigations on Human Subjects

When the human is the object of scientific study, care must be taken
that the conduct of the study is not demeaning of human dignity. No
matter how valuable the scientific results, a researcher may not deal
inhumanly with research subjects. To do so is to sacrifice one human
value for another.

The tradition of free inquiry involves more restraint than would at
first sight appear to be the case. Knowledge is not the top value. The
pursuit of knowledge is a compelling moral force, but it meets and must
accommodate itself to other values that have an equal or greater claim
to the scientist's allegiance—especially the preservation of human life
and human dignity.

Scientists can and should use human subjects for research purposes, but they may do so only if they are sensitive to people's rights to determine what happens to themselves. They may do so only if they treat them as human beings and not as objects. They cannot justify in terms of research results what is an insult to the human spirit in terms of research method.

The novel *Murder in a Hospital* is the story of a certain hospital in which a number of patients died mysteriously.[9] The suicide of a physician on the staff brought to light that the deaths had resulted from the physician's injecting a particular substance into the patients during a study of anaphylaxis, which, in the novel, was the problem of the day. The study had been nearly finished. A meeting of the hospital staff was called to decide what should be done with the physician's records of the study, which were before them on the table. One member—a pathologist—urged that they must be given to the world because they were of great importance. But the senior physician and presiding officer of the meeting—a clinician—held the opposite view and swayed the meeting to his position. The papers were destroyed in the presence of the group. The statement of the senior physician bears quoting: "May I remind you that our duty to our neighbor, our fellow man, comes before even our interest in science." We can ask ourselves how we would have voted if we had attended this meeting. Giving the clinical investigator's findings to the world would have been one way to give meaning to the death of those patients who died as a result of the experiment.

Physicians are unique in that they must be scientists as well as humanitarians. They stand perilously on these two pedestals, and when one is raised or lowered excessively, they are likely to be toppled into the same ugly morass in which the Nazi physicians found themselves as a result of their experimentation with humans during World War II.[45] His Holiness Pope Pius XII spoke to this issue: "Science itself, therefore, as well as its research and acquisitions, must be inserted in the order of values. Here there are well-defined limits which even medical science cannot transgress without violating higher moral rules. The confidential relations between doctor and patient, the personal right of the patient to the life of his body and soul in its psychic and moral integrity are just some of the many values superior to scientific interest."[51]

Experimentation on human beings has been an important and essential instrument in the development of medical skill since the beginnings of scientific medicine. When Hippocrates suspended upside down a group of patients who were suffering from intractable leg pain and thus established the differential diagnosis between what now is known as ruptured intervertebral disk on the one hand and cancer on the other, he performed the first experiment of this kind. Nobody questioned his legal right to perform it. Neither have the similar successful and un-successful efforts of many generations of physicians-scientists during the subsequent centuries been questioned from the point of view of le-gality. Paradoxically, the only legal regulation involved the use of dead bodies. The reason why the living human beings were unquestioningly entrusted to the good judgment and intentions of physicians was the generally held view that the ethics of physicians, reinforced by their dependence upon the continued regard and respect of their fellows, guaranteed greater safeguards than legal injunctions. The privileged position that doctors hold in society depends, in large measure, on the trust which people have in the purity of their motives. It was not until various governmental and nongovernmental administrative organiza-tions, staffed in part by nonscientists and hence not bound by the codes and the mutual approval-dependence of the medical-scientific frater-nity, became involved in the process of medical research, that a conflict of interests entered into the field, requiring legal regulation.

Some serious ethical problems arise in relationship to research with human subjects which may be overlooked. In all ethical systems the person has been judged as harshly by sins of omission as by sins of commission. Some capable investigators avoid research in sensitive areas where the risk of criticism is high and may join certain self-ap-pointed judges in criticizing and questioning the motives and method-ology of those constrained by their own concerns or by society to ex-plore dangerous frontiers. The unanswered questions in medicine are many. Cancer patients beg for wholeness. Chronic schizophrenics by the thousands wait for liberation and restoration. The crippled want to dance and the blind want to see. Answers to these problems will involve investigators who risk their necks. Patients and subjects may also take certain risks and be happy to do so for their own benefit and the benefit of others. Kierkegaard said: "To venture causes anxiety, but not to venture is to lose oneself."

The use of human subjects in research that is of some risk to them is not only morally justifiable but, in certain situations, morally re-quired.* Medical research affords abundant evidence that it is some-times required on moral grounds that humans be subjected to risk. The development and use of vaccines is one case in point. Vaccines involve statistically minimal but real risks to their recipients. The great bene-

---

* Many have urged that programs for compensation be developed, at the fed-eral government level, for any volunteer injured in biomedical or behavioral research. Unfortunately such a compensation program has not come to pass, although worthy and greatly needed, probably because of the costs and diffi-culties in administering it.[33]

fits derived from vaccines serve as the moral justification for what is done.

The use of humans in research is required because of the limitations of research with animals and the moral demand to alleviate suffering. That there is a moral imperative for physicians to attempt to alleviate suffering means that they have to try new methods. When the climate of human experimentation is such that clinical investigators are quickly blamed when things go wrong, they may decide to pursue the path of safety. This path of safety, however, will not advance human knowledge or alleviate human suffering.

Restraints imposed by FDA guidelines or those of other agencies or institutions may raise some overlooked ethical issues.[57] The investigator fears the easy bureaucratic "no" that springs from the possibility that the option to make exceptions to detailed guidelines may be denied by an administrator who brings to the problem one's own set of biases. One of these biases is the knowledge that the administrator will never be condemned for the unrealized benefit but only for the demonstrated harm. This situation makes it easy for the administrator to say no.

Persons who seek to do good by helping another run some risk of creating trouble for themselves. Those concerned foremost with protecting themselves, with keeping their skirts clean, should give some thought to the message in Albert Camus's *The Fall.* Camus has his hero, Jean-Baptiste Clamence, carry the message that a life that is not transcended in the service of another is a lie. Jean-Baptiste has devoted the last years of his formerly successful life to the pursuit of a strange profession, to be a *judge-penitent,* capturing his listeners through a confession of the lies of his own life, thus forcing them in the end to confess in their turn and be judged as miserable a liar as Jean-Baptiste himself. In his own account, he describes as the actual turning point in his life this incident: One night, walking home after midnight in a contented mood, while crossing a bridge he vaguely notes the form of a young woman, bent over the railing, seeming to contemplate the river. He stops but does not turn around. He hears a woman's cry, several times repeated, floating down the river, then an interminable silence. He learns something from this experience that radically changes his entire life: Refusal to act as your brother's keeper sometimes leaves you strangely crippled. The book ends with Jean-Baptiste delirious and dying, avowing his fervent hope that the young girl might throw herself into the river again and give him another chance to save her, and himself.

Another important ethical issue has been raised by biostatistician Robert Lewis. Given that informed persons agree to participate in a

medical experiment, they do so in trust that an effective use will be
made of their contribution, and particularly that it not be squandered
by inappropriate experimental protocol.[41] Lewis describes the participant's expectation: "The gift of person for medical experimentation is
filled with dignity and hope. In the eyes of the donor, the opportunity
to participate may provide for a great gift to mankind, and what is
given to the researcher in positive trust is expected to be used wisely
and for the benefit of others. The donor expects not only that the experiment be worthwhile in topic but that it be a scientific experiment if
such is implied. The donor trusts that the scientific utilization will be
effective and efficient."

The modern medical institution brings together a variety of abilities
for experimental design, the collection of data, and the analysis and re-
porting of results. Responsible investigators imply that these resources
will be used when they identify themselves and request the cooperation
of a patient. If they do not use them and if they are not personally responsible for an efficient design of experiment and a modern analytic
technique, then their assurance or implication of scientific merit is de-
batable. In the name of the institution, Lewis emphasizes, there are
real and implied guarantees to the donor that one's contribution would
be used to its full value and not squandered through fault or obsoles-
cence in the design of research.

Another area of ethical concern relates to the use of certain types of
volunteers for research purposes. For example, the use of prisoners in
human experimentation has had many vocal advocates as well as opponents. Opponents feel that groups such as prisoners may be easily ex-
ploited. This concern is justified and some protective procedures are
necessary. The other side of the coin, the right of the prisoner to volunteer and participate, is emphasized by surgeon and researcher John C.
McDonald, who has conducted experiments using prisoner volunteers.[44] Because a shortened sentence and financial reward are usually
not offered, they cannot be considered incentives. A practical dimension is that volunteering breaks the monotony of prison life and involves the prisoner in an activity of interest to all the prisoners, an activity directed by people outside of the prison. McDonald comes to the
heart of the matter, as far as the inmates are concerned, in stating that
the experiment serves also to help the inmates feel worthwhile—that
they are doing something useful for themselves and others. They volunteer for certain advantages that are clear to them, and they perse-
vere in the research program because their desires are largely fulfilled.

In summary, the ethical issues related to research with human subjects are many but not insoluble.[8, 14, 46] Laws and codes continue to pro-
liferate. Most of these mandates are promulgated for worthy reasons,

but their effect is not without drawbacks. Laws and regulations produce records and restrictions in a never-ending cycle. In a field as complex as research with human subjects, all rules are imperfect and susceptible to many interpretations, and these are not made perfect by additional rules. At the same time, they are not made useless by the presence of imperfections. Risk can never be eliminated completely unless all medical practice and research are abandoned. The real issue is well stated by heart surgeon and researcher Michael E. DeBakey: "Continued suffering and preventable death from curable disease are extravagances no code of morality can afford."[16]

It is difficult to improve upon the conclusion written by Claude Bernard almost a century ago: "So, among the experiments that may be tried on man, those that only harm are forbidden, those that are innocent are permissible, and those that may do good are obligatory."[10] This is in keeping with the pivotal moral and ethical guide of our major religions, stated succinctly in the Bible: "Thou shalt love thy neighbor as thyself" (Leviticus 19:18; Matthew 22:39; Mark 12:31).

OATHS AND CODES

At graduation exercises in recent years, some medical students have recited the prayer of Maimonides rather than the classical oath of Hippocrates. In switching to the prayer of Maimonides, these graduates are reflecting perhaps some movement away from time-honored traditions in the quest for what is described on today's campuses as "relevance in a modern world" or "that which is applicable to the twentieth century." At the same time, there has been a trend during the past two decades for more schools to use medical oaths as part of commencement rituals. In passing, a special vote should be registered in favor of the use of the Hippocratic oath, with or without the updating of certain words and phrases, as a symbol of continuity. There is much to be said for rehearsing the fact that the traditions of Western medicine are 2½ millennia old.

A survey of United States medical schools conducted by psychiatrist Ralph Crawshaw indicates that more than 90 percent of medical schools use some type of oath or pledge at commencement exercises.[15] The oath is seen as part of the rites of passage from student to practitioner. Although medical oaths at times may give the impression that they are charters for the protection and preservation of the profession, they represent sacred commitments by students just before they become physicians pledging that they will, as long as they live, protect not themselves nor their profession but their patients.

Crawshaw's survey shows that of the 90 percent of schools using oaths, 17 percent use the classical form of the Hippocratic oath. Another 29 percent administer a modified form of the Hippocratic oath. Some 24 percent of the medical schools employ the Geneva declaration* and 30 percent use oaths or pledges classified as "other." The majority of the others remain similar to the Hippocratic oath, with most changes confined to omitting or updating certain words or phrases.

The prayer of Maimonides, which is growing in popularity at commencement exercises, is named for Rabbi Moses ben Maimon, a Jewish philosopher and physician who lived during A.D. 1135–1204 and practiced medicine in Egypt. The prayer is as modern and relevant today as when it was written eight centuries ago:

> Thy eternal providence has appointed me to watch over the life and health of Thy creatures. May the love for my art actuate me at all times; may neither avarice nor miserliness, nor thirst for glory, or for a great reputation engage my mind; for the enemies of truth and philanthropy could easily deceive me and make me forgetful of my lofty aim of doing good to Thy children. May I never see in the patient anything else but a fellow creature in pain.

> Grant me strength, time and opportunity always to correct what I have acquired, always to extend its domain; for knowledge is immense and the spirit of man can extend indefinitely to enrich itself daily with new requirements.

> Today he can discover his errors of yesterday and tomorrow he may obtain a new light on what he thinks himself sure of today. Oh, God, Thou hast appointed me to watch over the life and death of Thy creatures; here am I ready for my vocation and now I turn unto my calling. Guide me in this immense work so that it may be of avail.

There are many codes in medicine, and two of the most prominent ones are the Nuremberg code and the Declaration of Helsinki. The Nuremberg code was formulated in response to experiments on humans done in the name of science by the Nazi regime. The Declaration of Helsinki was developed in 1964 by the World Medical Association and

---

* The Declaration of Geneva was drafted and adopted in 1948 by the Second General Assembly of the World Medical Association. The experiences of the German physicians under Hitler stimulated this formulation, a modernization of the Hippocratic oath. The emphasis of the Geneva declaration is upon the sacredness of human life, the brotherhood of man and the international fraternity, and obligations of physicians. The Declaration was revised in 1968.

revised in 1975. There have also been formulations by the American Medical Association (its new version was approved in 1980),* the British Medical Research Council, the United States Public Health Service and others. These codes evolved because of the complexity and the weighty responsibility of unprecedented medical decisions—particularly those related to the use of human subjects in research.[54] They represent general guides, not categorical imperatives, and the physician-scientist's self-discipline, judgment, and conscience must ultimately operate in individual decisions. Irvine H. Page, in commenting on medical ethics, makes this pointed statement: "In so fragile a relationship as that between physician and patient, it is character that calls the tune. I am under no illusion that regulations, codes and declarations are consulted before the physician and patient agree on a code of conduct."[50]

The codes and oaths which have developed in our country and in Western society generally stress those principles on which the majority agree and do not make normative those principles on which serious disagreement exists. Also, most codes or oaths are strongly influenced by situations prevailing at particular historical periods. For example, the codes which were set forth after World War II were deeply influenced by the Nuremberg trials of Nazi war criminals. Thus, over the years, adaptations are made in the principles, for the principles have difficulty speaking for all times.

All codes prove inadequate in some situations or often lack clarification in specific matters. At the same time, is it possible to study existing codes and oaths and extract general principles that will guide those in patient care and in research with human subjects? The answer is yes. In therapy and research, the ethical guidelines needed can be stated as six basic convictions or moral insights. These insights represent the essence of most codes or oaths that have been developed to guide us in the health field.

The first such insight calls for treating the individual as a person and not as a thing in all our actions and relationships. Thus, in therapy and research, there is a recognition of distinctive features of persons—namely, their right to self-determination, and, in turn, their freedom and human dignity.

The second moral insight calls for the treatment of the person as an end and not as a means to an end. This requires an acceptance of a form of Immanuel Kant's categorical imperative that we should always treat other persons as ends and never solely as means. This view is

---

* The series of codes set forth by the American Medical Association, beginning in 1847, have been revised five times—1903, 1912, 1947, 1955, and 1980.

bound up with conceiving other persons as having unconditional worth solely because persons are ends in themselves, determining their own destiny and are not to be treated merely as means. To treat persons merely as a means involves a violation of autonomy because persons so treated are being treated in accordance with rules not of their own choosing.

According to this principle, for example, health care ought to be based on voluntary and informed consent by a patient or subject of research, and not on coercion, deception, or brainwashing. In practice, this principle also says not to exploit patients, such as persuading them to have surgical procedures that they do not need, or in any way using them for aims that benefit the physician or someone other than the patient. Adherence to such a principle will cut down on the number of laboratory tests, especially those used primarily to make a patient's chart look good or complete, protect against malpractice, or benefit the physician economically.

While this principle has a treasured place in medicine, it has been challenged by some within and without the circles of medicine who speak of a consequentialist imperative to "achieve good." Some extreme versions of the "to achieve good" imperative seem to imply that ends at times justify means, perhaps to the extent of agreeing partly with the late labor organizer, Saul Alinsky, who held that those who worry about means in relation to ends usually wind up on their ends with no means at all.

The third basic conviction or moral insight states that in treatment or experimental situations, there ought to be operative the law of reciprocity—the willingness of a person to be treated the way he or she is treating another person. Would the therapist or investigator be willing for himself or herself, spouse, or child to have this procedure employed on them in the same way it is being used on the patient or research subject? Thus, the therapist and researcher should test their acts by the law of reciprocity. The physician who did the first cardiac catheterization adhered so closely to this principle that he was his own first human subject for the procedure.

The fourth conviction or moral insight declares that in controversies involving the individual *versus* the collective, generally dispute has to be resolved in favor of the individual. To some extent, the collective or broader social group is an abstraction and the only genuine reality is the concrete individual.

This moral insight does not preclude weighing the "value" of the whole in relation to the "value" of individual humans. It requires a careful understanding of the deontological and utilitarian and how the utilitarian may be considered without disregarding the deontological.

Deontology emphasizes individual rights and is concerned with giving the individual his or her due, while utilitarianism is community directed and concerned with achieving the greatest good for the greatest number. Respecting individual rights may limit some treatments or scientific research or make them more costly. The ethical imperative in the deontological approach is "to violate no individual rights."

While serving both patient and community, the doctor gives the individual patient first priority, according to the principle described above. For example, decisions of how persuasive or coercive to be in caring for the suicidal person must be done for the patient's sake and not on the basis of what equity the community or others have in the patient. Decisions regarding dying patients must be related to what the patient wants or what is in the patient's best interest and not what is in the best interest of "others." Special problems may emerge where the competence of patients to judge their own welfare is seriously questioned. Among such patients are children, the mentally ill (especially institutionalized ones), the critically injured, certain elderly persons, and dangerously ill or comatose patients. Whereas the exercise of paternalism in the care of such patients represents interference with a person's liberty of action, this interference is ethically justified by reasons referring exclusively to the welfare, good, needs, interest, or values of the person being cared for or even coerced. In this sense, the individual takes precedence over the collective, and the doctor's actions are guided by what is best for the patient and not what is best for some group or society in general.

Of course, often there is no conflict between the rights of the individual and those of the wider social group, and the best interest of one will serve the other. Sometimes the doctor may not be sure whose rights should come first. When such a question arises, the wisest course of action is to put the individual patient first.

The fifth basic conviction relates to the fidelity of covenant in the doctor-patient relationship. The practice of medicine or research in medicine involves a covenant of fidelity, a mutuality of trust in human relationships, as ably described by ethicist Paul Ramsey in many of his writings.[52, 53] Justice, fairness, canons of loyalty, sanctity of life, and *agape* (love) are some of the names given to the moral quality of attitude and of action owed to all persons by any person who enters into a covenant with another person.

The doctor-patient relationship is anchored in a covenant situation. Thus, our task in ethical decision making is to identify or find the actions and abstentions that come from adherence to covenant. In other words, what are the moral claims upon the doctor in crucial medical situations in which decisions must be made about how to show respect for, protect, and preserve the life of one's fellow human beings? Instead of covenant of fidelity, some may prefer the phrase "duties of fidelity" or Pedro Lain Entralgo's term "the medical friendship."[39]

The sixth ethical principle or basic conviction is the affirmation of accountability. The affirmation of accountability undergirds medicine's commitment to the conservation and preservation of life. Thus, intrusions into individual lives or into the course of biological development that could be destructive or irreversible should not be undertaken without exceptionally strong justification, as ethicist James M. Gustafson has repeatedly emphasized in his lectures and writings.[27, 28, 29, 30] Physicians are accountable for all of their actions.

Further, physicians may see in their practice and research that the affirmation of accountability may at times require a subordination of human ends to the well-being of the whole of creation. Certain human claims for individual rights and values may be overridden for the sake of the more inclusive well-being of a wider circle of life. For example, in the population explosion on this earth, circumstances have arisen in which the right to unlimited human procreation is a threat to the well-being of all life. The affirmation of accountability calls us in medicine to address a broad group of problems ranging from the lack of proper nutrition for particular groups or whole populations to the lack of adequate health care when the resources for such are available. In facing such problems, doctors are not switching from a deontological to a utilitarian aproach but promoting in their patient the responsibility and accountablity that accompany a patient's freedom and rights.

Further, the moral and ethical insights in most codes or oaths represent, in a sense, great Biblical admonitions or truths. Chief among these are: "Thou shalt love thy neighbor as thyself" (Leviticus 19:18, Matthew 22:39) and "Whatsoever ye would that others should do to you, do ye even so to them" (Matthew 7:12). Also, the insights in these codes or oaths can be further illuminated by three more scriptural statements from the mainstream of the Biblical tradition: "And my covenant shall be in your flesh as an everlasting covenant" (Genesis 17:13); "For thou hast made man a little lower than the angels . . . and madest him to have dominion over the works of thy hands" (Psalms 8:5-6); and "For unto whomsoever much is given, of him shall be much required" (Luke 12:48).

Moreover, it must be remembered that while one distills from codes and oaths their essence or basic convictions, one is not dealing with ironclad rules but general guides. As mentioned earlier, the physician-scientist's self-discipline, judgment, and conscience must ultimately operate in individual decisions. Also, in medicine, possibly the ancient

Roman definition of the field of ethics is a noble guide: *Honeste vivere nemini laedere, suum cuique tribuere*—live uprightly, hurt no one, give to each one's due.[37]

INFLUENCING THE STUDENT'S VALUES
AND POINT OF VIEW

In interviews with a number of senior medical students regarding values and decision making, almost all of them insisted that they made decisions in large measure on the basis of the values with which they came to medical school. More formal studies support this finding.[6, 11] One cannot escape the conclusion that good people make good doctors, and a person's "goodness" is largely determined prior to entering medical school.

If students are guided in their decision making by values which they brought to medical school, then medical schools do not possess as much power for shaping medical orientations as has been supposed. It has been shown, however, that if medical schools are to have a significant effect on value orientations of students, a direct rather than indirect approach holds the greatest potential. In other words, students can be changed over the course of four years, but these changes can only be brought about by conscious and direct efforts. Little has been accomplished by hoping that medical students will examine and reflect on their attitudes and those of their patients by being placed in the "right" situations. On the other hand, much is accomplished by discussing issues and attitudes directly in relation to specific medical contexts.[31] Since many attitudes in medicine are based on religious and philosophical considerations, issues should be discussed in such a way that the religious and philosophical dimensions of these issues are clearly identified. Medicine is a value-laden enterprise, and such a recognition makes it easier to consider the philosophical and religious as a part of the fabric of medical issues.

The problem at hand is to bring to bear in a meaningful and, hence, useful way reflections on ethical issues. These reflections include—but should not be confined to—abstractions from concrete detail. Instead, one thinks of how to deal with kinds of cases. This thinking then serves as a guide and check on thinking about individual cases as they arise. With reflection in mind as a central focus, what teaching-learning modalities can be adapted to almost any setting in training programs related to ethics and human values? A few are discussed here.

Lectures in medical ethics are useful in giving information, learning the language of the field, becoming acquainted with concepts, and learning much of the theoretical that prepares one for becoming an informed and reflective participant in ethical decision making. The lecture method has been criticized, however, because it is a limited instrument in bringing about behavioral change on the part of the student. Such a criticism is valid, but the lecture remains a useful teaching modality when combined with other methods.

The seminar approach involving reading in depth, reflection, and discussion is a good teaching-learning instrument, especially if used in conjunction with the case conference method, with the presentation of patients when appropriate. Also, ward rounds and grand rounds furnish impressive opportunities for demonstrating ethical decision making in the context of concrete situations.

Thus, the major educational tool is clinical in nature—the individual case situation. This approach avoids overly abstract methods, and emphasizes the uniqueness of each ethical or value-oriented decision as it relates to a specific patient and specific set of circumstances. Since the patient and the situation are presented, the students will not be dealing solely with the theoretical in ethics but with the concrete. They will then be guided in methods of ethical decision making in situations very much like those they themselves will encounter in their daily practice of medicine.

Another conscious and direct effort with great potential for bringing about change in students relates to furnishing them with proper models of conduct. Actually, students seek great models after which to fashion their lives as persons and as physicians. They want to be exposed to people who make education relevant by integrating compassionate study and informed conduct, by demonstrating a care and concern for what students can become, and by giving students a profound motivation for learning—the hope of becoming better persons. When we give to students great models who put into practice the highest ideals in their care of students and patients, students will learn much about empathy, about the rights and dignity of patients, and about the use of the self as an instrument in healing.

Great models who have a profound impact on students are usually not the authoritarian and dictatorial types. Authoritarian types often complicate students' growth in decision-making capacity. Of course, not all authority figures are authoritarian or rigid in their relationships; some are quite benevolent. The problem arises, however, particularly for the medical student and young physician because many aspects of medical training and practice are hierarchical in nature. Thus, the weight of authority may often be distracting in new situations which call for courageous action. Every advance in science has been made at the expense of someone's reputation as an authority. A question often asked is: How can one be stimulated by authority and not paralyzed by it?[38]

The history of anatomy offers an excellent example of how the weight of authority smothered and distorted new and correct observations. For about 1400 years following Galen, anatomists saw in their dissections only that which they were told to look for by Galen. When they found structures that were different from or missing in the descriptions of the great master, they called them "abnormal." In effect, the cadavers that did not confirm their expectations were considered to be "bad" cadavers. Not until the sixteenth century, in the work of Vesalius, was anatomy recognized as a science in which observation took precedence over authority. Only when anatomists began to look at the structure of the human body as it is, and not as they believed it should be, were they able to correct such Galenic errors (resulting primarily from the projection of pig, monkey, or dog anatomy into the human body) as the five-lobed liver, the seven-segmented sternum, the mandible consisting of two parts, the double bile duct, and the horned uterus.[2]

Vesalius, however, did not have an easy victory in insisting that observation take precedence over authority. His work received the most unkind reception from the conservative anatomy chair holders, and his own teacher, Sylvius (Jacques Dubois) of Paris, gave him the nickname of Vesanus (madman). To preseve the authority of his beloved Galen, Sylvius thought up the ingenious argument that the human body had changed since the time of Galen. For example, he mentioned that the differences in the curvature of the femur were due to the new fashion of narrow trousers.[2]

APPROACHES TO ETHICAL DECISION MAKING

There are several lines of approach to ethical decision making. Physicians tend to draw on one line in some situations and on another in other situations. Each of the principal lines of approach has a place in medical ethics, and each has merit.

The Characterological Approach.   This approach to ethical decision making may be summarized in the aphorism, "Good persons will make good decisions." People of good character—possessed of honesty, integrity, kindly inclination, and goodwill—will make decisions that are ethical. So long as persons' moral autonomy is supported and safeguarded, they will act in exemplary fashion, when motivated by a genuinely benevolent character.[63] *

Medicine in the West has been guided by the Hippocratic oath, which places the character, or "purity of heart," of the physician in a central position. Physicians are to subordinate personal interests and desires to the needs of their patients. Physicians are to respect and exemplify the purity, and even the holiness (in the sense of being beyond temptation), of their art and knowledge. The medical ethic set forth by Thomas Percival in 1803 emphasizes the same theme: clarity of vision, purity of commitment, and strictest temperance. Further, physicians are to show tenderness and concern for persons in terminal illness, and are to be motivated in relation to all patients by kindness and virtue rather than by avarice or the wish for adulation.

No comments about the shortcomings of the characterological approach can deny its essential virtues. Yet, the approach exhibits some inadequacies that need mentioning.[26, 34, 35, 40] Unfortunately, good persons do not always make good decisions, even when they are well informed. Humankind throughout its long history has noted the subtlety and ubiquity of evil, especially the capacity in the person often to diminish the distance between good and evil. A second weakness of the characterological approach, as Vaux has ably described, is its tendency to minimize the complexity of the actual situations in which decisions have to be made.[63] In its reliance in part on intuitive judgments, it may regard as unnecessary the process of rigorous and fine-grained assessment or appraisal of the problem, thus distorting by oversimplification the nature of the situation about which a decision is to be made.

The Formalistic Approach. The formalistic method proceeds from some view of general or comprehensive principles, in the light of which situations are examined. To a great extent, the procedure is deductive, although discerning the exact nature of the situation may be done with inductive care. In the evaluation of ethics, when it became clear that custom and character were insufficient to deal with the novel element in situations, there followed a search for principles on the basis of which decisions could be made. The formalistic approach to ethics with which American physicians are acquainted represents long-standing traditions in either religion or philosophy in the West.

The oaths and codes that have been developed within the medical profession are clear illustrations of the extent to which a formalistic

---

* I am indebted to Kenneth Vaux for his overview of the characterological and formalistic approaches in medical ethics.

approach influences clinical practice. Although a formalistic approach may be challenged, there is merit in awareness of the basic principles that one brings to actual situations.

The greatest difficulty with a formalistic approach in medical ethics is the tendency to read specific situations in light of the principles and to minimize the complexities in the actual situation. This is especially true because the method is mainly deductive, from principle to situation. Further, the principles are themselves influenced by historical immediacies and cannot speak for all time. Some ethicists believe that even in a dogmatic or self-contained set of principles, there was originally an interplay between many actual situations and development of the principles. Thus, new situations will continue to influence basic principles. A formalistic approach would not survive if it made no adaptations in its principles.

The Situational Approach. *   This ethical approach seeks to arrive at truth in the clinical situation by an inductive and empirical approach rather than the deductive approach. The approach is case-oriented. It represents an ethical approach used for centuries and called today situation ethics. In this moral strategy, the governing consideration is the situation. Situationists know the ethical maxims of their community and its heritage, and they treat them with respect as illuminators of the problems. They are prepared, however, to set aside any of these rules in the situation, if love and reason seem better served by doing so.†

Situation ethics accepts reason as the instrument of moral judgment and sees conscience as a function (verb) not as a faculty (noun)—a word for one's attempts to make decisions creatively, constructively, and fittingly. Thomas Aquinas has come close to the situationist's definition of conscience in declaring it "the reason making moral judgments." [3]

---

* The essence of this section in great measure has been drawn from the writings of Joseph Fletcher, as well as some personal association with him. The field of medical ethics has been profoundly enriched and illuminated by Fletcher's work. He has entered into dialogue with people from a variety of professional backgrounds to debate the complex issues under discussion, and has done so always with warmth, grace, and enthusiasm. [18, 19, 20]

† Daniel Callahan believes that Joseph Fletcher, the leading interpreter of situation ethics, sets up an unnecessarily sharp dichotomy between "rule ethics" and situation ethics, thereby ignoring many other middle-ground possibilities for structuring medical ethics. [13] One can respond by saying that possibly there is in Fletcher's position a way to move back and forth between concrete situations and some order of basic principles, and that each continues to inform the other.

Dietrich Bonhoeffer, the highly respected theologian who was executed for trying to do away with Adolph Hitler, expressed well the position of the situationist: "The question of the good is posed and is decided in the midst of each definite, yet unconcluded, unique and transient situation of our lives, in the midst of our living relationships with men, things, institutions and powers, in other words in the midst of our historical existence."[12]

A concrete example of situation ethics is found in Richard Nash's highly successful play, *The Rainmaker*. The key to the play, ethically, lies in a scene where the morally outraged brother of a lonely spinster threatens to shoot the sympathetic but not "serious" Rainmaker because he makes love to her in the barn at midnight. The Rainmaker's intention is to restore her sense of womanliness and her hopes for marriage and children. Her father, a wise old Texas rancher, grabs the pistol away from his son, saying, "Noah, you're so full of what's right you can't see what's good."

Fletcher summarizes situationism as a method that proceeds from (1) its one and only law, *agape* (love), to (2) the *sophia* (wisdom) of the church and culture, containing many "general rules" of more or less reliability, to (3) *kairos* (moment of decision, the fullness of time) in which the responsible self in the situation decides whether the *sophia* can serve love or not.[20] A simpler way of saying this is that law is reduced from a statutory system of rules to the love canon alone. Precepts are replaced with the living principle of *agape* in the sense of goodwill at work in partnership with reason.

Fletcher joins a host of others in emphasizing that the opposite of love is not hate but indifference.* The essence of moral guilt lies in the failure or refusal to respond to the needs or calls of others: it does not lie in the failure to obey an abstract rule or principle. It is impossible to be responsive to any principle; one can only respond to the calls and claims of others.[19] Responsibility is too much thought of in a forensic way, as answerability to laws or rules rather than as a response to people's calls and needs. The physician-writer Anton Chekhov prayed to God to defend him from generalizations, usually professed by people who have never been in trouble.

There are many situations in medicine where physicians may protect themselves by taking no action. They may have kept their "skirts clean" according to their code by failing to respond to another's need. "The ultimate norm in the moral realm and its only absolute law is

---

* George Bernard Shaw expresses this idea lucidly: "The worst sin towards our fellow creatures is not to hate them, but to be indifferent to them: that's the essence of inhumanity."

thus the law of intelligent responsiveness." Father Johann adds in his essay entitled "Love and Justice" that the precepts of code morality (such as the Ten Commandments) "can serve as guidelines in the making of moral decisions," but they "cannot be finally decisive in our moral choices."[36]

Buber always insisted that to be responsible means to respond, to hear the call or claim of others, and furthermore, that "responsibility cannot be laid down according to any set principles but must be ever again recognized in the depths of the soul according to the demands of each concrete situation."[21]

The moral narcissism of the neurotic conscience results in a tendency to put principles before persons, an unloving preoccupation with being right in all events irrespective of the effect upon persons, with the conviction that "La vertu excuse tout" ("Virtue excuses everything"). Such a negative and anxious viewing of life puts avoidance of guilt so much in the foreground that many human situations are not grasped in their humanness.

Such a conscience is identified by Mark Twain in his short story "Was it Heaven? or Hell?" The story tells of a pair of women who felt strongly about the evils of lying. When their doctor asks them whether they would tell a lie to shield a person from an undeserved injury or shame, their answer is no.

"Not even a friend?"
"No."
"Not even your dearest friend?"
"No."
"Not even to save him from bitter pain and misery and grief?"
"No. Not even to save his life."
"Nor his soul?"
"Nor his soul."
"I ask you both—why?"
"Because to tell such a lie, or any lie, is a sin, and could cost us the loss of our own souls—would, indeed, if we died without time to repent."
"Is such a soul as that worth saving? Reform! Drop this mean and sordid and selfish devotion to the saving of your shabby little souls, and hunt up something to do that's got some dignity to it! Risk your souls. Risk them in good causes; then if you lose them, why should you care? Reform!"[62]

Love and reason, as emphasized in situation ethics, may illuminate a knotty problem now under discussion in medical ethics: Should an unrelated living donor be allowed to give a kidney to a patient?* Many do not believe an unrelated donor's offer of a kidney should be refused if the prospective donor is of sound mind and clear of motivation. Of course, physicians who believe differently may not be able to participate in the transfer of the kidney, and their position should surely be respected.

Among the foundation pillars of medical ethics are "to do no harm" and "to carry out only those procedures which are intended to be of benefit to one's patient." These guidelines operate in the context of the doctor–patient relationship. The donor transcends this doctor–patient model and brings in a psychophilosophical dimension that operates in the broader context of human relationships. The issue here relates to what one person is willing to sacrifice for another. The motivation could differ from one donor to another but could well have the common denominator of altruistic love, which probably any human being is capable of. In this broader psychophilosophical context, the two foundations of medical ethics mentioned may still be applicable. In the relationship with the donor, the physician intends no harm, and the donor's gift may be of inestimable value to himself or herself. The testimony of many donors is that their act of altruism has had far-reaching constructive effects on their lives.

It seems appropriate at this point to define altruism. Altruism is devotion to the welfare of others, regard for others as a principle of action. Such a principle is not in conflict with self-love. The Biblical admonition to "love thy neighbor as thyself " implies that respect and love for another individual cannot be separated from respect and love for one's self. The Biblical scholar Leo Baeck has given a somewhat different translation of Leviticus 19:18, usually translated "Thou shalt love thy neighbor as thyself." The exact translation, he contends, would read, "Thou shalt love thy neighbor: he is as thou." Thus, one loves one's neighbor because one's neighbor is like oneself.[7] Many scholars have stated the concept similarly— the *other* is *thou*.

As humans in their development moved away from a simple life close to the earth and broke their primary bonds with nature, they experienced a separateness, an isolation, an aloneness. They have since tried to overcome their separateness and become at one. By trial and error, humans through the centuries have discovered that love banishes their

---

* Our present knowledge in the immunological matching of organs is such that a cadaver kidney may be almost as good a match as one from an unrelated living donor. Thus, does one have the right to take a kidney from an unrelated living donor? That is the critical and relevant question at this stage of our knowledge.

isolation and separateness, reunites them with their fellows, and yet permits them to retain their identity and integrity. In all relationships, giving is a major component. Herein, one of the great paradoxes of life is found: in love, giving means receiving. In love, one gives oneself.*

Fromm defines love as the active concern for the life and the growth of that which we love. He emphasizes that beyond the element of giving, the active character of love becomes evident in that it always implies certain basic elements common to all forms of love: care, responsibility, respect, and knowledge.[23] All of these elements of love are readily seen as related to altruism.

Love is the ultimate principle on which all ethical decisons should be made. Sheer survival, or adherence to a natural or supernatural law, cannot take precedence over *agape* love. What is needed is courageous examination of painful and ambiguous problems in the light of that love. Good things are always capable of evil deployment. One cannot refuse to do good because one fears the possible evil. Augustine was right to make love the source principle from which all else derives. He reduced his whole ethic to the single maxim *"dilige et quod vis, fac"*— "love and then what you will, do."[5] Kant's contention that the only good thing is a good will is what the New Testament means by love. Love is intrinsically good and no action apart from its foreseeable consequences has any ethical meaning at all.

Through the centuries there has been confusion between love and justice. Fletcher contends, however, that love and justice are the same, for justice is love distributed.[19] He amplifies this statement by giving the example of a resident physician on emergency service deciding whether to give the hospital's last unit of plasma to a young mother of three or to an elderly skid row alcoholic. He may suppose that he is being forced to make a tragic choice between love and justice. He may think that choosing the good of the mother and her children means ignoring love's impartial and "nonpreferential" concern for every neighbor. Fletcher goes on to say that love must make estimates, for it is preferential. To prefer the mother in that situation is the most loving decision, and therefore a just one. If love does not calculate the immediate and remote consequences, it turns irresponsible.

One of Richard Niebuhr's most fascinating themes was set forth decisively only toward the end of his life and includes in his posthumously published *The Responsible Self.*[47] Theological ethics require that one

---

* Maslow contends that one's higher nature contains the need for doing what is worthwhile and for preferring to do it well. Lower need gratifications can be bought with money, but when these are already fulfilled, then people are motivated only by higher kinds of "pay."[42]

ask, "What is my goal, my ideal, my telos?" The ethics of law require the question, "What is the law and what is the first law of my life?" Niebuhr goes on to say that guided by the ethics of responsibility, the individual asks, "What is going on? What is the most fitting response I can make to what is happening?" Here the fundamental social character of human existence is recognized: one is always in dialogue with and responsible to other selves.

CONCLUSION

The shift in medical ethics has been away from stern and ironbound do's and don'ts, from prescribed conduct and legalistic morality. This shift has brought both discomfort and insecurity to many physicians. Some prefer an ethical system of prefabricated morality, or firm rules to lean on. The contextual, situational, circumstantial case-centered method is too full of variables for them—they want only constants. As the new developments in medicine become increasingly complicated and wide-scoped, our ethical decision making grows more complex. In medical ethics we can no longer fit reality to rules but must fit rules to reality, for decisions ought to be made situationally, not prescriptively. The unchanging structures of life are fewer than previously thought.

A new appreciation of the role of personal conscience is emerging. This does not mean that decisions and actions are no longer to be guided and checked by rules, but that personal responsibility for decision can no longer be delegated to any other person or any institution, including the church.[43]

The love canon as a substantive principle, as set forth by Joseph Fletcher, appears most relevant in medical ethics. Fletcher proposes an ethic inspired by the practical considerations of four factors: the end, the means, the motive, and the consequence as they relate to any situation. He proposes that the principle of *agape* love replace the rigidity of legalism. His formula is clearly stated: always do the most loving thing in every situation. He defines love in terms of objective good achieved. Fletcher emphasizes that love and justice are always commensurable.

Possibly General Charles De Gaulle has expressed as well as any the core of ethical decision making: "Faced with crisis, the man of character falls back on himself. He imposes his own stamp on action, takes responsibility for it, makes it his own."[55] De Gaulle often stood in the midst of ambiguity and uncertainty, yet he seemed always able to act decisively in matters of the gravest import. His statement reveals his formula for action—a formula most relevant for the decision maker in medicine.

REFERENCES

1. A definition of irreversible coma: Report of the Ad Hoc Committee of the Harvard Medical School to Examine the Definition of Brain Death. JAMA 205:337, 1968
2. Ackerknecht EH: A Short History of Medicine, rev ed. New York, Ronald Press, 1968, pp 104–106
3. Aquinas T: De Veritate, Q 16, Art 1; Q 17, Art 1.
4. Augenstein LG: Come, Let Us Play God. New York, Harper, 1969
5. Augustine: *Ep Joan vii* 5 (MPL 35,2033)
6. Babbie ER: Science and Morality in Medicine. Berkeley, University of California Press, 1970
7. Baeck L: The Essence of Judaism. Translated by Howe I. New York, Schocken, 1948
8. Beauchamp TL, Childress JF: Principles of Biomedical Ethics. New York, Oxford University Press, 1979
9. Bell J: Murder in a Hospital. Baltimore, Penguin Books, 1941
10. Bernard C: An Introduction to the Study of Experimental Medicine, 1878. Translated by Greene, H.C. New York, Schuman, 1949, p 102
11. Bloom SW: Some implication of studies in the professionalization of the physician. In Jaco EG (ed): Patients, Physicians and Illness. Glencoe, Illinois, Free Press, 1958, pp 313–321
12. Bonhoeffer D: Ethics. London, SCM Press, 1955, p 214
13. Callahan D: A book review of Joseph Fletcher's Humanhood: Essays in biomedical ethics. Pharos 42:38, 1979
14. Childress JF: Ethical issues in the experimentation with human subjects. Conn Med 43:26, 1979
15. Crawshaw R: M.D. oaths—tradition vs. relevance. AMA News, August 16, 1971
16. DeBakey ME: Medical research and the golden rule. JAMA 203:574, 1968
17. Engelhardt HT Jr: On the bounds of freedom: From the treatment of fetuses to euthanasia. Conn Med 43:15, 1979. See also The ontology of abortion. Ethics 84:217, 1974
18. Fletcher J: Humanhood: Essays on Biomedical Ethics. New York, Prometheus Books, 1979
19. Fletcher J: Moral Responsibility. Philadelphia, Westminster Press, 1967
20. Fletcher J: Situation Ethics. Philadelphia, Westminster Press, 1966
21. Friedman MS: Martin Buber: The Life of Dialogue. New York, Harper & Row, 1960, p 145
22. Fromm E: Man for Himself. New York, Rinehart, 1947, pp 92–94
23. Fromm E: The Art of Loving. New York, Harper, 1965
24. Graubard M: The Frankenstein syndrome: Man's ambivalent attitude to knowledge and power. Perspect Biol Med 10:419, 1967
25. Gunn J: The Immortals. New York, Bantam, 1962, p 71
26. Gustafson JM, Laney JT: On Being Responsible—Issues in Personal Ethics. New York, Harper & Row, 1968

27. Gustafson JM: Can Ethics Be Christian? Chicago, University of Chicago Press, 1975
28. Gustafson JM: The Contributions of Theology to Medical Ethics. The 1975 Pere Marquette Theology Lecture. Marquette University Theology Department, April 6, 1975
29. Gustafson JM: Mongolism, parental desires, and the right to life. Perspect Biol Med 16:529, 1973
30. Gustafson JM: Protestant and Roman Catholic Ethics. Chicago, University of Chicago Press, 1978
31. Guttentag OE: A course entitled "the medical attitude": An orientation in the foundation of medical thought. J Med Educ 35:903, 1960
32. Halleck SL: Legal and ethical aspects of behavior control. Am J Psychiatry 131:381, 1974
33. Hamilton MP: Compensating victims of medical research. Christian Century, November 29, 1978, pp 1149–1150
34. Hauerwas S: Character and the Christian Life. San Antonio, Trinity University Press, 1975
35. Hauerwas S: Vision and Virtue. Notre Dame, Indiana, Fides Press, 1975
36. Johann RO: Love and justice. In DeGeorge RT (ed): Ethics and Society. New York, Doubleday, 1966, p 33
37. Jonsen AR, Hellegers AE: Conceptual foundations for an ethics of medical care. In Reiser SJ, Dyck AJ, Curran WJ (eds): Ethics in Medicine: Historical Perspectives and Contemporary Concerns. Cambridge, Massachusetts, MIT Press, 1977, pp 129–136
38. Knight JA: Conscience and Guilt. New York, Appleton-Century-Crofts, 1969
39. Lain Entralgo P: Doctor and Patient. New York, McGraw-Hill, 1969
40. Laney JT: Character and the Moral Life. (The Rice Rockwell Lectures) Baton Rouge, La, LSU Press (in press)
41. Lewis R: Medical ethics. Saturday Review, August 6, 1966, p 52
42. Maslow AH: Toward a Psychology of Being. Princeton, NJ, Van Nostrand, 1962
43. McCormack R: The new morality. America, June 15, 1968, pp 769–772
44. McDonald JC: Why prisoners volunteer to be experimental subjects. JAMA 202:511, 1967
45. Mitscherlick A, Mielke F: Doctors of Infamy. Translated by Norden H. New York, Schuman, 1949
46. Munson R: Intervention and Reflection: Basic Issues in Medical Ethics. Belmont, California, Wadsworth, 1979
47. Niebuhr R: The Responsible Self. New York, Harper, 1963
48. Osler W: Teaching and thinking. Montreal Med J 23:561, 1895
49. Outler AC: The beginnings of personhood: Theological considerations. In Jersild PT, Johnson DA (eds): Moral Issues and Christian Response. New York, Holt Rinehart & Winston, 1976, pp 378–386
50. Page IH: Medical ethics based on symposia. Modern Medicine, April 6, 1970, p 83

51. Pope Pius XII: The Moral Limits of Medical Research and Treatment. Washington, DC, National Catholic Welfare Conference, 1952
52. Ramsey P: The Patient as Person. New Haven, Yale University Press, 1970
53. Ramsey P: The nature of medical ethics. In Reiser SJ, Dyck AJ, Curran WJ (eds): Ethics in Medicine: Historical Perspectives and Contemporary Concerns. Cambridge, Mass, MIT Press, 1977, pp 123–137
54. Reiser SJ, Dyck AJ, Curran WJ (eds): Ethics in Medicine: Historical Perspectives and Contemporary Concerns. Cambridge, Massachusetts, MIT Press, 1977
55. Rider's Digest, 23:3, Aug. 23, 1971
56. Rosenfeld A: The Second Genesis—the Coming Control of Life. Englewood Cliffs, NJ, Prentice-Hall, 1969
57. Schwartz H: Medical costs and the drug industry. Wall Street Journal, April 21, 1980
58. Simons F: The Catholic church and the new morality. Cross Currents 16:429, 1966
59. Skinner BF: Beyond Freedom and Dignity. New York, Knopf, 1971
60. Skinner's utopia: Panacea, or path to hell? Time, September 20, 1971, pp 47–53
61. The genetic payoff—an editorial. Wall Street Journal, January 22, 1980
62. Twain M: Was it heaven? or hell? The Writings of Mark Twain, Vol 24. New York, Harper, n.d.
63. Vaux K: Ethical issues for the physician. In Hiltner S, Poole R (eds): Human and Religious Values in Medical Practice. In press. See also Biomedical Ethics. New York, Harper & Row, 1974, pp 37–45

14

COMING TO TERMS WITH ONE'S FEELINGS ABOUT DEATH

So teach us to number our days, that we may apply our hearts unto wisdom.
—Psalms 90:12

The medical student and physician confront death almost daily. This confrontation awakens an ancient impulse deep within the person—to move away from the dying. Moving away from the dying is not caring for the dying, which is a major professional and human responsibility. The task then is to work with our feelings about death so that we will be free to care for our patients and not be controlled by our fears and defensive behavior.

The ability to endure the presence of death in life is of paramount importance in human existence. To open oneself to death is to accept the aspect of becoming, that is, of transformation, which is the very essence of life. Because, however, medical students are suddenly flooded with an "excess of death" in anatomy laboratories, autopsy rooms, and dying patients in hospital wards, they may quickly shut themselves off from this aspect of life by putting aside all thought of death. This inhibits their own psychological growth and creates in its place an appearance of security which is, in fact, continually threatened by unconscious anxieties.

How does one relate to, and come to terms with, death, which seems to stand in irreconcilable contrast to life and to all one's experience of living things? The concern is not with one's intellectual response to physical defenselessness, but with the way in which the person, in the center of one's being, feels touched by the inevitability of death. Is one able to bring this fact into harmony with one's feeling for life?

From the dawn of consciousness, whenever humans have encountered and become aware of death, they have been horrified to the very core of their being. Their impending death or the death of others has brought almost equally the feeling of horror. Herzog has said that one can find a way of uniting life and death, of bringing them into harmony,

239

only if one is prepared to transcend the limits of one's existence: "This task is only possible if man can see that part of himself reaches into the unknown, and that it is from the unknown that order and meaning are given to life."[10]

The person, as a creature of time and space, is faced with the task of identifying himself or herself with eternity. The most helpful response will issue from basic philosophical, religious, or psychological deliberations about death already in one's possession. Most of us cannot endure pondering death without resources, be they transcendental, inspirational, or existential.

Regardless of the population studied, death is usually viewed as the extreme abomination in one's experience. Despite a host of defense mechanisms and stratagems, fear of finitude is never quite hushed. In the face of death, almost all patients—the terminally, seriously, chronically, and mentally ill—assess the world as good and not to be ceded if possible.

People have a legitimate need to turn away from death, but doctors have little opportunity to do so. Unfortunately, the doctors' work has been made more difficult because an excessive camouflage and eradication of the notion of death prevail in the United States, leading to a falsification of the essence of human beings. Energies used in continuing attempts to shelve and repress the concept of death could be more constructively applied to other aspects of living. Forster has commented penetratingly that "death destroys a man but the *idea* of death saves him."[8] This camouflage of death continues in spite of a flood of publications on death and dying.

Medical students, through their experiences with dying patients, are forced to recognize at some level of their consciousness the interrelation of the anticipation of death and the conduct of life. Although seldom emphasized in medical school, this interrelation has been recognized and commented upon by generations of philosophers and theologians.

ACCEPTING OUR FINITUDE

Humankind underwent a long process of development before it could accept death as essentially related to life and as an essential feature of the human condition. At first death must have seemed completely alien to life, and by no means a natural part of it. Yet one becomes conscious of life in its familiar reality only as a result of the contrast with death. This contrast gives life a value of its own by providing a dark background against which to reflect it more radiantly. Dante gives us remarkable insight into life and death through his picture of hell: "There they have not the hope of death."

Today, many people manage to repress death emotionally and acknowledge it only intellectually because they are dominated by a deep sense of the potential "omnipotence" of science. They regard death as a thing which really ought not to happen and take great comfort in the steady flow of newspaper articles about victories of science in the struggle against death or the conquest of death. Recent spectacular developments in medical technology have greatly augmented this wishful thinking on the part of many people, including physicians. Such an escapist attitude may help a little in the quest for assurance, but it is a remarkably close parallel to the attitude of our ancient ancestors who, in their drawings and paintings, represented death by an individual fleeing from a dead person in panic and horror.

The spectacular advances in surgery, genetics, and other fields have fostered visions of control over life and death, making any reminder of humankind's continuing finitude seem both incongruous and unacceptable. The responsibility afforded by greater and greater extensions of power over life (and over the boundaries, but not the fact, of death) is to be exercised in light of a *mortal* perspective and not from a vantage point above history as a timeless master.[15] Medical students or physicians caught up in this fantasy of doing away with death will be unable to reap for themselves and their patients the rich benefits growing out of the acceptance of one's finitude. Instead, their energies will be spent in yet another type of effort to quell their inner turmoil over their own fears of death.

WRESTLING WITH THE PARADOXES OF DEATH

Death is not a phenomenon that one can think about in a disinterested fashion. Because it is such a final event in one's life, anxieties about death continually threaten to distort attitudes and thoughts about it. Thus, death has a paradoxical character.

Although death is an inevitable and universal event, it is one which a person cannot take lightly, cannot demote to the status of a common, everyday happening. While death may be an ordinary event, for a particular individual death asserts itself as an *extra*-ordinary event. No one else can do one's dying, for one's own death is intensely personal. The awareness of death and the integration of this awareness into one's life are at the root of personality.

Another paradox surrounding death is that while we accept intellectually the fact that we are going to die, emotionally and experientially we have difficulty in believing it. There seems to be a factor in conscious experience that encourages us to avoid considering that which, in another sense, we know is our destiny. With the passing of years and experience with illness, this response gradually becomes chastened and tempered.

A third paradox is that death is both a biological and spiritual phenomenon. The sense in which death is biological is obvious, but a person has to face the question of what death means. The meaning of death has to do with the spirit and involves primarily consciousness and awareness. The real fear about death relates to the ultimate loss of consciousness, the end of all meaningful experience, the dissolution of one's personality. If meaningful involvement could continue, what happens physically would be of minor importance. In appearance, there is little difference between the dead body and one that is asleep, but in another sense we are overwhelmingly aware of the difference: consciousness with all it entails is gone forever.

Although death occurs as an end to life, its reality permeates the whole of one's existence. The awareness of the fact of death may impose a pattern on one's life of which one is often unaware. Intimations of mortality are a part of one's life from an early age, although these intimations are usually not kept in conscious awareness because they would be too anxiety provoking. Without saying much about it, one's realization of one's impending death, at some level of awareness, makes one long to leave an enduring mark on the world.

MADE FREE BY THE ANTICIPATION OF DEATH

The Psalmist has prayed: "So teach us to number our days, that we may apply our hearts unto wisdom." The courage and determination to make sense of life while it lasts and fulfill all its possibilities can come only when we accept our finitude, the fact that one day death will claim us.

Often when one fritters away life yet is constantly intimidated by symbolic threats of death, much time and energy are consumed in hoping that there will be no death. On the other hand, the realization of death places immediate and tremendous pressures upon the person. The continuing recognition of one's mortality suffuses life with a liberating sense of urgency and helps one avoid self-deception. The problem of the meaning of life becomes a problem of first importance.

When one is free of the fear of death or symbolic threats of death (loss of job, disruption of one's dependency on another person, sickness, loss of friends, and so on), one is usually able to see one's life as a total project, to look ahead toward a complete plan for life. The immediacy of death, the awareness that one has no time to waste, leads to honesty with oneself and the ability and courage to make important decisions. The person aware of a limited life span will usually concentrate on essentials and not waste time in useless details. Detail is often an excuse to avoid the real issues in life and keeps one from getting immediately to the point of one's life.

Many who learn that they have a very limited life span, like the persons who have been told they have about a year left, take stock of their lives after regaining their composure. They are now forced to decide what in life is important and what is not. They are compelled to face the question of the ultimate meaning of life and to face it *now*. Usually they will not procrastinate, and they may suddenly experience an extraordinary and almost inexhaustible surge of energy. An old proverb declares that in victory, no one is tired. The individual with limited time to live has the power and the motivation to make a success of life and now realizes that one cannot escape from the obligation to fulfill one's life. Authentic success and the full meaning of life can probably be achieved only when one has clear insight into the fact that every individual has been condemned to die, including oneself.[11, 12, 13]

Death must be faced irrespective of religious commitment. The believer and the disbeliever in immortality are subject to the vicissitudes and the vitality of death. One may handle the fact of death by becoming deeply religious. If one does, this may help one cut through the pseudo goals of one's life such as status, sex, and money, and direct one's mind to the ultimate problem. If one acquires a steadfast conviction in immortality, then one can spend some time in the preparation for immortality, whatever the mode of immortality to which one subscribes.

The outlook on life as stressed here corresponds well to these words of Cyril Connolly in *The Unquiet Grave:* "Melancholy and remorse form the deep leaden keel which enables us to sail into the wind of reality; we run aground sooner than the flat-bottomed pleasure-lovers, but we venture out in weather that would sink them." Thus, it is not difficult to see that a primary task of the person is the recognition that the threat of death—real and symbolic—is inevitable and inescapable. One must acknowledge and accept the truth that "time is running out." Peter Koestenbaum, philosopher and psychotherapist, is one of the most articulate and insightful persons of our time in guiding us to a better understanding of the vitality that comes from an acceptance of one's finitude.[11, 12, 13]

LEARNING HOW TO DIE

Martin Heidegger claims the authentic life to be the life that is lived in the presence of death. He is convinced that it is only by unblinkingly facing one's eventual annulment that a person can be delivered from the trivial cares of the normal daily round and enabled to dedicate himself or herself to projects whereby a human career may be given some really high significance.

The reality of death that presses in upon the medical student and doctor every day invites them compellingly to deepen their self-understanding and to reach for some greater profundity in their grasp of what it means to be human. The awareness that death lends a special quality to living has had various familiar expressions throughout the history of humankind. A deep-wrought consciousness of the limits of life, of the shadow of the sphinx, acts like a charge and lends a richness to life. This theme appears in the prefatory essay to Wescott's volume of stories, *Good-Bye Wisconsin*. Wescott explains why he and his expatriates went to Europe in the 1920s: "It is the Greeks and Romans and the traditions preserved in Europe by the translations of Petrarch and by Montaigne and Goethe which, if one is an American, exasperate the imagination. Traditions of the conduct of life with death in mind."[31]

In response to Wescott's comment, one cannot help thinking of two remarkable customs that existed in ancient Rome. During great banquets or special feasts, a visitor would appear briefly in the banquet hall, carrying a skeleton and a sign which read: "Remember, all must die." Another custom related to the victorious warrior who returned home from his conquests to be honored by his people. As he rode through the city in his chariot, with the shouting throngs lining the streets, a servant stood behind him in the chariot holding a golden crown over his head and whispering in his ear: "All glory is fleeting."

Often, a young person busily engaged in building a philosophy of life has been most courageous in coming to terms with death as an essential prerequisite for coming to terms with life and vocation. Thus, it is not astonishing that William Cullen Bryant wrote "Thanatopsis," Edna St. Vincent Millay wrote "Renascence," and Franz Schubert wrote his lieder of death, all while they were teen-agers.

Psychiatrist-philosopher Karl Jaspers has expressed succinctly the decisive task facing all of us: "If to philosophize is to learn how to die, then this learning how to die is actually the condition for the good life. To learn to live and to learn how to die are one and the same thing."[5] Possibly Thomas Mann was expressing a similar thought when he said: "All interest in disease and death is only another expression of interest in life."[21]

Death and tragedy are both great teachers. Philosophy begins when we recognize the fact that all are mortal, and faith is probably born when we deal with the meaning of our finitude. Such was the experience of Willie Keith in *The Caine Mutiny*.[32] One of the sailors aboard the ship went to his battle station. A bomb from the kamikaze plane hit the sailor's station and blew him to bits. The novel continues: "With the smoke of the dead sailor's cigar wreathing around him, Willie passed to thinking about death and life and luck and God. Philosophers are at home with such thoughts perhaps, but for other people it's actually torture when these concepts—not the words but the realities— break through the crust of daily occurrences and grip the soul. A half hour of such racking meditation can change the ways of a lifetime. Willie Keith crushing the stub in the ashtray was not the Willie Keith who had lit the cigar."

Many young people in contemplating their finitude and the brevity of life have been challenged to fill their limited life span with noble and unselfish living. The intimation of a rendezvous with death led Countee Cullen, an 18-year-old black youth and a senior in a New York City high school, to speak about man's rendezvous with life:

> I have a rendezvous with Life
> In days I hope will come,
> Ere youth has sped and strength of mind,
> Ere voices sweet grow dumb;
> I have a rendezvous with Life
> When Spring's first heralds hum.[6]

Adaptation to death is a necessary part of maturation, and deficiency in this adaptation is an integral factor in neurosis. Stern, through the use of extensive clinical material from his psychiatric practice, postulates that fear of death is fear of the repetition of mortal terror experienced in early ubiquitous biotraumatic situations defined as object loss or being abandoned by the mother, and that underlying mortal terror—the response in trauma—is primarily depression, a state of sensorimotor retardation.[27] The amalgamation of anxieties of the past with the fear of the inevitable final trauma perpetuates the impact of early conflicts and reinforces the clinging to infantile dependency, according to Stern.

Some rich rewards can come to the medical student and physician in their care of the dying. Being therapist to a dying patient resensitizes one to the uniqueness of each person—and to one's own finitude. Work with the dying person can provide the therapist with an invaluable entryway to further understanding of who one is. Furthermore, it can be a liberating experience, not only for the patient, but for the one involved in the treatment as well.

NO PERSONS LIVETH UNTO THEMSELVES

The most significant explorations of death must always treat persons in their relatedness. Because no persons live completely unto themselves, the problem involves more than the finitude of the person. Theologian Joseph Haroutunian contends that the anxiety regarding death can be understood only when "man" is seen as a "fellowman." "Man" is a being who exists as a "fellowman" by virtue of his acknowledgment of others as existing with himself, thus making his own life possible by their communications with him. Knowledge of oneself as destined for physical death emerges in one's life in togetherness with others.[9] One is self-conscious as a being who is conscious of his neighbor. In other words, consciousness of oneself and others is a function of the actual presence of others and of the daily transactions that take place between one another. We die as human beings because we live as human beings, that is, by our communion with one another. In communion, the decisive thing is love.

It has been said that one is most alone when one dies. In a sense this is true, for that person alone dies. It does not follow, however, that one dies alone or that one's death is simply the end of the individual organism. "A man dies as a fellowman, and the sting of death is his separation from his fellowmen, or the end of life which is the loss of fellowmen. It is love that provides the peculiar shock of human death, and the only way not to feel the sting of death is to deny the love which is our life."[9]

Possibly Segal's *Love Story* struck a responsive chord in the hearts of millions simply because the reader caught a glimpse of how the human meaning of death is bound up with the question of love. In the midst of death, Jenny and Oliver cherished every precious moment given them together. In the presence of such love, there was no thought of the living wanting to flee from the dying—but only the thought that in such communion there could be no separation.[25]

A task for every individual is to experience a sense of participation in the whole of humankind. Such a sense is deeply reassuring in the face of the knowledge of death. The living and the dead and the generations yet unborn make up that enduring communion of humanity that shares the adventure of life upon this earth. William Cullen Bryant's poem "Thanatopsis" beautifully conveys this sense of participation:

> Yet not to thine eternal resting-place
> Shalt thou retire alone, nor couldst thou wish
> Couch more magnificent. Thou shalt lie down
> With patriarchs of the infant world—with kings,

The powerful of the earth—the wise, the good,
Fair forms, and hoary seers of ages past,
All in one mighty sepulchre . . . .[3]

DEFENSES USED IN DEALING WITH DEATH

The outstanding characteristic of protoplasm is a persistent tendency to remain intact in spite of being surrounded by media that ensure its ultimate destruction. It is generally accepted that along with the acquisition of speech and the use of tools, the awareness of death was among the first truly human characteristics.

A group of defenses gradually developed to deal with death and its awareness. These form a phylogenetic progression or steps up the ladder of conquering the fear of death: denial, projection, propitiation, flirtation, substitution, and sublimation.[22]

Ceremonial burial was practiced early in human history. (Out of sight is out of mind.) Denial of the loss of the capacity to function in death inspired the burying of food and tools with the corpse. This custom developed, however, at a somewhat later date.

The early Hebraic attempt to reconstruct in writing the beginnings of all things led to the story of Adam and Eve who were driven from the Garden of Eden because they had acquired a forbidden knowledge of good and evil—that is, life and death. Humans now became aware that they must die. As a penalty for acquiring this bitter knowledge, the man must work and the woman must bear her children in pain, according to the Genesis story. Upon the pillars of accomplishment and compassion civilization has been built.

When denial was no longer possible except symbolically, personification of death made possible its physical projection. In a futile effort to thrust death from oneself by giving it away or forcing it upon another, Cain killed his brother Abel, thus establishing the prototype of the "aimless" murder. After killing Abel, Cain's first impulse was to hide. When early humans first began their mad raids of killing to project death from themselves, they became the epitome of death to others. They were hunted and they hid. They hunted and they hid. Hiding as a defense against death from nonhuman agencies, as well as human, became common, for the two were only dimly differentiated.

Sacrifice of the most valued one next to the self, the firstborn son, softened gradually in time to the substitution of the criminal or a prized animal. The projection of death onto some "other" had the effect of mitigating, temporarily, the dread of death. Stylized and surrounded by ceremonies, these performances were part of the development of the world's religions. Thus, propitiation was a giant step forward in humankind's dealing with the fear of death.

Flirtation and escape as a method of recapturing the joy that follows a brush with death is difficult to locate in the sequence of humankind's emerging defenses. To beard the lion in the den, to be involved in daring encounters with natural hazards, to be involved in dangers when one appears to die, and then, to come alive or to be "born again" provides a new and stimulating lease on life. On the psychic level, these experiences "prove" the individual's immunity to death. The story of the hero who escapes death, preferably through his own efforts, remains the number one plot. Stories of successful sexual conquest run a poor second. The "flirt and escape" devotee remains with us as the test pilot, stunt person, athlete, daring explorer, and mountain climber.

Substitution is comparable to displacement and refers to an unacceptable emotion, goal, or object which is replaced by one which is more attainable or acceptable. A form of substitution would be listening to the stories of the hero's escape from death. The vicarious pleasure in listening to such stories provides a weak but satisfactory copy of the original sensation.

Socrates learned from Diotima, to whom the Athenians offered sacrifice, that "to the mortal creature, generation is a sort of eternity and immortality . . . . Marvel not then at the love which all men have of their offspring, for that universal love and interest are for the sake of immortality." Diotima went on to say "there certainly are men who are more creative in their souls than in their bodies . . . . Such creatures are poets and all artists who are deserving of the name inventor. But the greatest and fairest sort of wisdom by far is that which is concerned with the ordering of states and which is called temperance and justice."[23] Sublimation in its highest form becomes the desire to leave the world richer in knowledge and compassion than the individual found it. To ease, extend, and enrich the lives of others is the inspiration for the choice of occupations of doctors, educators, and scientists.

A SENSE OF IMMORTALITY

The human has a need to maintain a sense of immortality in the face of inevitable biological death. This need is related to a compelling universal urge to keep an inner sense of continuous symbolic relationship, over time and space, to the various elements of life. It is part of the organism's psychobiological quest for mastery, part of an innate imagery that has apparently been present in the mind since the earliest periods of history and prehistory.[4, 20]

Otto Rank has written of the human's long-standing need of "an assurance of eternal survival for his self," and further stated that "man creates culture by changing natural conditions in order to maintain his spiritual self."[24] One cannot ignore the important psychological perspective which sees the quest for immortality as inherent in human psychology and human life. Although one is capable of denying the fact of death, the sense of immortality is much more than such a denial. More basic is the quest for a way of experiencing one's connection with all human history, with the continuity of life. Probably no person has been more lucid and informed in discussing psychologically the topic of the continuity of life than Robert J. Lifton, psychiatrist and clinical researcher. We are indebted to him for his great work and illuminating insights.[16, 17, 18, 19, 20]

According to Lifton, the sense of immortality may be expressed through any of several modes.[18, 19] First, it may be expressed biosocially by means of family continuity, living on through one's sons and daughters and their sons and daughters, by imagining an endless chain of biological attachment. This mode of immortality never remains purely biological but extends into social dimensions in the sense of surviving through one's organization, religious body, nation, or even species.

Second, a sense of immortality may be achieved through a theologically based idea of a life after death as a form of survival and as a release from this life to existence on a higher plane. This concept has been present in the world's great religions and throughout human mythology. The theological mode need not rely upon a concrete vision of afterlife, and no such vision is prominent in many forms of Jewish and Buddhist belief. Christianity has perhaps been most explicit in its doctrine of life after death, but intra-Christian debate over interpretation of doctrine has never ceased, with present thought tending toward a stress upon transcendent symbolism rather than literal belief. Lifton contends that what is basic is a symbolic conquest of death on the part of the religion's hero and founder. He goes on to say that Buddha, Moses, Christ, and Mohammed transcended individual death through various combinations of moral attainment and revelation and left teachings by which their followers could strive to do likewise.[19]

The third mode of immortality may be achieved through one's creative works or human influences—through one's art, writings, inventions, thought, and lasting influence of any kind upon human beings. Lasting influences upon individuals, who in turn transmit them to their posterity, can be an important mode of immortality for teachers, clergymen, and physicians.

The fourth mode of immortality may be achieved through being survived by nature itself: the perception that natural elements—limitless in space and time—remain. The renewed interest in the natural environment may be a form of clinging to those natural forces that preceded us and that we have always counted upon to outlast us. This theme often emerges in memorial services, particularly those for physicians that are conducted by physicians. A typical example is a recent memorial service in which one of the participating physicians emphasized: "Man, with all his diverse gifts, is fully part and product of the nature that is his home. He is cousin to all other living forms. Thus, beyond our kinship with our fellowmen, there is always our kinship with the natural world that stamps its pattern of constant change on every existing thing. . . . Life and death are different and essential aspects of the same creative process. In this sense life affirms itself through death. In death as in life we belong to nature."

Lifton identifies the fifth mode of immortality as experiential transcendence that depends entirely upon a psychic state of ecstasy or rapture to break the ordinary bounds of existence, of the senses, and of mortality itself. It is encountered in religious and secular mysticism, but ecstatic experiences have emerged in song, dance, battle, sexual love, childbirth, athletic effort, mechanical flight, contemplation, and artistic and intellectual creation—sometimes with the aid of drugs, fasting or starvation, and other ordeals. Such experiences involve a profound reordering of the symbolic world that we inhabit. These experiences bring a sense of connectedness and significance not ordinarily available to the individual. Also, there is at least a temporary move beyond the problems of time and death. This immortalizing element is probably at the root of both its intensity and its capacity to produce enduring inner change.

One may ask, what does this discussion of the modes of immortality have to do with one coming to terms with one's feelings about death? I believe that Lifton is right in emphasizing that the controlling image in human psychology is that of death and the continuity of life. As symbol-forming beings, we have a need for connectedness with something beyond ourselves, for an inner sense of continuous symbolic relationship over time and space to larger and more enduring forms than the individual self. The medical profession today seems to have great difficulty coming to terms with ideas on death and even greater difficulty with the tenacious human insistence upon some form of life outlasting death. Doctors often tend to dismiss the impulse as superstition or to consider it a matter of private belief well outside professional concern.

Unfortunately, at a time when the theologically based mode of immortality is less attractive to many people, some of the other modes of immortality are threatened by nuclear weapons and our capacity to destroy the earth. The bomb, the body counts in our unending wars, and the killings on our highways and in our streets have made death a daily part of our symbolism. Further, other events can be mentioned—Three Mile Island, the Love Canal, Agent Orange, as well as genetic effects of LSD and marijuana. The terror probably comes less from the fear of individual death than from the lost sense that anything can be permanent. Yet, in this atmosphere the doctor must care for patients, ministering meaningfully both to the living and the dying. The mythological theme of death and rebirth takes on particular pertinence now for doctor and patient, and every constructive effort that can be made to grasp something of the doctor's and the patient's relationship to death becomes, in its own way, a small stimulus to rebirth.

TOLSTOY, IVAN ILYICH, AND EACH PERSON'S STRUGGLE

Count Leo Tolstoy's *The Death of Ivan Ilyich,* a double story of the decomposing body and awakening soul, is one of the most powerful works in the literature of the world. Tolstoy's original idea had been simply to write a diary of a man struggling with and then abandoning himself to death. Gradually he saw, however, what the story might gain in tragic depth by being told in the third person.[29]

Tolstoy employs the same precision in his clinical analysis of the disease (cancer of the abdominal region) as in his description of the successive stages passed through by the dying man's soul.* Ivan Ilyich, the dying man, is in no way exceptional, or even likable, but we identify with him because through him we imagine what our own death will be. While Ivan Ilyich moans in his pain and draws up the balance sheet for his life, our own lives pass in review. At the end of his torment, two things are at the forefront: the terror of what is coming and the emptiness of what has been. "No philosophical dissertation can ever equal in depth this simple 'documentary'—unemotional, sharp, cruel, devoid of all artistic effect—of a sickroom."[29] The story is a classic literary expression of anticipated death as a test of the integrity of one's entire life, of the cohesion and significance of the life one has been living.

It has been said that the theme of Ivan Ilyich is related to Tolstoy's struggle against an obsessive fear of death and the conclusion that he

---

* Kubler-Ross's clinical observations in *Death and Dying* are quite similar to Leo Tolstoy's artistic perceptions in *The Death of Ivan Ilyich.* Tolstoy describes the same stages and criticizes the same attitudes toward death that Kubler-Ross abhors in her book.[14] Although Tolstoy did not spend much time in hospitals, his artistic sensibilities allowed him to perceive the same behavior and attitudes associated with death that Kubler-Ross noted under clinical conditions almost a century later.[26]

had wasted his life, a struggle which culminated for him in a spiritual rebirth. His struggle was not too different from that of every person who at some level and at some time must work through one's feelings about death. Hopefully, one will face the confrontation creatively, recognizing one's failures, shattered dreams and lost opportunities, and emerge from the experience not in despair but spiritually renewed and reborn. This is why Tolstoy's portrayal of the life and death of Ivan Ilyich strikes such a responsive chord in each individual who reads the story. Here is one of the finest examples in all literature of this basic existential theme of discovering through death the meaning of life, portrayed with such realistic understanding that one perceives immediately its universal significance.

Ivan Ilyich, trained in law, is a judge and a perfect example of the conscientious official. His rise through the ranks of the administration keeps pace with the increasing boredom of his marriage. His material circumstances are vastly improved by an unexpected promotion. He is able to move into a luxurious apartment perfectly suited "to his rank," and he becomes totally absorbed in decorating and furnishing it. When there is nothing left to decorate, he and his family become bored again. While hanging curtains, however, Ivan Ilyich falls from a ladder and, after a time, the pain begins to grow worse instead of better. This is the prelude to a period of constant anguish for the judge. He senses that something dreadful has been going on inside of him—something more important than everything that has happened to him until then.

He consults doctors who reassure but cannot cure him. His wife and daughter refuse to take him seriously or feign cheerfulness in order to diminish his worrying. A chasm opens up between him and all people who have their health. They are only play acting or role playing. Of course, Ivan Ilyich had been a master at playing roles. He understood his role as a judge and treated everyone precisely according to his position in society, never deviating except when, with a show of virtuosity, he went beyond the role just so he could come back to it. He treated his wife and children the same way. In his illness, when physicians and everyone else treat him in the same way that he had treated others, he learns the bitter fact that he was only a case:

> Ivan Ilyich's great misery was due to the deception that for some reason or other everyone kept up with him—that he was simply ill, and not dying, and that he need only keep quiet and follow the doctor's orders, then some great change for the better would be the result. He knew that whatever they might do there would be no result except more agonizing suffering and death. And he was made miserable by this lie, made miserable at their

refusing to acknowledge what they all knew and he knew, by their persisting in lying to him about his awful position, and in forcing him too to take part in this lie. . . . Apart from this deception, or in consequence of it, what made the greatest misery for Ivan Ilyich was that no one felt for him as he would have liked them to feel for him. At certain moments, after prolonged suffering, Ivan Ilyich, ashamed as he would have been to own it, longed more than anything for some one to feel sorry for him, as for a sick child. He longed to be petted, kissed, and wept over, as children are petted and comforted. He knew that he was an important member of the law-courts, that he had a beard turning grey, and that therefore it was impossible, but still he longed for it . . . . Ivan Ilyich longed to weep, longed to be petted and wept over.[28]

Ivan Ilyich's servant boy Gerasim and his own young son Volodya are the only two whom he feels understand him and are genuinely sorry. Gerasim does all the nursing chores cheerfully, willingly, and spontaneously. Of all those around Ivan, this servant boy is the only one who can accept death as natural. Once he says to Ivan, "We shall all of us die," and goes on to reassure him that the nursing chores are no trouble at all.

As Ivan grows steadily worse, the strength and honesty of Gerasim nourish him, for he feels that the members of his family are hypocrites who choose to pretend that he is not dying. Death to his family is not part of the same decorum he, too, had once revered and is therefore hidden as unpleasant and shameful. Only the peasant boy Gerasim can understand his pain because only he admits that death is real and natural.

Ivan retreats into his private anguish and begins to wrestle with the question "Where shall I be when I am no more?" As his illness wears on, he begins to feel more alone, less understood, less loved. His presence is a weight upon his family, for he is preventing them from being happy, amusing themselves, and going about their business. In trying to recall his former pleasant life, he is appalled to discover that all the memories he took for gold are nothing but false coin. Only memories of childhood reveal true happiness. Yet, if he had always lived correctly, why was this happening to him and what really was one's purpose on earth? Gradually it dawns on him that all the time he thought he was succeeding in his career, he was actually failing in his life. Suddenly he knows that the scarcely detected urges he had consciously stilled in order to do as people thought proper had been the true impulses, in fact the only authentic expressions of his life. Since he had not known the truth about life, he also had not known the truth about death. His sorrow increases as he thinks of the irrevocable choices he had made. His lament in the face of approaching death is that of wasted opportunity. ("I have lost all that was given me and it is impossible to rectify it") and existential guilt related to the awareness of the enormous gap between what he had been and what he feels he might have been.

The priest comes and the sacrament eases him and gives him hope momentarily. Soon his wife's presence reminds him of the deception that his life has been. He is seized with terror and screams for three days, unable to relinquish the illusion that his life has been good. Then the struggle ceases. He grows calm and begins to listen attentively. In that instant it is revealed to him that although his life had not been what it ought to have been, it still can be set right. Opening his eyes, he sees his wife and son weeping by his bedside, and his son holding and kissing his hand. Deeply aware of them now and of their feelings, he feels sorry for them. As he asks their forgiveness, everything becomes clear to him. He must not hurt them, must set them free and be free himself of his agonies. At this point for Ivan Ilyich, death disappears: "Death is finished . . . it is no more!" The pain and fear of death are no longer present; instead there is only light and joy. "So this is it!" he suddenly exclaims aloud, "What joy!"

Death had meant emptiness and the termination of a life without significance. Death is transcended through a sudden spiritual revelation which revivifies Ivan Ilyich's sense of immortality by transporting him, even momentarily, into a realm of what he can perceive as authentic experience. In this realm, also, he feels in contact with eternal human values of pity and love.[20]

Significant in Ivan Ilyich's search for meaning in his life is his disgust for the evasiveness of those around him concerning the nature of his illness. In spite of his yearning for an end to this falsity, his family members are incapable of acting otherwise because their deception is also self-deception, their own need to deny death. Why? Because they are immersed in their own guilt over why they are being permitted to live while he is dying—guilt made particularly intense by their hypocrisy and relief that death is claiming him and not them.*

The one voice of integrity around Ivan Ilyich is that of his servant Gerasim, who makes no effort to hide from him the fact that he is dying but instead helps him understand that death is natural and, after all, the fate of everyone. Here Gerasim, the living, lessens the emotional

---

* Bruno Bettelheim, a survivor of the Nazi concentration camps, emphasizes a cause of "survivor guilt" often overlooked. One is glad that "it was he who died and not I." This feeling of gladness, Bettelheim contends, is the source of personal guilt that a survivor finds hard to free himself of.[1]

gap between himself and Ivan Ilyich, the dying, by stressing their shared destiny. This in turn enables the dying Ivan Ilyich to see his experience in relationship to the larger rhythm of life and death, and thereby awakens his biologically linked mode of immortality.

We who work with the dying patient may serve functions similar to that of Ivan Ilyich's servant Gerasim. K.R. Eissler in *The Psychiatrist and the Dying Patient* speaks of helping the patient during the "terminal pathway" to "accomplish the maximum individualization of which he is capable."[7] Weisman and Hackett, in numerous papers, similarly stress psychiatric intervention to help the dying patient preserve his or her identity and dignity as a unique individual, despite the disease, or, in some cases, because of it. Lifton emphasizes that achieving these goals depends also upon restoring the patient's sense of immortality through any of the various modes available to him.[18] Weisman and Hackett describe a "middle knowledge" or partial awareness which patients have of their impending death, and find that patients' relatives and attending physicians, like those of Ivan Ilyich, because of their own conflicts over death, often have a greater need to deny this outcome than patients themselves. A situation is thus created in which patients are unwilling to admit their "middle knowledge" to those around them, for fear that they will move away from them and leave them alone and isolated from those who have given their life a sense of continuity and connection.[30]

CONCLUSION

In summary, how can one accept one's finitude and come to terms with one's feelings about death? There is no easy answer to be given by others, for the solution lies in a deep personal struggle to understand something of one's own nature and destiny. In this search, the medical student has often found the dying patient an excellent teacher. Keeping company with the dying can be a fulfilling and rewarding experience for one who demonstrates concern by caring for patients in the full sense of the word. With the help of such patients one can begin one's own preparation for death. It is interesting that the great physician William Osler always thought of himself as a student of the art and act of dying; and patients saw Osler as one who had looked deeply into the eyes of death and understood something of the mystery of death—its impenetrable mystery.

A further step is to read great literature and see how those portrayed there faced death and sought its meaning. For example, as mentioned earlier, Leo Tolstoy's *The Death of Ivan Ilyich* is probably the greatest masterpiece on death that has been written in either ancient or modern times. Other writings include Alexander Solzhenitsyn's *Cancer Ward,* John Gunther's *Death Be Not Proud,* Albert Camus' *The Plague,* and Helmut Gollwitzer's *Dying We Live.*

Also, we should seek in history how others have handled death or maintained a mortal perspective. We can learn much from the ancient Greeks' tragic sense of life and much from the Romans who repeatedly reminded themselves that all glory is fleeting and that all must die.

One of the most ancient of all admonitions declares that since there is no remedy for death then we should prepare for it. Preparation and acceptance go hand in hand. May we be guided by the words with which the seventeenth-century physician Sir Thomas Browne closed his book of self-revelation, *Religio Medici:* "Bless me in this life with but the peace of my conscience, command of my affections, the love of thyself and my dearest friends, and I shall be happy enough to pity Caesar. These are, O Lord, the humble desires of my most reasonable ambition, and all I dare call happiness on earth: wherein I set no rule or limit to thy hand or providence. Dispose of me according to the wisdom of thy pleasure. Thy will be done, though in my own undoing."[2]

It is only in daring to accept one's death as a companion that a person may really possess life. Doctors are no exception. They, like their patients, will guard their Thermopylae, and they deserve honor if they are able to foresee that Ephialtes will finally appear, and in the end the Medes will go through.

REFERENCES

1. Bettelheim B: The ultimate limit. Reflections 4:22, 1969
2. Browne T: Religio Medici. Edited and annotated by Winney J. London, Cambridge University Press, 1963, p 96
3. Bryant WC: Thanatopsis. In Hill CM (ed): The World's Great Religious Poetry. New York, Macmillan, 1944, pp 699–701
4. Campbell J: The Masks of God: Primitive Mythology. New York, Viking, 1959, pp 30–49, 461–472
5. Choron J: Death and Western Thought. New York, Collier Books, 1963, p 228
6. Cullen C: I Have a Rendezvous with Life. In Cullen (ed): Caroling Dusk. New York, Harper & Row, 1927
7. Eissler KR: The Psychiatrist and the Dying Patient. New York, International Universities Press, 1955
8. Forster EM: Aphorism. In Auden WH, Kronenberger W (eds): The Viking Book of Aphorisms. New York, Viking Press, 1962
9. Haroutunian J: Life and death among fellowmen. In Scott NA Jr (ed): The Modern Vision of Death. Richmond, John Knox Press, 1967, pp 79–96

10. Herzog E: Psyche and Death. Translated by Cox D, Rolfe E. New York, Putnam, 1967, p 17
11. Koestenbaum P: Is There an Answer to Death? Engelwood Cliffs, NJ, Prentice-Hall, 1976
12. Koestenbaum P: The New Image of the Person: The Theory and Practice of Clinical Philosophy. Westport, Conn, Greenwood, 1978
13. Koestenbaum P: The Vitality of Death. Westport, Conn, Greenwood, 1971; See also The vitality of death. J Exist 5:139, 1964
14. Kubler-Ross E: On Death and Dying. New York, Macmillan, 1969
15. Laney JT: Ethics and death. In Mills LO (ed): Perspectives on Death. New York, Abingdon Press, 1969, p 236
16. Lifton RJ, Olson E: Living and Dying. New York, Praeger, 1974
17. Lifton RJ: On death and the continuity of life—a psychohistorical perspective. Omega 6:143, 1975
18. Lifton RJ: On death and death symbolism: The Hiroshima disaster. Psychiatry 27:191, 1964
19. Lifton RJ: Politics of immortality. Psychology Today 4:70, 108, 1970
20. Lifton RJ: The Broken Connection: On Death and the Continuity of Life. New York, Simon & Schuster, 1979
21. Mann T: The Magic Mountain. Translated by Lowe-Portey, H.T. New York, Knopf, 1946, p 495
22. Maurer A: The child's knowledge of nonexistence. J Existent Psychiatr 2: 193, 1961
23. Plato: Symposium. The Portable Plato. New York, Viking, 1948
24. Rank O: Beyond Psychology. New York, Dover, 1958, pp 62–101
25. Segal E: Love Story, New York, Harper, 1970
26. Soudek IH: Waiting for the end—a study of the similarities between Elizabeth Kubler-Ross's On Death and Dying and Leo Tolstoy's The Death of Ivan Ilyich. Pharos 43:9, 1979
27. Stern MM: Fear of death and neurosis. J Am Psychoanal Assoc 16:3, 1968
28. Tolstoy L: The Death of Ivan Ilyich. Selected Tales. Washington, DC, National Home Library Foundation, 1935
29. Troyat H: Tolstoy. Translated by Amphoux N. Garden City, New York, Doubleday, 1967, pp 460–462
30. Weisman AD, Hackett TP: Reactions to the imminence of death. In Grosser GH, Wechsler H, Greenblatt M (eds): The Threat of Impending Disaster. Cambridge, Mass, MIT Press, 1964, pp 300–311
31. Wescott G: Good-Bye Wisconsin. New York, Harper, 1928, p 34
32. Wouk H: The Caine Mutiny. New York, Doubleday, 1954

15

SO NOBLE
A HERITAGE

May God give you
not peace but glory.
—Miguel de Unamuno

The transformation of a medical student into a physician is a rugged
and remarkable endeavor. The student's educational experience in
medical school is probably the most intense and emotion laden of all
educational experiences. In each stage of the student's training, the sick
person's presence is real or implied; and this presence brings a special
human dimension that permeates every aspect of the student's learning.

While the major focus of this book is the philosophical and emotional
growth of the medical student, I am aware that an essential aspect of
medical training is the house staff phase. The partial neglect of the residency phase is not to minimize its importance. At the same time, my
preoccupation with the "magic years" of medical school grows out of
the firm belief that the foundation is laid in medical school for much of
what the doctor will be in the future. If the foundation is solid, the doctor's house staff training, as well as a lifetime of continuing education,
will have the proper support and undergirding necessary for effective
development.

Medical students are cognizant of the heavy demands being placed
upon their profession by a society now awakened to the reality that all
its people deserve and should receive adequate health care. Also,
today's medical students seem as determined as any who have gone
before them to make central in their lives the medical profession's primary reason for existence—service to the patient. The students now
entering medical school are likely to bring with them humanistic concerns and a deep social consciousness. As emphasized at many points in
this book, students espouse a point of view similar to the message of
Hamlet: "What a piece of work is a man! How noble in reason! How in-
finite in faculty!" When humanistic values are nurtured and reinforced
in the students' training, these values stand a better chance of survival
after graduation.

As this book is brought to a close, the thought uppermost in my mind
is the marvelous heritage in which medical students are immersed.

How can they be helped to experience a sense of continuity with all who have gone before them and who have left them their knowledge, dedication, and vision? In a sense, they should be able to experience this continuity whenever they try to help a sick person and find themselves a part of the drama of healing.

While frequently overwhelmed by the tragic aspects of suffering and disease, students find renewal and encouragement when healing does take place. Even when victories are not won over illness and death, meaning and purpose in their efforts sustain them. Such was the situation recently with a student assigned to the kidney transplant ward. Over a period of weeks all efforts to help one of the patients had been of no avail. The patient had received a kidney transplant from his sister. The surgical procedure of transplanting the kidney had been made almost impossible by the patient's generalized arteriosclerotic blood vessels. After the transplantation, the grafted kidney did not function. Later, the patient's right leg had to be amputated because of ischemic gangrene. Shortly thereafter he died of large emboli in both lungs. In the middle of all this pain and disappointment stood the patient's sister and his wife. His sister had "lost" her kidney while "failing to help" her brother. His wife, almost in a state of exhaustion, was rarely permitted by him to leave his bedside because of his terrible fear of death. When all was over, the student remarked, "Although we lost every battle, what a privilege to have worked and struggled for this patient's recovery."

Soon this student will be graduating, and a very special group of privileges and prerogatives will be granted him and the other graduates. With the rights and privileges of the degree Doctor of Medicine will go enormous responsibilities. The ideas and ideals that should guide their lives could scarcely be more saliently expressed than in a prayer written by Augustine: "Oh Lord, who hast warned us that Thou wilt require much of those to whom much is given, grant that we, whose lot is cast in so goodly a heritage, may strive together the more abundantly to extend to others what we so richly enjoy. And as we have entered into the labours of other persons, so to labour, that, in their turn, other persons may enter into ours, to the fulfillment of Thy holy will."

INDEX